Richard Rorty

Philosophy Now

Series Editor: John Shand

This is a fresh and vital series of new introductions to today's most read, discussed and important philosophers. Combining rigorous analysis with authoritative exposition, each book gives clear and comprehensive access to the ideas of those philosophers who have made a truly fundamental and original contribution to the subject. Together the volumes comprise a remarkable gallery of the thinkers who have been at the forefront of philosophical ideas.

Published

John Searle
Nick Fotion

Charles Taylor
Ruth Abbey

Thomas Kuhn
Alexander Bird

Robert Nozick
A. R. Lacey

W. V. Quine
Alex Orenstein

Richard Rorty
Alan Malachowski

Michael Dummett
Bernhard Weiss

Richard Rorty

Alan Malachowski

PRINCETON UNIVERSITY PRESS
PRINCETON AND OXFORD

Published in North and South America by
Princeton University Press, 41 William Street,
Princeton, New Jersey 08540. All rights reserved.

First published in 2002 by Acumen
Acumen Publishing Limited
15a Lewins Yard
East Street
Chesham
Bucks HP5 1HQ, UK

Library of Congress Control Number 2002107397

ISBN 0-691-05707-9 (hardcover)
ISBN 0-691-05708-7 (paperback)

Designed and typeset in Century Schoolbook
by Kate Williams, Abergavenny.
Printed and bound by Biddles Ltd., Guildford and King's Lynn.

www.pupress.princeton.edu

10 9 8 7 6 5 4 3 2 1

Contents

In memory of my father

Alan Malachowski

(1928–2002)

Preface and acknowledgements

This book has some personal history behind it that may help explain its overall approach. Towards the end of my teenage years at school in the late 1960s, after various unsatisfactory infatuations with the classics, literary criticism, mathematics, psychology, economics and history, I discovered poetry. Or rather, that of Ezra Pound in particular. There was something tremendously exotic about both Pound's use of language and his subject matter, something that transported me, in imaginary time and place, far beyond the confines of my local council estate. For here was a poet who had delved deep into the resources of culture and history, who, as Thom Gunn later pointed out, had learned from Browning "to speak through the mouths of others: a troubadour-warrior, a Chinese river merchant's wife, Sextus Propertius, or an Italian Renaissance prince" (Gunn 2000: ix).

Furthermore, there was something sufficiently numinous about the lines to light up the deeper parts of my mind, parts that, despite my nodding acquaintance with Freud and Jung, I never knew to exist, yet alone expected to inhabit. Images from the *Selected Poems* in lines like "Grey olive leaves beneath a rain-cold sky" (Gentildonna) and "A wet leaf that clings to the threshold" (Liu Ch'e) flooded the kind of incandescent light into my awakening sensibility that it seemed would be everlastingly inextinguishable. For this light lingered soothingly at the core of consciousness throughout even the darkest adolescent ponderings.

Before long, however, reading Pound became disturbingly problematic. When I moved enthusiastically on to his enticingly large epic, the *Cantos*, I struggled valiantly to make the whole text cohere

– a difficulty disconcertingly echoed by Pound himself in the *Drafts & Fragments* section (CX–CXVII):

> I am not a demigod,
> I cannot make it cohere.
> (CXVI)

As I lay with my hard cover edition of the *Cantos* open on the white pillows each night, I failed to weave any of its various threads together before drifting off into sleep. The mind's inclination towards a narrow, self-regarding centre of gravity was still challenged:

> When the mind swings by a grass-blade
> an ant's forefoot shall save you
> (LXXXIII)

Luminosity still flashed from the page:

> A blown husk that is finished
> but the light sings eternal
> a pale flare over marshes
> where the salt hay whispers to tide's change
> (CXV)

But I could make little sense of the overall project. Threads were left hanging all over the place. To push things forward, I began to 'read around' the poem, haunting the city's central library to find out more about Pound himself and follow the trail of his wide-ranging interests.

Further exposure to central Poundian themes such as usury and key Poundian characters like Jefferson, Confucius and Cavalcanti only made things worse. Indeed, it shifted the problematic focus from the *Cantos* to Pound himself. I had naïvely assumed that someone whose pen emitted such ineffably sublime light would be supremely wise, or at the very least intellectually infallible. But the Pound I looked to for guidance outside the field of literature turned out to be hopelessly lost in a swirling fog of ideas. These were at best quirky and at times morally unswallowable. No amount of wider reading in economics, history and so on could put the *Cantos* in 'proper context' and thereby make sense of the whole. The poem reflected the chaos of Pound's half-baked thinking. Perhaps the very light he enabled my mind to in some measure absorb had at a certain point cracked his own. Whatever it was, he appeared fatally flawed.

So, by association, did poetry itself. Hence I looked for something more reliable than the luminescent experiences it had proved it could engender. Fortunately, I appeared to find it in philosophy, and while still at school. Bertrand Russell's 'On Denoting' was my first model. What apposite tools of analysis it appeared to provide at the time. The propositional function seemed a thing of wonder! Clear thinking would surely cut through rhetorical dissembling straight to the chase for truth, thus preventing the kind of psychological and moral fractures of the mind that ruined Pound. However, my attempts at it also shut out all but the narrowest shafts of forensic light. Unnourished, the wider, warmer, inner glow of adolescence finally began to expire. It never occurred to me to take the *Cantos* back down off the shelf and read shafts of the poem *just* for their fragmented insights and inspirational beauty. That is until, a great many more intellectual heroes and heroines down the road, I encountered the writings of Richard Rorty.

The first encounter in 1981 was unpromising. I was now researching and teaching philosophy at the University of East Anglia (UEA). Alan Hobbs, a colleague and one of my former tutors, was fired up at the time (he later cooled down pretty quickly) by a recent controversial critique of the prevailing analytic tradition. This was Rorty's seminal book *Philosophy and the Mirror of Nature*. He urged me to read it. I did so eagerly. But, when reporting back on my reactions, I found myself reduced to one truculent word: "decadent". Rorty had offended against my underlying sense of philosophical purpose. Despite plenty of fair weather exposure to the later Wittgenstein, an instinctive leaning towards Brouwer's intuitionism in mathematics and some sympathy for Dummett's anti-realism in the philosophy of language, I believed that, in the end, philosophy should sail under a realist flag, that those on board should strive to express the truth about the nature of reality and our place within it. Rorty apparently derided that sort of hankering after that sort of truth. Nevertheless, something in his writing must have struck a chord. And in any case, the thought that *Philosophy and the Mirror of Nature* had caused far too many other philosophers, including myself, to protest far too much aroused the sneaking suspicion that Rorty might be on to something. Serendipity also played its part.

When I arrived at UEA, Bob Newell, then a senior lecturer, casually invited me to sit in on his undergraduate course *American Philosophy: The Rise of American Pragmatism*. Those were the happily unrealistic days before the complete hegemony of big business values, before market forces and the concomitant marketing practices of bureaucratic self-inflation had yet started to exert their insidious, strangulating grip on higher education in the UK and elsewhere. The very brief one-page course outline would probably provoke sharp administrative retaliation these days. But it made an incisive gesture towards content and relevance before wisely referring us back to primary sources – the classic texts of Peirce, James and Dewey, yet also, not so far back, W. V. Quine's.

Although I say "us", only two students actually signed up and class discussions were agreeably intense. There were no formal lectures as such. Bob enthused over the texts as we tried to keep up with him. One day, for example, we found him excitedly reading something hot off the press. An article by Quine on morality – a topic he had not apparently tackled in print before. The elegance of presentation was of the usual sparkling vintage, but it turned out to be a damp squib as far as new ideas were concerned.

Because I knew something about current developments in areas such as logic, the philosophy of language, cognitive science and epistemology, Bob seemed to think I knew a lot about philosophy itself (I guess I probably conveyed the impression that I thought the same at the time). Hence he often asked me to comment on sticky passages or tricky issues. In reply, I invariably stumbled. He was generous in both smoothing things over and not pointing out the reasons for my ineptitude. But two of the main reasons must have been glaringly obvious anyway. Both made a return to Rorty pretty much inevitable.

In the first place, the tried and tested methods of dealing with philosophical topics that I had become familiar with simply did not work. They missed the mark by a mile every time. By the same token, though a separate reason, my preconceived picture of pragmatism as one of philosophy's long-dead ducks quickly collapsed. This picture was largely inherited from Russell. It depicted James as a vigorous, but insufficiently *philosophical*, polemicist, Dewey as a woolly, if well-intentioned, thinker who spawned masses of correspondingly flabby prose and Peirce as someone whose brilliant, but haphazard, work on signs had been supplanted by more precise themes and techniques derived from the Frege–Russell tradition.

The mismatch between standard analytical criticisms and the disobliging pragmatist target somehow suggested that Rorty's conception of intellectual change – in which metaphorical motivation and the unruly spread of contingent events do much more work than the more regimented march of theorizing or reasoned argument – required serious reconsideration. Furthermore, the emergence of an image of pragmatism that fed so seamlessly into Quine's naturalistic approach to philosophy and, at the same time, resurrected Dewey as a figure to be reckoned with, replicated key features of Rorty's own portrait. The resemblance was all the more indicative because Bob had apparently fostered this image from his own studies of pragmatism, quite independently of Rorty.

The return to Rorty involved organizing a series of faculty seminars on *Philosophy and the Mirror of Nature* and then using the results as the basis for putting together an ambitious collection of critical essays that were published by Blackwell under the astute, but encouraging, eye of Stephan Chambers in 1990. A title was not difficult to choose: *Reading Rorty*. Three UEA philosophers figured in the final selection: David Houghton, the late Martin Hollis and myself. Martin Scott-Taggart had given a spirited talk to round off the seminars. This casually fostered the impression that Rorty still had plenty of catching up to do as far as some of the key figures in both the continental tradition and pragmatism were concerned. But it never materialized into publishable form. I was fortunate in being able to secure just about everyone on my wish list of other contributors: an excellent combination of fresh talent and old hands. Most were immediately keen to take part in the project, and the rest came graciously on board after some gentle persuasion. Convivial discussions with Rorty himself, first during a break at a conference in Cambridge and then on a visit to his home in Virginia, won his seal of approval and clarified some details about his career as well as the development of his thinking. I left Rorty's university office in Virginia armed with a large pile of publications related to his work. However, preparation for writing the introduction to *Reading Rorty* was nearly spoiled by the kind of mistake I had made some 25 years earlier with regard to Pound.

Like Pound's, Rorty's interests were breathtakingly wide. Thus his writing performed a task analogous to that performed by Pound's. It lifted me out of my parochial intellectual environment. I started to read thinkers who did not appear on analytic philosophy's list of the usual suspects – especially thinkers in the continental tradition like Hegel, Nietzsche, Heidegger and Derrida. But I was reading them for the wrong reasons: to get that final fix on Rorty. It took some time before I realized my mistake. Then I adopted a more relaxed stance. Fortunately, the modest introduction betrayed few signs of any wider struggle to pigeon-hole Rorty.

After reading early drafts that Rorty sent me of his forthcoming book *Contingency, irony, and solidarity*, poetry, literature and indeed the arts in general became much more alive for me. The Lazarus touch was probably Rorty's suggestion to stop trying to beat private aesthetic delights into social shape, into consistently worthy public projects. It encouraged my explorations of these areas of culture for personal insight and pleasure. I also came to appreciate the various 'contingencies' of my previous dealings with artists like Pound. This was an 'appreciation' that I should have formed much earlier after coming across the works and writings of John Cage and especially Marcel Duchamp. But it took Rorty to force my hand. A picture of Pound on the cover of a small book by G. S. Fraser in a series called *Writers and Critics* had first attracted my attention. Then the quotations inside from Pound's poems sparked a desire for more intimate encounters. Contingencies abounded. Perhaps some other picture on some other book would have taken me in a different direction. Perhaps if I had known in advance of Pound's association with fascism, I would never have given him serious consideration. Perhaps the beauty of Pound's words would simply have passed me by on another occasion. In any case, what Pound's shimmering lines did for me, they singularly failed to do for some of my friends, despite my earnest prompting. Most probably, what I was looking for, when it came to the task of tackling the *Cantos*, was a rational explanation of the accidental nature of my seemingly profound experiences with Pound's poetry – a precise formula for understanding the vicissitudes of aesthetic bliss. In short, I unwittingly wanted to make art subservient to philosophy. Rorty showed how they could live side by side in fruitful interaction.

I still delved into multifarious sources derived from the published evidence of Rorty's voracious reading habits, sources that ranged from novels like Neal Stephenson's *Snow Crash* to historical monographs such as James Kloppenberg's *Uncertain Victory: Social Democracy and Progressivism in European and American Thought, 1870–1920*. Sometimes this kind of delving generated useful light on Rorty's position that was not already clearly present in his own writing. A case in point, discussed in Chapter 5 of the present book, concerned his emphasis on the links between 'liberalism' and 'the avoidance of cruelty'. Reading Judith Shklar's *Ordinary Vices* helped explain the choice of emphasis. But more often my general approach to such sources was simply to enjoy the inspiration they provided irrespective of their prospective influence on my interpretation of

Rorty as a philosopher. This was just as well because, unlike Pound, Rorty is no Humpty Dumpty figure. Despite the fears, and sadly at times jibes, of his critics, his philosophical heart is solid and in the right place. He does not need putting back together again.

I thus gave up on the search for the 'real Rorty', the one that could be deduced from the sum of all the authors he had read, the one that could be called up squarely before the tribunal of the tradition he attacked. But I continued to take his increasingly large body of work seriously, if in a lighter spirit. This volume is the outcome.

For the most part, it hacks away the contemporary thickets of controversy that Rorty has generated and offers a way of 'appreciating' him as a valuable, far-sighted thinker who throws up new ideas, puts an interesting spin on some old ones, and helps broaden the philosophical canon and redefine the course of philosophical history. It is necessary to cut these 'thickets' away because many of Rorty's critics, especially in philosophy, fail to read him carefully and thus tend to misrepresent his views. This failure brings to mind William James's comment on comparable misrepresentations of John Dewey's work: "It seems incredible that educated and apparently sincere critics should so fail to catch their adversary's point of view" (James 1978: 175). The whole approach of such critics is puzzling. They contend that Rorty's views are *obviously* absurd, but seem unperturbed by the fact that they are unable to demonstrate this by using the very tool whose absence, they claim, makes those views absurd: reasoned argument. Instead, they seem to spend most of their time deploying heavy-handed rhetoric to try to do the kind of thing to Rorty they criticize him for trying to do to them: make his views look bad when compared to their own. We return to this puzzle in Chapter 6. The handling of Rorty's critics in that chapter may seem rather rough, less polite, certainly, than Rorty's own measured responses. Apart from the occasional sign of exasperation, these generally tend to exhibit the solicitousness of wise therapists towards their patients' persistent follies. On his view, presumably, his critics deserve some sympathy because analytic philosophy shot itself in the foot years ago and has been stamping around, unaware of the self-inflicted causes of its agitation, ever since. But in my view the critics in question deserve some harsher treatment, not least because they dish it out so frequently themselves (I will not burden the reader's sensibility with examples of their distasteful claims), and invariably on the basis of shallow, inadequate readings of Rorty's texts. Their approach seems to incorporate an unconscious, inverted principle of charity that engenders a very perverse image of Rorty: the clearer, more provocative and more telling his point, the worse his intentions and the weaker his overall position.

This book was written in roughly equal parts in three separate countries: England, South Africa and America. The manuscript was more or less finished just as the catastrophic events of 11 September 2001 occurred in America. It is impossible to predict how some of the views canvassed here on self-creation, solidarity, liberal utopia and so on will fare in the light of complex world events yet to unfold. But, already the situation resonates with Rorty's account of how contingent historical events cause new metaphors and images to spring up that in turn reshape the intellectual and political landscape. As I write, James Poniewozik claims in *Time Magazine*: "So much that we could say casually a month ago rings empty, even cruel, today. Our metaphors have expired. Pleasure seems mocking and futile. The language that artists, comedians, storytellers and actors use to explain us to ourselves now seems frivolous, inappropriate or simply outdated." Whether he should have included 'philosophers' here is a key issue raised by Rorty's work, and one that probably now takes on a greater sense of urgency even for those who will insist to their grave that philosophy's greatest metaphors have no expiry date.

All books probably warrant more extensive acknowledgements than their authors are inclined to voice. I hope those I have left out here will forgive the oversight. I must thank John Shand, and Steven Gerrard of Acumen, for inviting me to write the book in the first place, Richard Rorty for his unfailing kindness in promptly answering my sporadic queries over the years, Tim O'Hagan, Bruce Lyons, Rupert Read, David Houghton and Gerry Goodenough for long-term moral support at the University of East Anglia, Tom Sorell for some characteristically insightful, fair-minded comments on a late draft, and Matthew Festenstein for similarly useful comments. I should also thank John Arthur for inviting me to teach a course on Rorty at Binghamton University, where the American portion of the present text was written. I am indebted to the Binghamton faculty and the staff of the Ramada Inn, Binghamton, for providing a quiet, friendly atmosphere that was very conducive to both writing and thinking. I am also most grateful to the Binghamton students for their great warmth, for responding so enthusiastically to unfamiliar material, and for showing me that one of my hunches about Rorty was mistaken. I thought that, for all its merits, Rorty's approach was 'motivationally inadequate', that once his pragmatist advice was heeded, there would be little incentive to create and explore new thoughts. But, when I asked the Binghamton students to identify and discuss issues in purely Rortyean terms, foreswearing such notions as 'correspondence to reality', they found masses of interesting and useful things to say. There seemed to be plenty of wind left in their sails after throwing the whole analytic agenda overboard. This provided much food for thought while writing the present volume.

The people of Kleinmond in South Africa have been extremely hospitable. Of these, I should above all mention Piet and Mardi Pelser, Wayne and Beverly Saunders, Sarie Meiring and all the staff at the nearby Arabella Country Estate. Their friendly resourcefulness has helped my wife and me create an ideal second home there in recent years. Although it still has grave social and economic problems as well as its fair share of political infighting and trivial disputes, South Africa seems to provide a glowing example of the kind of political pragmatism Rorty advocates. It is a country inspired by 'social hope' and held together by 'solidarity'. The traditional proverb *umuntu ngumuntu ngabantu* (A person is a person through persons) echoes both Rorty's politics and the public side of his approach to personal identity. Furthermore, South Africa's current emphasis on 'practical experimentation' and the pursuit of concrete social and economic goals leave little time for the sort of politics of 'detached spectatorship' and 'high theorizing' that Rorty so rightly decries.

Finally, and most of all, I should thank my whole family for putting up with my quixotic ways over the years, especially my wonderfully supportive wife Lesley and our dear son Jannie, who lovingly overcame the trials and tribulations that this writing project imposed on them.

What is philosophy today – philosophical activity I mean – if it is
not . . . the endeavour to know how and to what extent it might
be possible to think differently, instead of legitimating what is
already known?   Michel Foucault

There is no vantage point, no first philosophy.   W. V. Quine

Old questions are solved by disappearing.   John Dewey

A note on the text

A key to the abbreviations employed to identify individual quotations from Rorty's writings is given on p. xxi. The sources for other quotations that are not identified in this way can be found in the bibliographical material. In the interests of 'accessibility', footnotes have been avoided throughout. However, by way of compensation to those who may feel the need for more 'context', some brief advice on further reading is given at the end of the book. Additional recompense comes in the form of the quotations from Rorty himself. These serve two purposes. They help confirm the account of his views that is given here and they bypass the critical storm that Rorty's work has provoked so readers can get a more direct 'feel' for his unique style, one of the attractions of his way of doing philosophy.

Rorty sometimes uses double, or full, quotation marks where single would normally be used. Single quotation marks have been substituted for 'double' in places where Rorty's usage might cause confusion (for example: when the term or phrase already occurs within double quotation marks).

Abbreviations

AOC *Achieving Our Country: Leftist Thought in Twentieth-Century America*. Cambridge, MA: Harvard University Press, 1998.

CP *Consequences of Pragmatism*. Minneapolis, MN: University of Minnesota Press, 1982.

CIS *Contingency, irony, and solidarity*. Cambridge: Cambridge University Press, 1988.

EHO *Essays on Heidegger and Others: Philosophical Papers II*. Cambridge: Cambridge University Press, 1991.

LT *The Linguistic Turn* (ed.). Chicago, IL: University of Chicago Press, 1967. Second enlarged edition 1992.

ORT *Objectivity, Relativism and Truth: Philosophical Papers I*. Cambridge: Cambridge University Press, 1991.

PMN *Philosophy and the Mirror of Nature*. Princeton, NJ: Princeton University Press, 1979.

PSH *Philosophy and Social Hope*. Harmondsworth: Penguin, 2000.

TP *Truth and Progress: Philosophical Papers III*. Cambridge: Cambridge University Press, 1998.

WO "Trotsky and the Wild Orchids". In PSH, pp. 3–20.

WWL "The World Well Lost". In CP, pp. 1–19.

Introduction

> I have spent 40 years looking for a coherent and convincing way
> of formulating my worries about what, if anything, philosophy is
> good for.   (PSH: 11)

Richard Rorty was once described by the distinguished American
literary critic Harold Bloom as "the most interesting philosopher in
the world". A thinker whose writing attracts such lofty praise from
such elevated sources should normally need little or no introduction.
But Rorty is a notable exception.

As a *philosopher*, he represents a profession that now exerts, for
reasons his own work attempts to diagnose, a very modest impact on
public opinion and world events. Although Rorty has made admirable efforts to cross the barriers of excessive technicality and abstrac-
tion that his chosen profession has erected around what he considers
to be, in any case, a largely anachronistic definition of its subject
matter, his writing is not yet well known to the general reader.
Furthermore, even inside philosophy and those other areas of intellectual endeavour, such as literary theory, where Rorty's ideas have
exerted a sizeable influence, the significance of that writing tends to
be misunderstood.

In philosophy, where Rorty's thinking has gained some notoriety
for trying to turn the subject upside down, his writing is generally
underestimated. It is frequently viewed as the work of a rather slip-
shod iconoclast. Rorty is seen, in this vein, as something of an 'anti-
philosopher' who leaves himself open to the most superficial objections.
Thus some fellow philosophers hold that Rorty a grossly
irresponsible relativist, someone who believes no intellectual position

1

Richard Rorty

is ultimately better than any other such position. Others take him to be an out-and-out nihilist about truth, someone whose own views on that very topic are therefore self-defeating, if not incoherent (because, by his own lights, *they* cannot be deemed true). And, in those spheres outside philosophy where Rorty's work is often given greater prominence, it is frequently celebrated on the wrong basis, as if it purports to lend more philosophical credibility, and hence more theoretical kudos, to the discipline in question even when one of Rorty's most firmly held views about philosophy is that, when properly understood, it can no longer be expected to shore up or underwrite extra-philosophical claims.

Overall, there is no denying Rorty's impact. Nevertheless, his controversial work has generally been more influential than understood – a fate that justifies an 'introduction' such as this, but one that can also be viewed with some irony, given, as we shall see, Rorty's de-intellectualized view of progress in the history of philosophy.

So much for some of the general reasons why Rorty needs an introduction. But, what *kind* of 'introduction' does he need? We will later have more to say about the main ways in which, despite his influence, Rorty is misunderstood, especially by his critics in philosophy itself. Clearly any overview of his work must at least attempt to steer past the worst errors of the latter. But this does not mean that it should strive to present the 'real Rorty', the thinker behind the texts that these critics have, in their various modes of blindness, simply failed to recognize.

Rorty is vehemently opposed to 'essentialism'. This is the age-old philosophical notion that reality and the things comprising it have an *intrinsic* nature – something our understanding of the world has to discern and remain faithful to if we are to acquire anything like genuine knowledge. As a pragmatist, Rorty holds that:

> There is no such thing as a nonrelational feature of X, any more than there is such a thing as the intrinsic nature, the essence, of X. So there can be no such thing as a description which matches the way X really is, apart from its relation to human needs or consciousness or language. (PSH: 50)

It would therefore be ironic to impose what amounts to an 'essentialist interpretation' on his own work, one that professes to depict what it all *really* adds up to.

Ironic, perhaps, but would it be wrong? The answer to this question seems to depend, for a start, on the viability of Rorty's global strictures against essentialism. If those are correct, then *nothing* has an essential nature and terms like "really" are redundant in contexts where we describe what the world, including even something like Rorty's philosophical contribution to it, is like. But this initial thought threatens to ditch us into some very murky waters. For how are we actually to determine the standards of 'correctness' here?

Happily, however, our intimation that an introduction to Rorty's work should eschew any concept of 'the real Rorty' does not have to prejudge the weighty issue as to whether Rorty is actually *right* to reject essentialism and is hence himself automatically invulnerable to essentialist interpretations. The guiding thought behind the intimation is very simply this: an introduction to Rorty needs first to take him at his own word and then try to maximize the coherence of the results. It needs, in short, to be a far more charitable enterprise than his critics are usually prepared to countenance. To do this requires a close look at Rorty's major texts and at the picture of his aims and approach that emerges from them. In that picture, a deep and far-sighted thinker can be detected, one who does not actually want to make new moves *within* the traditional philosophical arena, but rather wants to help redefine that 'arena' – to change our conception of what philosophy is, what it involves, the ways in which it ought to be practised and the topics that it should deal with. These features of Rorty's enterprise are interesting enough without any rhetorical flourish to the effect that they constitute anything like the 'true nature' of his philosophy.

Non-essential Rorty

Some readers may well be disappointed to discover that the present book does not even attempt to portray the 'real Rorty'. This is likely to be the effect of an unconscious hankering after the kind of 'rhetorical flourish' that was just now rejected. Books, even sober academic ones, are often sold on the strength of enticing, though exaggerated, claims to reveal the 'real truth' about their subject. Few authors are willing to stop at the stage of pointing out that they have an interesting, fresh 'take' on their subject. Most want to go much further and stake a claim to the 'real truth of the matter'.

But, there could also be a more substantial worry here. If a supposed general introduction to a thinker explicitly states that it is not going even to try to explain what that thinker's work *really amounts to*, then why should we trust what it says? Surely what we look for in an introduction to an intellectual figure is first and foremost an authoritative account of the significance of their work. How can an account that does not aim to capture what a thinker is 'really saying' be in any sense *authoritative*?

This question raises exactly the kind of issues provoked by Rorty himself. He wants us to scrap much of the rhetoric closely associated with many of traditional philosophy's most cherished notions, such as "reality", "truth", "knowledge", "mind", "rationality" and "morality". But what makes him so provocatively 'interesting' is that he maintains we can do this without thereby having to lose our grip on effective standards of inquiry, useful norms of behaviour and so on. An introduction to Rorty's work that makes no claim to a 'definitive interpretation' occupies a correlatively provocative position if it also denies any consequent loss of 'authority'. But, how can such a 'denial' be credible?

An interpretation – or 'reading' – of Rorty can gain 'authority' from its manifest familiarity with the relevant texts and their connections with other texts, but also from how 'useful' the resulting portrait of Rorty is. The present 'introduction' seeks no 'authority' beyond that gained on these criteria – with the 'usefulness factor' being cashed out in terms of helping readers appreciate more clearly what Rorty is trying to do and encouraging them to think a bit harder, and perhaps a bit more creatively, constructively, and in a less tradition-bound way, about the many important issues raised by his work. Some will no doubt complain that this approach is, itself, far too 'Rorty-like' – that the present book is just going to turn out to be 'Rorty squared', when, for objectivity's sake at least, it needs to be more independent, more like 'Rorty divided' or even 'Rorty with errors subtracted'. Let me then say something further in defence of 'Rorty squared'.

Readers of this book do not have 'the essential Rorty' in their hands. Nevertheless, what they do have is intended to be more than 'sufficient' in the sense that it provides a comprehensive interpretation of Rorty's thinking – an interpretation that sympathetically maps out the development of his written work so that the 'usefulness' of its major themes can be explored and assessed without distractions. Such an interpretation is needed because hyper-critical approaches, those that have unfortunately become the norm, tend to obscure Rorty's aims and prevent fruitful discussion of what is most philosophically adventurous in his writing.

Notice that the assumption here is not that what I call 'hyper-critical approaches' are bound to be mistaken – it would be silly to assume Rorty is totally immune to this kind of criticism (we return to this point below). The supposition is rather that a hyper-critical approach would not serve such a useful *introductory* purpose. This still requires a bit more unpacking. We have abandoned any claim to the production of a definitive account of Rorty's work and yet, at the same time, we seem to want to hang on to the contentions that other approaches 'obscure' key aspects and contain errors of interpretation. Furthermore, one of Rorty's own favoured notions – that of 'usefulness' – has already become ubiquitous even though its definition remains vague. The objections implicit in these remarks are again reminiscent of two general objections commonly voiced against Rorty himself:

1. Without an anchor in determinate reality or at least a conception thereof, 'anything goes' (i.e. wild relativism).
2. Without a precise definition, the notion of 'usefulness' is itself incapable of serving any worthwhile philosophical purpose.

However, they also miss the mark for much the same reasons in each case.

The first objection crudely presupposes that the whole vocabulary of 'critical assessment' is inextricably tied to a certain metaphysical picture, namely: realism. And here, the leading thought is that if the attempt to focus on what is actually the case (the benchmark focus demanded by realism) is abandoned, then it will not be possible to make genuine distinctions between 'what is better' and 'what is worse', 'what is correct' and 'what is incorrect', 'what is accurate' and 'what is inaccurate', 'what is the right interpretation' and 'what is the wrong interpretation', and so forth. Against this, Rorty holds that such distinctions can be made – indeed, can *only* be made – on the basis of other, non-realist, criteria. These are *pragmatic* criteria. Thus, for example, one interpretation may be better than another because it more effectively satisfies certain desires or fulfils such and such a purpose. In our present case, it is reasonable for us to talk about, say, 'errors in the interpretation of Rorty's work' without committing ourselves to further talk about what his work 'really signifies'. For errors can be identified relative to a variety of practical considerations extraneous to conceptions of 'the real meaning' of an author's words. These include the goals and purposes of reading the relevant texts.

As for the complaint that, until it is defined more precisely, the notion of 'usefulness' is empty, Rorty's own response is salient. He claims he does not want to employ this notion as a blanket theoretical notion, one that requires a prior, fixed meaning. He prefers to think of its significance as something that fluctuates according to the demands of particular cases. In our case, we have already outlined some general criteria for 'usefulness' regarding the approach taken in this book. The approach is designed to be 'useful' to the extent that it:

* facilitates appreciation of what Rorty is trying to achieve
* encourages exploration of important issues raised by Rorty's key writings
* clears the path to a proper consideration as to how socially and intellectually useful Rorty's main themes are.

However, even if these criteria are accepted, it remains to be seen why a less sympathetic, or even 'hyper-critical', approach could not also satisfy them.

Falling out of sympathy with Rorty

Plenty of philosophers in particular have already so 'fallen'. Indeed, as Jonathan Rée points out, the publication of *Philosophy and the Mirror of Nature* (PMN), Rorty's first book, "lost him the sympathy of nearly every pukka philosopher in the English-reading world" (Rée 1998: 7). But, we need to ask of those who have taken this unfavourable stance whether it is likely that their understanding of Rorty has been impaired in the process. At first blush, the very posing of such a question may seem outrageous. If it is anything, or so this indignant kind of response goes, philosophy is a 'critical discipline' in which lack of sympathy with viewpoints is a 'tool of the trade' and commonly a reliable symptom of appropriate 'understanding'. Philosophers pride themselves on their ability to pick holes in arguments, deflate unnecessary distinctions, undermine positions and pinpoint anomalies in belief structures. To suggest that when they turn their critical gaze on Rorty's writing they may thereby betray a 'lack of understanding' seems to put Rorty in the company of those whose alleged thoughts are beyond rational evaluation and therefore philosophically irrelevant. But the suggestion is subtler than that.

To fall out of sympathy with a thinker because one has digested their views and found those views wanting is one thing. Our suggestion has no quarrel with this. It concerns something quite different: the obstacles to understanding that a *premature* lack of sympathy can create. Some philosophers dismiss Rorty on 'hearsay' without reading his work in any detail. Others seem only to read Rorty when they are already primed to dispute his views so that nothing he has to say gets much of an airing. What we called the 'hyper-critical approach' takes this to an extreme: Rorty's ideas are knocked to the ground *before* they have been given a chance to demonstrate whether they can fly.

Proponents of the 'hyper-critical approach' would baulk at all this. On their view, the very fact that Rorty's ideas *can* be swiftly knocked to the ground shows that those ideas do not deserve to fly. Hyper-critical scrutiny is simply a reasonable test that all philosophically sound ideas have to pass. Such scrutiny facilitates 'understanding'. As far as philosophy 'proper' is concerned, 'premature lack of sympathy' is a myth.

Against this background orthodoxy, the claim that Rorty's ideas can best be understood from an initially sympathetic vantage point is going to look like special pleading – the kind of pleading that only the gullible or disreputable friends of dubious irrationalists indulge in. But an introduction to Rorty's work needs to risk the charge of 'special pleading'. The reason for this is that Rorty is attempting to launch philosophy on a path that takes it into new territory that is *incommensurable* with present-day 'hyper-critical philosophy'. This 'incommensurability' means that hyper-critical philosophy probably does not possess the appropriate tools for making much sense of the territory in question, that its accustomed lines of criticism, however appropriate in other cases, may be irrelevant.

This is a very controversial suggestion. For, according to hyper-critical philosophers, their methods have *universal* jurisdiction so there can be no such 'new territory'. If Rorty is setting philosophy on a path to anything that supposedly resides beyond the authority of these methods, it is a path to one form or another of intellectual oblivion. Some of Rorty's critics therefore also argue that he is intent on destroying philosophy.

In later chapters, the claim that Rorty is philosophy's self-appointed undertaker is denied. But no attempt is made to engage with the details of other hyper-critical objections to his work. The complaints of some harsh critics in philosophy are discussed in

Chapter 6, but the aim there is to expose the gap between their criticisms and the target, not to adjudicate the substantive issues that they believe are at stake. This, too, is a Rorty-like omission. For Rorty's general response to the prospect of such 'complaints' is to 'change the subject'. He wants to sideline such objections for the same reasons that, in his seminal book *Philosophy and the Mirror of Nature*, he attributes to the philosophers Wittgenstein, Heidegger and Dewey in their 'setting aside' of 'epistemology' and 'metaphysics' as "possible disciplines":

> I say "set aside" rather than "argue against" because their attitude toward the traditional problematic is like the attitude of seventeenth-century philosophers toward the scholastic problematic. They do not devote themselves to discovering false propositions or bad arguments in the works of their predecessors (though they occasionally do that too). Rather they glimpse the possibility of a form of intellectual life in which the vocabulary of philosophical reflection inherited from the seventeenth century would seem as pointless as the thirteenth-century philosophical vocabulary had seemed to the Enlightenment.
>
> (PMN: 6)

To further clarify why it is best to introduce Rorty's ideas in relative protective isolation from conventional, hyper-critical reactions, we will later occasionally hark back to the following illuminating analogy with the progress in the arts.

When an extraordinarily innovative move is made within the arts, for example in music or poetry, the results may well offend against established, well-proven, critical standards. Hence the phenomenon – that can seem puzzling in retrospect – of great works of art being treated with derision by otherwise cultured, perceptive and intelligent cultural critics. Those critics are inclined to believe that the current standards of aesthetic taste 'rationally determine' the constitution of 'good art'. And they often assume such standards can be elevated to 'principles' that demarcate the essential nature of art itself. Thus in those cases where these standards are clearly inappropriate (because no attempt has been made to meet them – think, for example, of the way in which the composer John Cage's infamous 'silent' piece made no effort to satisfy conventional notions of musical appreciation), the critics high-handedly rule that these "are not art".

Now imagine that we want to explain the significance of something that has been ruled against in this way. We could proceed by trying to show that the putative work of art *does* satisfy the very standards on which it has been condemned – perhaps by arguing that it meets more exacting or elevated standards that can be derived from or are somehow implicit in the originals: "Although Picasso appears to display a poor grasp of pictorial composition, if you look more closely at his work, you will see that he is finessing the compositional breakthroughs of painters like Cezanne." Such ploys are frequently successful because great artists tend to 'create' from a springboard of great competence in conventional skills (e.g. Picasso was an excellent draughtsman). This makes it easier for advocates to weave a narrative plea that reveals links between what is 'innovative' about the works in question and more orthodox perceptions. Then the boundaries of art can be extended accordingly. However, "ploy" is the right term. For what is most compelling about many great works of art is the dazzling sense of 'uniqueness' that they convey, the ways in which they convince us that there has never been anything quite like them on the face of the earth before. When we start to 'see' posited links with previous creations, our understanding appears to deepen, but something important may also be lost. For when the works in question can be assimilated by the tradition they tried to escape, or radically transform, they lose some of their vitality and are ready, as Marcel Duchamp once so aptly put it, 'for the museum'.

Progress in the arts generally occurs within a tradition, but *great progress* is usually a matter, in the end, of breaking with tradition, of extending conventional 'boundaries'. Sometimes there are 'quantum leaps' of creativity, when a fresh way of doing things catches on and the ploy of taking this 'freshness' away by digging up links with the past does not work – even if it can, in theory, be done, the results are too inconsequential or boring. When poets began to write in 'free verse', there were hostile cries of "this is not poetry" from the old guard and corresponding attempts to legitimize it by citing historical precedents. But, as poets enjoyed exploring this unleashed way of writing and audiences responded in kind, the debate over artistic status quickly subsided. Now nobody gets hot under the collar over whether *The Waste Land* or *Cantos* are 'really poetry'.

This introduction to Rorty is written on the premise that his work may represent something of an analogous 'quantum leap' in philosophy. It does not seek to show conclusively that some hyper-critical genius cannot spring up to undermine Rorty's claims and at the same time revive interest in the themes he would have us set aside. But it does try to convey why it would take 'a genius' to do this, as it would have taken a talent of at least Shakespearian stature to fend off the transition to free verse and keep ongoing culture intrigued by matters of metre and rhyme.

From this sympathetically 'agnostic' position, it seems best not to wait for genius, but to take the possibility of a 'quantum leap' seriously. This leap could carry philosophy into territory where traditional methods and problems are irrelevant, where new, 'post-pragmatist' themes emerge. To engage with Rorty's writing by making detailed hyper-critical objections to its every move right now would be like trying to force the genii of a particular artistic innovation back into the dusty bottle of conventional standards. Even if this could be done, it would betray a lack of understanding of the original enterprise (as a conventionally rationalized squashing of the first impulses to write free verse presumably would have done). Should Rorty's various ways with philosophy catch on, it will be difficult for intellectuals of the future to take the present hyper-critical fear and resentment of him seriously. They will see him as a thinker who freed intellectual culture from some stale, parochial obsessions, encouraged new ventures in 'self-creation' and launched a set of socio-political themes that made philosophy more relevant to the demands of post-twentieth-century living. Furthermore, they will be probably be puzzled as to why a thinker who introduced 'compassion' into a subject hitherto so proud of its 'cool' approach – a thinker who often said things like "*all* human relations untouched by love take place in the dark" (ORT: 205) – was treated so harshly by so many other members of his profession.

Points of emphasis

This introduction does not seek to present the 'real Rorty', but it does offer a *particular* Rorty, one that emerges from its own slant on his work. It is time to explain in more detail what this 'slant' involves.

Rorty's writing covers a great deal of ground. The following account of that writing is 'comprehensive' in that it deals with texts spanning the whole of his career so far – some forty years or so. But a *fully* comprehensive treatment that deals with the wide range and vast quantity of written material Rorty has produced is ruled out by limitations regarding both the availability of space and the intellectual level of exposition. Such limitations, common to most 'introductions', have necessitated some hard choices about overall 'emphasis'. Since different emphases may have conveyed a very different picture of Rorty, readers deserve some preliminary guidance on these choices. They involve five resulting features of the book's general approach:

1. Rorty's 'early works' are not explored in any great detail.
2. Rorty's important connection to 'continental' philosophers is briefly alluded to from time to time, but not explored in depth.
3. The relationship between Rorty's views and natural science is largely ignored.
4. For the most part, the 'accuracy' of Rorty's account of the history of philosophy is not discussed.
5. Very little attempt is made to adjudicate large substantive issues (for example (as above): whether Rorty is *right* to reject essentialism).

Each of these choices about 'emphasis' warrants some further explanation at this stage, not least to clarify how it is possible to abjure so much material and yet still lay claim to a genuine measure of 'comprehensiveness'.

1. Early Rorty

Periodization is one familiar way we get to grips with important cultural figures. Thus we come to speak of 'late Beethoven', 'early Pound', 'late Heidegger', and so on. Sometimes these descriptions seem to be dictated to us by the timing and content of relevant works – so, for example, differences between his *Tractatus* and *Philosophical Investigations* apparently force us to talk of an 'early' and a 'late' Wittgenstein. Scholars and commentators then tend to have a field day disputing these 'natural divisions' by finding 'continuities' or 'deeper differences' that override them.

In this book, Rorty's work is subjected to what we might call 'reticent periodization'. "Reticent" in that it is both compatible with our professed lack of interest in tapping 'the real Rorty' and fallible. There is 'compatibility' because the 'divisions' are made to map out a useful, manageable interpretation of Rorty's progress, no more. And there is 'fallibility' because these 'divisions' could be cancelled out by other 'useful' interpretations. 'Early Rorty' refers to works before *Philosophy and the Mirror of Nature* and related writings such as his important article "The World Well Lost" (WWL, reprinted in

Consequences of Pragmatism (CP): Ch. 1). We outline some broad features of the early period that blur its boundaries. But, again this is a modest undertaking that simply posits some 'continuities'. It is carried through only to show that the picture of Rorty as an analytic philosopher turned traitor after *Philosophy and the Mirror of Nature* is something of a caricature. We do not examine the early works in their own right, placing emphasis instead on the sequence of books that earned Rorty his notoriety: *Philosophy and the Mirror of Nature*, *Consequences of Pragmatism* and *Contingency, irony, and solidarity* (CIS). These, along with his 'collected papers', are the published texts that he now seems to regard as providing his philosophical centre of gravity. He rarely mentions his articles on topics like 'eliminative materialism', 'privileged access' and 'transcendental arguments'. At some later stage, I hope to explore the possible connections between such articles and the Rorty that dominates these pages. Meanwhile, it is left for others to carry out a more thorough investigation of the 'early Rorty' that may provide grounds for giving greater prominence to his considerable accomplishments during the period in question, and hence for a corresponding reassessment of his achievements thereafter.

2. Rorty and continental philosophy

Rorty has done much to help heal the rift between 'analytic' and 'continental' philosophy – although both sides are reluctant to admit this. Analytic philosophers like to affect a tough stance, as if too much Rorty-inspired 'rapprochement' will weaken their resolve to tackle the 'hard problems' of philosophy inherited from great thinkers on their side of the fence. These are problems such as how the existence of consciousness in an otherwise material world can be explained and whether, when they make unconstrained choices in life, human beings possess such an intangible but important thing as free will.

In point of fact, many more analytic philosophers are taking Rorty's lead and actually reading thinkers like Heidegger, Foucault and Derrida while at the same time retracing their historical steps to determine whether key figures such as Hegel and Nietzsche should have been marginalized on the say-so of shallow and self-serving analytic commentators such as Bertrand Russell or A. J. Ayer.

Continental philosophers are inclined to adopt a distanced, superior tone when contemplating Rorty's treatment of thinkers such as Heidegger and Derrida. They seem to begrudge Rorty's ability to make such philosophers more accessible to those of analytic persuasion, and complain bitterly that he distorts what is deep and profound in their work when he puts his habitual pragmatist gloss on the best efforts of thinkers like Heidegger and Derrida. Nevertheless, there are signs that the increased analytic interest in the continental tradition is being reciprocated. And comparisons are springing up in the literature between representative thinkers on each side such as Davidson and Derrida. Rorty has encouraged such 'comparisons' with his own couplings of otherwise strange bedfellows such as 'Dewey and Heidegger' (CP: 37–59).

Within the continental tradition, Hegel, Nietzsche, Heidegger and Derrida have exerted the most obvious influence on Rorty. But it would take another, very different, kind of book than this one to explain the significance of their influence. Furthermore, even such a venture would come up against Rorty's personal adherence to a distinction he makes much of in *Contingency, irony, and solidarity*. This is the distinction between the 'public' and 'private' realms. The public nature of the influence that the continental tradition has exerted on Rorty – the influence that can be observed by the community of readers at large – shows up most clearly in his tendency to view philosophical ideas as *historical* phenomena, his correlative scepticism regarding any claim to have fixed the human philosophical agenda once and for all, and his conception of the self as a 'culturally created' entity. But the lessons here are not unique to Rorty's reading of continental philosophers; he also finds them in Dewey, Wittgenstein, Sellars, Quine and Davidson. Although Dewey is a hybrid case (because of his absorption of Hegel's historicism), the others belong squarely in the analytic camp. By the same token, Rorty derives similar inspiration from literary figures and other non-philosophical thinkers such as Freud.

As for the 'private' influence, Rorty has testified to the immense excitement and stimulation that his encounters with Heidegger and Derrida in particular have generated. But to extrapolate the results of this personal exhilaration beyond an evident loosening of the analytic grip on Rorty's style and an increased confidence in his ability to flex his imagination on less traditional themes would take someone with greater specialized expertise than I could ever hope to possess. For these reasons, I therefore offer no more than some suggestive brushstrokes to stimulate the reader's interest in the fascinating saga of Rorty's continental excursions.

3. Rorty and science

> In our culture, the notions of "science", "rationality" and "truth" are bound up with one another. Science is thought of as offering "hard", "objective" truth: truth as correspondence to reality, the only sort of truth worthy of the name. (ORT: 35)

Many of Rorty's more curmudgeonly minded hyper-critical commentators believe science is the hard case that shatters the pretension of his whole philosophy. The grounds for their verdict are straightforward: science shows that Rorty's central substantive views are false, and that his alternative to traditional philosophical thinking is therefore built entirely on sand.

For science discovers the nature of reality – like the chemical composition of water or the distances between the planets. The results of such 'discovery' – that water is made of hydrogen and oxygen or that Mars is such and such a distance from the Sun – involve mind-independent 'truths' (e.g. it is true that water is so constituted regardless of what human beings happen to believe about it). Some of these pick out 'essential features': given that water is made up of hydrogen and oxygen, then for something to be water it *must* have the same kind of composition. Something that is qualitatively indistinguishable from water (i.e. that looks, tastes and feels like water) but has a different chemical composition *cannot be* water. Moreover, the 'truths' discovered by science are *truths* in virtue of corresponding to how things really are ('Mars is such and such a distance from the Sun' is true because Mars really is that distance from the Sun: truth matches actuality). Good science dramatically and reliably increases the community's yield of such reality-matching truths.

This description of science looks like a *prima facie* refutation of Rorty's whole philosophy because it makes very good sense of claims that Rorty appears to deny: that there are mind-independent truths, that such truths are discovered, that some of them concern 'essences', that they are true because they depict the ways things really are, and so on.

What Rorty has to do, on this understanding, is demonstrate that the claims involved are false, that this description of science is fundamentally flawed. Of course, the assumption here is that Rorty's task is impossible because the account of science is so obviously correct in its fundamentals. By the same token, what a suitably rigorous and informative introduction to Rorty's work has to do is examine whether his views can withstand the challenge presented by science.

There is room, indeed, for an investigation of how Rorty's philosophy lines up alongside science as conceived above. But, such an investigation is beyond the scope of an introductory text. And it is unsuitable for the present 'sympathetic' approach in any case. To stage a confrontation between Rorty and science would be to risk losing expository sight of what he is trying to do.

Rorty is not the slightest bit interested in interfering with the practice of science itself. His only concern is to dispatch overblown, philosophical misconceptions *about* science, to dispatch the incipient 'scientism' of philosophical culture in the West. But, even here, Rorty is not intent on 'demonstrating falsehoods'.

He prefers to offer a picture of intellectual culture in which 'freedom' and 'solidarity' in the mutually enhancing form of 'unforced agreement' shape the norms of 'objectivity'. In this picture, old-fashioned, harder-nosed conceptions of science that appear to contradict Rorty's philosophical preferences simply fall by the wayside – as do expectations that philosophy should mimic science by, for example, taking on board its particular standards of intellectual rigour.

Reconsider the above 'description of science' from Rorty's perspective. It consists of a series of platitudes concerning the achievements of science that nobody would wish to deny. The trouble starts when those platitudes are worked up into an elevating philosophical explanation and justification of science, when prosaic terms like "discover" are given a deeper, 'realist' interpretation. For then the description begs all the important issues: that it makes sense to talk about mind-independent truths, that reality has an essential nature, that the idea of truths 'corresponding' to reality has explanatory power, and so on. Although Rorty does frequently challenge the cogency of such presuppositions, his main strategy seems to be to cast just enough doubt upon them to generate interest in the prospects of an alternative picture in which they cease to play such a vital role.

Rorty's inspiration for thinking that 'alternative pictures' do not need to stand in a relationship of direct intellectual contest with what they seek to replace, matching argument with argument against a background of shared assumptions as to what constitutes 'success' in such a conflict, comes mainly from Thomas Kuhn, the distinguished and influential philosopher of science:

Kuhn's major contribution to remapping culture was to help us see that the natural scientists do not have a special access to reality or to truth. He helped dismantle the traditional hierarchy of disciplines, a hierarchy that dates back to Plato's image of the divided line. That line stretched from the messy material world up into a near immaterial world. In the hierarchy Plato proposed, mathematics (which uses pure logic, and no rhetoric at all) is up at the top and literary criticism and political persuasion (which use mostly rhetoric, and practically no logic) are down at the bottom. Kuhn fuzzed up the distinction between logic and rhetoric by showing that revolutionary theory-change is not a matter of following our inferences, but of changing the terminology in which truth candidates were formulated and thereby changing criteria of relevance.   (PSH: 176)

If Rorty devoted more time to 'challenging' presuppositions that seek to bolster the philosophical self-esteem of science, he would end up engaging with his critics on their own territory where the kind of moves he wishes to make are automatically sealed off in advance. Furthermore, by responding as if science represented the 'toughest case' for him to crack, he would also unwittingly reinforce the view that it occupies a special place in culture – that scientific discourse is to be emulated because of its proximity to reality. Since he believes that the rhetoric of 'science capturing the truth about the world' is no more than 'rhetoric', and hence no more intellectually justified than the rhetorical pats on the back modern politicians tend to award themselves, Rorty channels more of his energies into producing an account of culture in which the intellectual profile of science is flattened out – blended into the rest of the scenery so that it does not symbolize a pinnacle of achievement that all other disciplines should aspire to. Hence, for expository reasons, science is given a correspondingly low profile here. The main aim is to provide the kind of background material that enables readers to give a fair hearing to Rorty's own more nuanced discussions of science in articles like 'Science as solidarity' (ORT: 35–45).

4. Historicism and history

We have said that Rorty does not wish to argue in detail against assumptions of analytic tradition that he finds unfruitful or anachronistic. He does, however, seek to undermine their authority by suggesting ways in which they derive from history. To show that they are rooted in history has a destabilizing effect because historical events are *contingent*. Such events do not have the brute 'necessity' of their *having to take place* built into them. They need not have occurred – something else could have happened instead. Philosophical problems and their 'solutions' have been treated as non-contingent, ahistorical phenomena, as considerations that transcend 'time and chance'. Thus, for example, the problem as to how mind and matter are related – one way of characterizing the so-called 'mind–body problem' – is regarded as an issue that is bound to arise as soon as one reflects on the nature of these two concerns. For mind and body must *somehow* be related (because of the obvious causal traffic between them), but it is difficult to see how they *can* be related given that mind, having no discernible physical properties, appears to be immaterial. How is it possible for matter (e.g. in the brain) to exert a grip within the purely mental sphere of consciousness? Rorty's stress on the historical nature of philosophical problems – his 'historicism' – is designed to dispel the air of 'inevitability' that surrounds them. If, *as it could have done*, history had followed a different path, problems that now look as if they have forced themselves upon us by the sheer weight of their intrinsic intellectual difficulty and importance might never have surfaced. To achieve his aims, Rorty does not have to provide a definitive account of the relevant history; he merely has to tell a plausible story in which the 'possibility' that things might have been different is raised. For this reason, it is not worth taking time out in the present context to assess the 'historical accuracy' of Rorty's narratives concerning traditional philosophers such as Descartes, Locke and Kant. Once more there is plenty of room in serious scholarship for such assessment, but again not in an introductory text. It is more important to discuss whether the phenomenon of 'contingency' that he invokes via such narratives, accurate or otherwise, has the implications he presupposes. We take up this line of critical discussion in Chapter 4.

5. Substantive issues

If philosophy is all about confronting certain traditional, substantive issues, such as whether or not a person who has good, and relevant, reasons for believing something that is in point of fact true thereby takes possession of 'knowledge', then to avoid confronting those issues, to put them to one side as Rorty suggests, is to avoid actually doing philosophy. But, since Rorty challenges what philosophy 'is all about', we cannot simply exclude him from its realms when he neglects traditional issues. Furthermore, we cannot hope to get a clear view of what Rorty is seeking to achieve if we keep trying to tie the noose of such issues around his neck all the time he is talking to us. For the broad structure of his vision of an intellectual culture in which such issues are rendered obsolete to have a chance of emerging intact, he has to be given free rein.

The very obsession with evaluating particular 'substantive issues' according to traditional standards of correctness (which involve correlative conceptions of 'truth', 'knowledge', 'rationality', and so on) is one of Rorty's main 'therapeutic' targets, something he dearly wishes to free us from. Whether Rorty is thereby, knowingly or otherwise, tempting us to leave all non-arbitrary standards of correctness behind in the process (he claims he is not, that he is merely asking us to substitute more useful and relevant, pragmatist criteria) can only be clearly seen if we come out from behind that fixation.

In expounding Rorty's views without constantly pinning them to or comparing them with the backcloth of potential 'solutions' to traditional substantive issues, this book gives the reader a taste of what Rorty thinks life can be like when we do step out in this way into the philosophical fresh air. Our strategy incorporates some 'criticisms' – it does not throw the baby of independent assessment out with the bath-water of obstructive hyper-criticism. But it attempts to do so in a manner that cautiously acknowledges Rorty could very well be describing himself when he 'concludes' of Heidegger that he:

> has done as good a job of putting potential critics on the defensive as any philosopher in history. There is no standard by which one can measure him without begging the question against him. His remarks about the tradition and his remarks about the limitations the tradition has imposed on the vocabulary and imagination of his contemporaries, are beautifully designed to make one feel foolish when one tries to find a bit of common ground on which to start an argument.   (CP: 39)

Because of the widespread misunderstanding as to what Rorty is seeking to achieve, more of his critics tend to 'look foolish' than know that they do and hence ever actually 'feel foolish'. The misapprehension stems not just from the compulsion to locate everything Rorty says on the map of traditional philosophical concerns, but also from unwillingness, or perhaps inability, to take his staunch refusal to propound substantive claims seriously.

Hence, for example, when Rorty explicates his negative attitude to 'essentialism', he tends to be immediately saddled with 'anti-essentialist claims', the kind that directly counter 'essentialist claims', that rekindle traditional philosophical issues as to which set of claims is *really true*. But Rorty wishes to sidestep all of this. Essentialist claims – that human beings (or whatever) have an inherent (biological, genetic, psychological, or whatever) nature, and so on – are not things that Rorty wants to 'counter': he simply wants us to be rid of them, to conduct our lives without giving them much thought:

> To say that there is no such thing as intrinsic nature, is not to say that the intrinsic nature of reality has turned out, surprisingly enough, to be extrinsic. It is to say that the term "intrinsic nature" is one which it would pay us not to use, an expression which has caused more trouble than it has been worth. (CIS: 8)

The claims that Rorty *does* make are pitched, as in the passage just quoted, in very general terms and at a level where they are incommensurable with, and hence not reducible to, the kind of substantive claims that perpetuate traditional philosophical disputes. What level is this?

It is tempting to say 'the meta-philosophical level', that Rorty is making claims *about* philosophical claims rather than, as it were, *at them*. But to say *just this* would be wrong. The meta-philosophical level is not an incommensurable platform. Claims made there can still be engaged by moves that belong within traditional debates (for example: "What empirical evidence does Rorty have for claiming *of* essentialist claims that they have caused more trouble than they have been worth?") The same goes for the 'meta-linguistic level' – where Rorty is taken to be making claims about the words used to express claims (as opposed to the claims themselves).

Rorty's 'claims' may have the appearance of 'substantive' claims, but they are intended to serve a different *function*. They are not designed to instil a fresh set of beliefs derived from literal content of the statements they encapsulate, but rather to *prod* us, by way of 'edification' (Rorty's term for the "project of finding new, better, more fruitful ways of speaking" (PMN: 360)), into exploring fresh ways of describing things. So the 'level' in question is a sort of *extra-*

philosophical, performative level, a place outside traditional philosophy from which words are issued to change what is going on there.

The process involved here sounds mysterious, and to the extent that it succeeds in operating outside the realms of 'normal philosophizing', it must do. But there are prior models for the kind of thing Rorty is depicted as doing here. He himself instructively cites Wittgenstein and Heidegger:

> Edifying philosophers have to decry the very notion of having a view, while avoiding having a view about having views. This is an awkward, but not impossible position. Wittgenstein and Heidegger manage it fairly well. One reason they manage it as well as they do is that they do not think that when we say something we must necessarily be expressing a view about a subject. We might just be *saying something* – participating in a conversation rather than contributing to an inquiry. Perhaps saying things is not always saying how things are. Perhaps saying *that* is itself not a case of saying how things are. Both men suggest we see people as saying things, better or worse things, without seeing them as externalising inner representations of reality. But this is only their entering wedge, for then we must cease to see ourselves seeing this without beginning to see ourselves as seeing something else. We must get the visual, and in particular the mirroring, metaphors out of our speech altogether. To do that we have to understand speech not only as not the externalising of inner representations, but as not a representation at all. We have to drop the notion of correspondence for sentences as well as for thoughts, and see sentences as connected with other sentences rather than with the world. We have to see the term "corresponds to how things are" as an automatic compliment paid to successful normal discourse rather than as a relation to be studied and aspired to throughout the rest of discourse. To attempt to extend this compliment to feats of *abnormal* discourse is like complimenting a judge on his wise decision by leaving him fat tip: it shows a lack of tact. To think of Wittgenstein and Heidegger as having views about how things are is not to be wrong about how things are; it is just poor taste. It puts them in a position which they do not want to be in, and in which they look ridiculous. (PMN: 371–2)

Philosophical propaganda

I have no proposition, and therefore I have no fallacy.
(Nagarjuna, trans. 1978)

The philosopher C. W. Huntington has also suggested a much older, and perhaps, for that reason, more illuminating precedent for Rorty's 'viewless' approach.

In his book *The Emptiness of Emptiness: An Introduction to Early Indian Madhyamika* (1989), Huntington outlines the goals and practices of Madhyamika philosophy in terms that resonate instructively across cultures and centuries with Rorty's approach. Having described Madhyamika philosophy as a subtle form of critique that "rejects our most fundamental empirical propositions and the matrix of rationality in which they are cast as matters of strictly normative and ultimately groundless belief" (1989: 10), Huntington invokes a context that corresponds to Rorty's own: "The Madhyamika sets itself in opposition to a philosophical tradition which was preoccupied with the search for more and more precise technical terminology and had neglected the practical application of philosophical theory" (1989: xii). He then makes some further interesting comments regarding one of Madhyamika's chief scholars, the Buddhist monk Candrakirti:

> Although Candrakirti has no fixed position to defend, it does not follow that his arguments are mere sophistry, for genuine meaning and significance are to be found in their *purpose*. The critical distinction here is between systematic philosophy, concerned with the presentation of a particular view or belief, and edifying philosophy, engaged in strictly deconstructive activity (the Madhyamika *prasangavakya*). The central concepts of edifying philosophy must ultimately be abandoned when they have served the purpose for which they were designed. Such concepts are not used to express a view but *to achieve an effect*. They are a means (*upaya*). (1989: xiii)

Huntington refers to Madhyamika thought, with its great stress on 'achieving effects', as 'soteriological philosophy' or 'philosophical propaganda'. He uses these phrases for two reasons: first, to encourage recognition that "this philosophy cannot, even in theory, be disassociated from a concept of practical application"; and second, "so that it might be more clearly distinguished as a radical departure from the type of philosophical enterprise through which one endeavours to discover or define an objective, value-free view of truth or reality" (1989: xiii). Rorty's enterprise could be characterized in the same terms, and for very similar reasons. Indeed, one of the main aims of the present book is to show that Rorty's views, and hence his 'position-free position', are 'edifyingly' presented 'to achieve an effect', that they should not be 'tastelessly' interpreted as further, if oblique and controversial, contributions to philosophy's age-old quest for the final, truthful picture of reality.

Chapter 1
Platonic yearnings

'Platonism' in the sense in which I use the term does not denote the (very complex, shifting, dubiously consistent) thoughts of the genius who wrote the Dialogues. Instead, it refers to a set of philosophical distinctions (appearance–reality, matter–mind, made–found, sensible–intellectual, etc.): what Dewey called 'a brood and nest of dualisms'. These dualisms dominate the history of Western philosophy, and can be traced back to one or another passage in Plato. Dewey thought, as I do, that the vocabulary which centers around these traditional distinctions has become an obstacle to our social hopes.   (PSH: xii)

I wanted very much to be some kind of Platonist, and from 15–20 I did my best. But it didn't pan out.   (WO: 9)

Richard Rorty's philosophical career is epitomized by the tensions between these two quotations. He is frequently depicted as an analytic philosopher, originally of no mean talent, who unfortunately strayed from the fold to become, in Jonathan Rée's catchy phrase, "the bad boy of American philosophy" (Rée 1998: 7). This common characterization tends to trap Rorty in an incessant crossfire. For many philosophers now strenuously maintain that he strayed too far – beyond, even, the bounds of academic respectability. Then there are others, equally vocal, who continue to claim that Rorty did not stray nearly far enough, that, while still hostage to an outmoded and politically suspect analytical agenda, he is far less 'bad' than he ought to be.

Rorty's own, relatively late, account of his intellectual develop-ment and philosophical motivation discloses a more complex and, in the end, much more interesting, picture. It is a picture in which such incendiary disputes over his status regarding analytic philosophy fade quietly into the background.

Orchids and the oppressed

The account comes in the form of an engagingly frank and, at times, uncustomarily intimate essay: "Trotsky and the Wild Orchids" (WO), first published in *Wild Orchids and Trotsky: Messages from American Universities* (Edmundson 1993). In this intriguingly entitled piece, Rorty tells us that he came to philosophy enthused by a prior purpose, only to find it could not be fulfilled: "I have tried to say something about how I got into my present position – how I got into philosophy and then found myself unable to use philosophy for the purpose I originally had had in mind" (WO: 5). As his account unfolds, we find a bookish and yet very passionate Rorty emerging. We discover a precocious, idiosyncratic individual whose interests, even by his early teens, already prefigured the main themes of his much later writings such as *Contingency, irony, and solidarity*.

This Rorty just *knew* when he was twelve years old: "that the point of being human was to spend one's life fighting social injustice" (WO: 6). But, at the same time, he had various "private, weird, snobbish, incommunicable interests" he just could not let go of. These included an obsession with the mysterious 'orchids' of his title:

> I was not quite sure why those orchids were so important, but I was convinced that they were. I was sure that our noble, pure, chaste North American wild orchids were morally superior to the showy, hybridized, tropical orchids displayed in florists' shops. I was also convinced that there was a deep significance in the fact that they are the latest and most complex plants to have been developed in the course of evolution.   (WO: 7)

Rorty felt an increasingly uncomfortable tension between the urgency of his political concerns for the plight of the 'oppressed', such as union organizers, sharecroppers or coloured firemen, and the seductively timeless pull of his "dubious esotericism":

> I was uneasily aware, however, that there was something a bit dubious about this esotericism – this interest in socially useless flowers. I had read (in the vast amount of spare time given to a clever, snotty, nerdy only child) bits of *Marius the Epicurean*

and also bits of Marxist criticism of Pater's aestheticism. I was afraid that Trotsky (whose *Literature and Revolution* I had nibbled at) would not have approved of my interest in orchids.

(WO: 7)

Hence by the time he escaped the clutches of the "playground bullies" and went on to the University of Chicago, he longed to find a way of unifying these disparate concerns, to square his interests in both Trotsky and the orchids: "I wanted to find some 'intellectual' or aesthetic framework which could let me – in a thrilling phrase which I came across in Yeats – 'hold reality and justice in a single vision'" (WO: 7). The 'reality' Rorty gestures towards by way of Yeats's 'thrilling phrase' was irredeemably *esoteric*. It was the blissful focus of his 'socially useless', private interests:

> By 'reality' I meant, more or less, the Wordsworthian moments in which in the woods around Flatbrookville (and especially in the presence of certain coralroot orchids, and of the smaller yellow lady slipper), I had felt touched by something numinous, something of ineffable importance. (WO: 7–8)

Failures of reconciliation

What were Rorty's options? As he recalls things, "much of the University of Chicago" was "enveloped in a neo-Aristotelian mystique" (WO: 8). Ironically, given his later predilections, this helped to make Dewey's pragmatism, with its forthright eschewal of all 'absolutes', seem far too superficial for Rorty's high-minded project of 'reconciliation'. Furthermore, since Dewey was revered by the people Rorty had grown up with, pouring intellectual scorn on him was "a convenient form of adolescent revolt" (WO: 8–9).

In the light of T. S. Eliot's "suggestions that only committed Christians (and perhaps only Anglo-Catholics) could overcome their unhealthy preoccupations with their private obsessions, and so serve their fellow humans with proper humility" (WO: 9), even religion seemed a better bet.

But only briefly. A "prideful inability" to take the recitation of the General Confession seriously led Rorty to abandon his unwieldy "attempts to get religion" (*ibid.*). After this spiritual disappointment, Rorty "fell back on absolutist philosophy" (*ibid.*), and on Platonism in particular.

Richard Rorty

He had read through enough Plato during his "fifteenth summer" to persuade himself that Socrates was right to equate virtue and knowledge. However, when looking back, Rorty also suggests his view was deeply coloured by a stubborn perception that, because there was no other way of bringing 'numinous reality' and 'social justice' into harmony, there was but one choice: "Socrates *had* to be right" (WO: 9). On that noble, but perhaps rather unstable, basis, Rorty was moved to major in philosophy:

> I figured that if I became a philosopher, I might get to the top of Plato's 'divided line' – the place 'beyond hypotheses' where the full sunshine of Truth irradiates the purified soul of the wise and good: an Elysian field dotted with immaterial orchids. It seemed obvious to me that getting to such a place was what everybody with any brains really wanted to do. (WO: 9)

True to his fluctuating form up to this point, Rorty's 'Platonic phase' did not last very long. The conflicts that inveigled him there in the first instance resurfaced with a vengeance. He was unable even to conceive how a Platonic philosopher could ever proceed without striving for *either* "argumentative power over others" *or* "a sort of incommunicable, private bliss" (WO: 10). To Rorty, *both* goals "seemed desirable", but he still "could not see how they could be fitted together" (*ibid.*). On top of this, he was seriously bothered by another, more general problem, one that appeared to threaten "the whole Socratic–Platonic idea of replacing passion by reason" (*ibid.*). This 'predicament' would later resonate in various related forms throughout much of his work in philosophy. The problem was simply, and yet devastatingly, this: How can *any* philosophers ever furnish objective, "non-circular justification" of their views?

Without such 'justification', it seemed that traditional philosophy, the ambitious kind of thinking that derived from the Greeks, would have drastically to trim its sails. And Rorty had begun to doubt seriously whether this kind of 'justification' was possible: "The more philosophers I read, the clearer it seemed that each of them could carry their views back to first principles which were incompatible with the first principles of their opponents, and that none of them ever got to that fabled place 'beyond hypotheses'" (WO: 10). By now, as he moved from Chicago to take a PhD at Yale, Rorty was irksomely aware that, with his grand fixation on 'reconciliation', he had painted himself into a tricky corner.

It appeared that his choice of views and corresponding intellectual positions *as a philosopher* would always be unstable. They would be vulnerable to attacks on their 'foundations' and exposed to the ravages of time for as long as they survived such attacks. At any juncture, such choices might be devastatingly undermined simply by being made to look 'arbitrary'. There was little prospect of finding a *position-independent* source of justification for particular philosophical views because "there seemed to be nothing like a neutral standpoint from which alternative first principles could be evaluated" (WO: 10). And this meant – or so it appeared to Rorty then – that no significantly principled philosophical position could be demonstrated to be 'objectively' (or 'in reality') better than any other such position. Furthermore, the 'immaterial orchids' were left dangling. The hallowed places where they sprang up could not be reached, it had apparently transpired, by mere philosophizing. Chained, as Nietzsche described it, "by the Socratic love of knowledge and the delusion of being thereby able to heal the eternal wound of existence" (Nietzsche 1967: s. 18), a philosopher must forever forfeit the illumination of orchidaceous bliss. It would be some time before Rorty conceived of a utopia, the vanguard of which would be constituted by 'ironists', those who had carved out a personal space for bliss and also learned to live with, perhaps even celebrate, 'philosophical instability'.

Hegelian detour

Rorty has never achieved the kind of ideal *philosophical* reconciliation of personal and public interests he sought in youth. But he began to 'see through' the whole project when he 'rediscovered Dewey'. A lengthy detour, starting with Hegel's monumental *Phenomenology of Spirit*, a book that had greatly influenced Dewey himself, prepared much of the ground.

Rorty took Hegel to be saying the sort of things that chimed very congenially with his own growing sense of how philosophy should be done absent the very possibility of impartial justification or 'neutral ground': "Granted philosophy is just a matter of out-redescribing the last philosopher, the cunning of reason can make use even of this sort of competition. It can use it to weave the conceptual fabric of a freer, better, more just society" (WO: 11).

Since Rorty sensed he had something of a "flair for redescription" (WO: 10), he also felt he could freely turn his philosophical hand to matters of social justice. Perhaps he could even "do what Marx wanted done – change the world" (WO: 11). As for those ineliminable orchids, Rorty hit on an *ad hoc* solution by moving on to an agreeable substitute in the shape of the similarly esoteric and refined pleasures of Proust's *Remembrance of Things Past*:

> Proust's ability to weave intellectual and social snobbery together with the hawthorns around Combray, his grandmother's selfless love, Odette's orchidaceous embraces of Swann and Jupien's of Charlus, and with everything else he encountered – to give each its due without feeling the need to bundle them together with the help of a religious faith or a philosophical theory – seemed to me as astonishing as Hegel's ability to throw himself successively into empiricism, Greek tragedy, Stoicism, Christianity and Newtonian physics, and to emerge from each, ready and eager for something completely different.   (WO: 11)

Here, it seemed, Rorty had at last begun to achieve an acceptable degree of harmony in his outlook without having to put a reconciliatory squeeze on his personal interests: "It was the cheerful commitment to irreducible temporality which Hegel and Proust shared – the specifically anti-Platonic element in their work – that seemed so wonderful" (WO: 11).

Rediscovering Dewey

Rorty returned to Dewey roughly twenty years after he "decided that the young Hegel's willingness to stop trying for eternity and just be the child of his time, was the appropriate response to disillusionment with Plato" (WO: 12). In Rorty's belatedly opened eyes, Dewey could now be seen as a philosopher who showed that it was possible to take on board everything Hegel had taught about the advantages of setting aside 'certainty' and 'eternity' without needing to compensate by way of anything grand and unscientific like 'pantheism'. Over the years, he became Rorty's "principal philosophical hero" (PSH: xii).

From Derrida to Heidegger

We will discuss Rorty's response to Dewey in a bit more detail when we examine his 'pragmatism' in Chapter 3. Meanwhile, we should

note that while Rorty was 'rediscovering Dewey', he also had his first
encounter with, on the face of it, a very different kind of thinker:
Jacques Derrida. This encounter led him "back to Heidegger" (WO:
12). Some forty years later, Rorty generously praised the role that
the philosopher Hubert Dreyfus played in facilitating his encounters
with 'European' thought:

> My own acquaintance with European philosophy owes almost
> everything to Dreyfus. Back in the late 1950s, when I was at
> Wellesley and Dreyfus was at Harvard, he encouraged me to
> read Merleau-Ponty and tried to convince me that Husserl was
> not nearly as pointless as I thought. Had I not been intrigued by
> his account of Husserl's break with Descartes, I should never
> have taught *Cartesian Meditations*. By helping John Wild and
> others translate the early portions of *Sein und Zeit* and letting
> me reproduce copies of the result, Dreyfus made it possible for
> me to assign bits of that book to my Wellesley classes. (This
> underground, unauthorised, mimeographed translation was the
> basis for most teaching of Heidegger in the United States prior
> to the publication, in 1962, of the Macquarries and Robinson
> translation. People whose German was weak but knew Dreyfus
> had a head start.) Toward the end of the 60s, when I started
> reading Derrida, Dreyfus was one of the few friends with whom I
> could hash over *La Voix et le Phenomène* and who could explain
> to me what was going on in Paris.   (Rorty 2000: ix–x)

Such encounters instigated a chain of perceived 'similarities' in
Rorty's readings of various philosophers. These enabled him to eventually weave together a number of threads in his thinking:

> I was struck by the resemblances between Dewey's, Wittgen-
> stein's and Heidegger's criticisms of Cartesianism. Suddenly
> things began to come together. I thought I saw a way to blend a
> criticism of the Cartesian tradition with the quasi-Hegelian
> historicism of Michel Foucault, Ian Hacking and Alasdair
> MacIntyre. I thought that I could fit all these into a quasi-
> Heideggerian story about the tensions within Platonism.
>   (WO: 12)

The 'story' – "the result of this small epiphany" (WO: 12) as Rorty
modestly describes it – was published in 1979 as *Philosophy and the
Mirror of Nature*, Rorty's first major book-length work. This text questions the dominance of 'theory of knowledge' in Western philosophy

and thereby opens up the horizons of its practice to an extent that may never have been achieved before. This "large-scale, frontal assault on representationalist epistemology and metaphysics" (Ramberg 2000: 351) is the main focus of Chapter 2.

Changing the subject

> To see keeping a conversation going as a sufficient aim of philosophy, to see wisdom as consisting in the ability to sustain a conversation, is to see human beings as generators of new descriptions rather than beings we hope to be able to describe accurately. (PMN: 378)

In the commonly held picture of Rorty's intellectual development we invoked at the outset, *Philosophy and the Mirror of Nature* usually signals his attempt to put analytic philosophy firmly behind him and strike out into fresh territory. When exploring this territory, it would no longer be necessary for him to be concerned about whether there were any Platonic landmarks or vantage points for "understanding the world . . . from a position outside time and history" (WO: 11).

In the opinion of the first set of critics we alluded to – those who were scandalized by his attempted departure from analytic philosophy – his leap into new realms was all too successful. Thereafter, in their view, Rorty's brand of 'philosophizing-without-landmarks-or-vantage-points' could make no significant contribution to the progress of analytic philosophy or any of its recognized progeny. In Rorty's hands, philosophy's 'horizons' were opened out on to a vacant lot. The other batch of critics may allow that Rorty crossed a few bridges, but they think he should have done something more radical – like blowing *all* such bridges up – to mark his commitment to new philosophical territory. Rorty's own account of his underlying motivation and his lofty ambitions indicates that he was never a real, dyed in the wool, analytic philosopher – any more than he was a genuine Christian or a fully fledged Platonist, and that both sides here have therefore missed the point. But should we trust Rorty's own account on this score?

First instincts and circumstantial evidence may suggest we should not. Autobiography is notoriously a charter for dissemblance and rationalization. Furthermore, the author of "Trotsky and the

Wild Orchids" is a self-confessed, and provenly able, 'redescriber'. Not only that; he is an arch sceptic about the notion of 'truth as accurate representation' who holds that the best and, ultimately, *only* non-deceptive, way to establish a philosophical point is to 'make it look good' relative to the closest competing alternatives. This should surely make us very cautious about attributing literal truth to his claims. Caution regarding such truth aside, it seems that Rorty did enough sustained work in analytic philosophy *before* he published *Philosophy and the Mirror of Nature* – on eliminative materialism, Strawson's attempt to improve upon Kant's central argument of the *Transcendental Deduction*, and so on – to make his personal agenda irrelevant to debates concerning the accuracy of the targeting of familiar complaints that he is a 'turncoat'.

Suppose that someone who once worked in logic and produced solid publications in that field later moved away from the discipline and then, still later, announced, in a self-revealing autobiographical account, that all the time they had been doing logic they were trying to make it conform to some conflicting, extra-logical, private purposes for which it could never be suited? Would we want to say that this person was never a 'real logician'?

The parallel case we are alluding to – for saying that, at one stage, Rorty's writings earned him the tag 'analytic philosopher' whether he now likes it or not – has similar surface plausibility. But closer inspection of Rorty's actual published work during the period in question suggests that his whole relationship to analytic philosophy was far more tenuous than the conferral of such a tag normally implies. It further suggests that this 'tenuousness' is perhaps best explained by recognizing the degree to which the relationship was infected by the instability of Rorty's motivation for entering philosophy in the first place, as reported in "Trotsky and the Wild Orchids". Thus, on this view, Rorty's reflections in 'Trotsky and the Wild Orchids' look much more like plain honest 'description' than opportunistic 'redescription'.

The publications of Rorty's so-called 'analytic period' manifested a sensitivity to the historical context of 'philosophical problems', a lack of confidence in any notion of a unilateral 'philosophical method', an empathy with classic American pragmatism and an abiding interest in meta-philosophical issues, all of which went against the established analytic way of doing business. On the 'Rorty-as-an-analytic-philosopher-gone-bad/-not-bad-enough' scenario, one of Rorty's most important publications of that time – a now 'classic' collection, *The*

Richard Rorty

Linguistic Turn: Essays in Philosophical Method (LT) – ought to constitute a *celebration* of the achievements of analytic philosophy. And indeed, in a retrospective essay, "Twenty-Five Years Later" (LT 1992), Rorty takes himself to task for treating "the phenomenon of the 'linguistic turn'" far too seriously in the following 'celebratory' passage from his original 'editorial introduction':

> Linguistic philosophy, over the past thirty years, has succeeded in putting the entire philosophical tradition, from Parmenides through Descartes and Hume to Bradley and Whitehead, on the defensive. It has done so by a careful and thorough scrutiny of the ways in which traditional philosophers have used language in the formulation of their problems. This achievement is sufficient to place this period among the great ages of the history of philosophy. (LT: 371)

Of this last sentence, Rorty says it is one he is "startled, embarrassed, and amused to reread". He then further comments that it:

> now strikes me as merely the attempt of a thirty-three-year-old philosopher to convince himself that he had the luck to be born at the right time – to persuade himself that the disciplinary matrix in which he happened to find himself (philosophy as taught in most English-speaking universities in the 60s) was more than just one more philosophical school, one more tempest in an academic teapot. (LT 1992: 371)

What Rorty overlooks in this somewhat bemused self-assessment is the incipiently subversive framework of discussion within which his formerly triumphant sentiments are voiced. For Rorty begins his introduction with what, for any straightforwardly analytic philosopher, would be an uncharacteristically *historicist* – virtually 'Hegelian' – account of 'revolutions' in philosophy. Moreover, although he does not express open hostility to 'linguistic philosophy', he demonstrates that he has thought uncommonly long and hard about the potential cracks in its self-congratulatory image. Rorty is thus correspondingly guarded about both the degree of linguistic philosophy's success and its long-term prospects.

In putting forward this historicist account and then reflecting on successive, abortive attempts to introduce 'presuppositionless methods', Rorty again raises the threat of 'circularity'. He does this in the very terms that were later to be echoed by his recollected worries about 'non-circular justification' in "Trotsky and the Wild Orchids":

To know what method to adopt, one must already have arrived at some metaphysical and some epistemological conclusions. If one attempts to defend these conclusions by the use of one's chosen method, one is open to the charge of circularity. If one does not so defend them, maintaining that given these conclusions, the need to adopt the chosen method follows, one is open to the charge that the chosen method is inadequate, for it cannot be used to establish the crucial metaphysical and epistemological theses which are in dispute. Since philosophical method is in itself a philosophical topic (or, in other words, since different criteria for the satisfactory solution of a philosophical problem are adopted, and argued for, by different schools of philosophers), every philosophical revolutionary is open to the charge of circularity or to the charge of having begged the question.   (LT: 1–2)

He also speculates that if, after having failed in its pretensions to become "a strict science" and having taken up "a merely critical, essentially dialectical function" (LT: 33), linguistic philosophy still manages to 'dissolve' all traditional problems in the sense "that no one is able to think of any formulations of these questions which are immune to the sort of criticisms made by linguistic philosophers" (*ibid.*), the future of philosophy might unfold in one of six possible ways. Rorty describes these in a bit more detail than is relevant here, but in short they come down to:

1. Analytic philosophy is regarded "as having led to a dead end" because a branch of philosophy springs up which does "not involve the reduction of questions about the nature of things either to empirical questions or to questions about language" (LT: 34). Phenomenology is a suggestive example here.
2. Philosophy "grows closer to poetry". Heidegger's later essays might be an example of this – "an attempt to do philosophy in an entirely new way" (*ibid.*).
3. Philosophers concern themselves with "the creation of new, interesting and fruitful ways of thinking about things in general" (*ibid.*). They could do this on the scale of "the great tradition of philosophy as system building – the only difference being that the systems built would no longer be considered *descriptions* of the nature of things or of human consciousness, but rather *proposals* about how to talk" (*ibid.*).
4. Philosophy might be regarded "as a cultural disease which has

been cured". It might come to an end with any residual concerns being taken over "by the arts, the sciences, or both" (*ibid.*).

5. "It might be that empirical linguistics can in fact provide us with non-banal formulations of the necessary and sufficient conditions for the truth of statements, and non-banal accounts of the meaning of words. Granted that these formulations and accounts would apply only to our present linguistic practices, it might be that the discovery of such formulations and accounts would satisfy at least some of the instincts which originally led (us) to philosophise" (LT: 35).

6. "It might be that linguistic philosophy could transcend its merely critical function by turning itself into an activity which, instead of inferring from facts about linguistic behavior to the dissolution of traditional problems, discovers necessary and sufficient conditions for the possibility of language itself (in a fashion analogous to the way in which Kant purportedly discovered the necessary and sufficient conditions for the possibility of experience)" (*ibid.*).

This catalogue of possibilities, of 'what might be', is fairly generous towards 'linguistic philosophy', but it is hardly the product of a mind that is entirely happy to work within the confines of this tradition's ideology and preferred 'methods'. The 'moral' that Rorty himself draws from his discussion of philosophy's future is uncannily predictive of his own: "The only moral that may be drawn, I think, is that the meta-philosophical struggles of the future will center on the issue of reform versus description, of philosophy-as-proposal versus philosophy-as discovery" (LT: 38).

What should we make of all this? Probably that our original assessment of Rorty's account of his intellectual development in 'Trotsky and the Wild Orchids' pointed the way forward, that 'disputes over his status regarding analytic philosophy' *should* be allowed to 'fade into the background'. Perhaps some commentators will be able to show that we can come to a better understanding of Rorty by contrasting him, either positively or negatively, with particular analytic philosophers or uncovering interesting developmental connections between specific articles Rorty published during his so-called 'analytic' period and his later writings – so that they have something more interesting to propose than our suggestion that the trail of Rorty's alleged defection from analytic philosophy leads right back through most of his early work. Meanwhile, we should concede that in this respect, at least, and for present 'introductory purposes', Rorty has convinced us to 'change the subject'.

To what? Well, we need to discuss the significance of what we called Rorty's 'first major, book-length work': *Philosophy and the Mirror of Nature*. Then we ought to examine the kind of 'pragmatism' he thinks should supplant the philosophical problems, methods and traditions he criticizes in that book. After that, we should review *Contingency, irony and solidarity*, the book in which, to pick up the plot again from "Trotsky and the Wild Orchids", Rorty at last set aside every vestige of his quest for 'reconciliation', and tried to show "what intellectual life might be like if one could manage to give up on the Platonic attempt to hold reality and justice in a single vision" (WO: 13). Finally, we can then turn to the main fruit of much of Rorty's labour: his political philosophy, with the main focus on his conception of 'liberalism'. Each of these subjects is considered consecutively over the next four chapters before we take some time out in Chapter 6 to consider the reactions of Rorty's critics and then bring things to a close in Chapter 7 with some concluding reflections on his 'legacy'.

Chapter 2

Conversation

> If we see knowledge as a matter of conversation and of social practice, rather than as an attempt to mirror nature, we will not be likely to envisage a metapractice which will be the critique of all possible forms of social practice. (PMN: 171)

In *Philosophy and the Mirror of Nature*, Rorty contends that, from Plato onwards, Western philosophy has viewed itself as just such a 'metapractice'. He argues that it should now cease to do so because there is no longer much point in 'seeing knowledge' as anything more than 'a matter of conversation and social practice'. Rorty's critics tend to sneer at the contention because they singularly fail to grasp how much is packed into the notions of 'conversation' and 'social practice'. For this reason, they cannot help substituting a derogatory, reductive "merely" for "anything more than". This chapter shows how to avoid such a crass lack of understanding of Rorty's position.

He only ever makes occasional, modest, low-key references to it in his later writings, but PMN was a major achievement by any standards. It had great influence on Western philosophy by opening up new areas for discussion and highlighting the work of thinkers hitherto marginalized (e.g. Heidegger), ignored (e.g. Foucault and Derrida) or simply forgotten (e.g. Dewey). But it also had a big impact on intellectual culture as a whole. Its revisionary conception of epistemic justification "as a social phenomenon rather than a transaction between 'the knowing subject' and 'reality'" (PMN: 9) provided much provocative food for thought in diverse areas ranging from literary theory to legal studies.

The book signalled a turning point in Rorty's career. Indeed, after its publication in 1980, neither the author nor philosophy itself would ever be quite the same again. There had been other critiques of analytic philosophy, but none with the combined range and depth of Rorty's – and certainly none that interpreted analytic philosophy as a "variant" on a succession of traditional attempts – from Plato onwards – "to escape from history" (PMN: 9). For, as Cornel West points out, "Rorty's story constitutes the first major effort of analytic philosophers to engage critically in historical reflection and interpretation of themselves and their discipline" (West 1989: 199).

The project

Rorty's project is remarkably ambitious: to liberate much of Western philosophy from its bankrupt and self-deceptive past. And he wants to do this by showing how traditional philosophical concerns are both *problematic* and *optional*.

These concerns are 'problematic' in the sense that they are pragmatically unfruitful, tend to lead to stalemate situations and depend, in any case, on hopeless, vainglorious 'representational' assumptions (e.g. that the mind can only come to know reality by representing it correctly). They are 'optional' because they are the product of what, in Rorty's later work, he calls 'time and chance' rather than some form of rational inevitability. To display their 'optional status', Rorty describes how these concerns emerged from a sequence of historical moves that began with Plato's contention that differences in the degree of certainty to which things are known must correspond to differences in those things themselves, were modified by Descartes's methodological scepticism and his correlative epistemic conception of the mind as something that knows itself better than it knows anything else, were then transformed into the Lockean empirical project of determining the scope and limits of human knowledge by discerning the capacities of the mind and finally revolutionized by Kant's view that the knowable aspects of *all* objects of empirical knowledge, both 'inner' and 'outer', are shaped by the mind's inherent cognitive constitution. This special knowledge, of the mind's essential role in the acquisition of knowledge, can be studied by non-empirical means, and it puts epistemology – the *theory* of knowledge – in the driving seat of philosophy while, at the same time, giving the latter an apparently privileged position in culture as a whole. Nothing that comes later, such as developments in the philosophy of language, displaces episte-mology because nobody challenges the larger preconceptions that make the whole sequence of events in question look like an *inevitable* unfolding of the only rational line of inquiry. In fact, as we will shortly see, Rorty thinks that some of those who play a big part in 'what comes later' sow the dialectical seeds of the destruction of this sequence, leaving epistemology stranded.

The details of Rorty's aims are carefully outlined in the "Introduc-tion" (PMN: 3–13), an intensely provocative text which, like his earlier opening piece in *The Linguistic Turn*, is worthy of study in its own right (not least in this case, as we shall shortly see, to dispel the mis-conceptions which tend to arise concerning what the author of PMN set out to achieve). Rorty candidly informs the reader that "The aim of the book is to undermine the reader's confidence in 'the mind' as some-thing about which one should have a 'philosophical view', in 'knowl-edge' as something about which there ought to be a 'theory' and which has 'foundations', and in 'philosophy' as it has been conceived since Kant" (PMN: 7).

To grasp the significance of this large, 'confidence-breaking' undertaking, we need to do at least three things that, for whatever reason, many of Rorty's fiercest critics seem to have neglected to do. First, we need to see how his chosen targets, 'mind', 'knowledge' and 'philosophy' – the three topics that structure the whole book – are connected. What brings *them* together in his field of fire? Secondly, we need to recognize the unique way in which Rorty intends to attain his stated aims. And finally, we need to be completely clear about what Rorty wants to do when he has achieved his aims. For after Rorty has destroyed the kind of 'confidence' he refers to, he has no plans to rebuild anything of a kindred spirit. Let us now look a bit more closely at these considerations.

Mind, knowledge and philosophy

Once upon a time, in some out of the way corner of that universe which is dispersed into numberless twinkling solar systems, there was a star upon which clever beasts invented 'knowing'. That was the most arrogant and mendacious minute of 'world history', but nevertheless, it was only a minute. After nature had drawn a few breaths, the star cooled and congealed, and the clever beasts had to die. (Nietzsche 1967: 1)

Rorty's notion of 'traditional philosophy' provides the link between his three main 'targets'. The notion is thoroughly 'epistemologized'. It depicts philosophy as the 'will to knowledge' of 'clever beasts'. On this understanding, philosophy "as a discipline" has always been inclined to view "itself as the attempt to underwrite or debunk claims to knowledge made by science, morality, art or religion" (PMN: 3).

'Mind' makes up the second part of the whole package here because it is so intimately involved in the way traditional philosophy has convinced itself that it can assess 'knowledge claims': "it purports to do this on the basis of its special understanding of knowledge and of mind" (PMN: 3).

The 'special understanding' of knowledge comes in two principal forms. It comes, first, as a grasp of what knowledge is – its *essence*: knowledge is *reality truly represented* ("to know is to represent accurately what is outside the mind" (PMN: 3)). And secondly – given this account of what knowledge actually is – it comes as comprehension of the proper criteria for determining 'accurate representation'.

Special understanding of the mind has two analogous modes. The first involves an understanding of the essential nature of mind itself as the mirror-like locus of representations: "The picture which holds traditional philosophy captive is that of the mind as a great mirror, containing various representations – some accurate, some not – and capable of being studied by nonempirical means" (PMN: 12). And the second mode of understanding concerns the genesis and correlative 'conditions of possibility' of such representations. It fields questions like: "Where did 'representations' come from?", "How were they 'formed'?", and "Under what conditions *could* they be so formed?"

In each instance, the 'special understanding' tends to derive from a prior, broader cultural outlook, one that *already* brings 'knowledge' and 'minds' together. It does this by assuming they are tailored for one another in *some* sense (e.g. God carves out the appropriate representations in the mind, ensuring an innate epistemic link with reality (rationalism) or the world causally imprints itself on the mind, forging just such a 'link' (empiricism)). It goes without saying that to discover this sense of a mind–knowledge 'fit' is to discover something of great and everlasting philosophical value.

Though purists, those who desperately want to believe that 'knowledge' is only philosophically interesting when considered *in its own right and on its own terms*, like to deceive themselves to the contrary, the 'value' concerned is not solely *intellectual*. It is also *practical* – perhaps primarily practical. For such a 'discovery' gives philosophy the right and the power to oversee all other disciplines and thus remain at the pinnacle of culture where the Greeks so properly and presciently placed it.

Things can work out like this, squarely in philosophy's self-interest, because "culture is the assemblage of claims to knowledge" – which means that philosophers are able to use their 'special understanding' and its concomitant 'valuable discovery' to "adjudicate such claims" (PMN: 3). In this way, the discipline of philosophy thinks it can achieve what Rorty believes it has invariably regarded as its 'central concern': "To be a general theory of representation, a theory which will divide culture up into areas which represent reality well, those which represent it less well, and those which do not represent it at all (despite their pretense of doing so)" (*ibid.*).

Rorty's approach

Rorty's approach is multifaceted. He uses a great variety of '*ad hoc* techniques'. For our introductory purposes, these can nevertheless be subsumed under the following customized headings: 'argument', 'historical recontextualization', 'appropriation' and 'narrative'. In short, he uses whatever seems appropriate to achieve his aims.

The very phrase '*ad hoc* techniques' acknowledges Rorty's robust scepticism about methodology. He does not have much faith in the efficacy of standard philosophical techniques as such. Moreover, he is disenchanted with the whole idea of philosophers devising special 'methods' to give their discipline an edge over the rest of intellectual culture. In 'Keeping Philosophy Pure: An Essay on Wittgenstein', published in 1976 a few years before PMN, Rorty remarks that "*Philosophers are forever claiming to have discovered methods which are presuppositionless, or perfectly rigorous, or transcendental, or at any rate* purer *than those of nonphilosophers*" (CP: 19, original emphasis). And, in a contemporaneous article, "Method, Social Science, and Social Hope", he suggests that the illusion that there is some uncommon philosophical method and accompanying 'terminology' out there, waiting to be discovered, will be dispelled "If, with Dewey, one sees vocabularies as instruments for coping with things rather than representations of their intrinsic nature" (CP: 198). None of the customized labels for Rorty's *ad hoc* measures is entirely transparent. Hence a few words of explanation are required.

The reader should bear in mind that, even though we describe these 'techniques' separately, they are deployed *interdependently* in Rorty's text. A good example of this 'interdependence' is Rorty's hybrid use of 'argument' and 'appropriation'.

Rorty regards himself as carrying "the dialectic within analytic philosophy . . . a few steps further" (PMN: 7). But these are radical steps which will, he thinks, "put us in a position to criticise the very notion of 'analytic philosophy', and indeed of 'philosophy' itself as it has been understood since the time of Kant" (PMN: 7–8). To illustrate this dialectic, Rorty focuses on certain 'internal critiques' of assumptions at the heart of the analytic tradition. Thus, for example, he homes in on Sellars's celebrated attack on 'the Myth of the Given' – the idea that knowledge can reside in isolation as a personally identifiable *ingredient* of particular experiences, that there are "self-authenticating non-verbal episodes" (Sellars 1963: 167). An example would be a 'raw feel'. In the process of 'identification' for this previous case, we may "think of the [Inner] Eye simply turning inwards and spotting a raw feel" and then: "The whole complex of social institutions and behavioural manifestations which surround reports of such raw feels seems irrelevant" (PMN: 108). When Rorty appeals to Sellars's arguments, and to his alternative social–contextual account of knowledge, he is both using argument to further his aims and appropriating the work of another philosopher. The result is a position on knowledge that Rorty calls "epistemological behaviorism", the thrust of which is the explanation of "rationality and epistemic authority by reference to what society lets us say, rather than the latter by the former" (PMN: 174).

Rorty says he prefers to call this position "epistemological behaviorism rather than 'pragmatism' because the phrase is less 'over-laden'" (PMN: 176). However, although the relevant chapter (i.e. Chapter 4) is pivotal and Rorty makes some passing references to this epistemic form of behaviourism later in his career, "pragmatism" soon finds favour again after PMN, overladen or not.

Argument

Because of his sceptical stance on philosophical methodology in general, Rorty's dependence on 'argument' – the most conventional component in his overall approach – is curtailed by considerations of 'utility', and deliberately so. He does not believe there is anything wrong with arguments as such (so he is not vulnerable to the simplistic charges of 'irrationality', 'self-refutation' and 'incoherence' that are often thrown his way). His general position is simply that 'argument' is not the be all and end all of philosophy. If a particular argument looks as if it will do the trick effectively – that is, quickly and without the need for too much elaboration – Rorty is happy to employ it. But his overall strategy is intended to circumvent any requirement for the kind of sustained, detailed lines of argument that characterize previous philosophical ventures.

To argue in detail and at length against the tradition he wishes to debunk and, in the end, move away from would be to risk entrapment. Rorty regards the history of that tradition as a series of such 'entrapments' – where those who consider themselves to be making 'progress' by 'arguing against' the positions of their predecessors are actually *continuing* the tradition by shoring up its common ground and unwittingly confirming its underlying principles and presuppositions. He therefore wants to 'set aside' both the 'problems' and 'methods' by which traditional philosophy has defined its self-image – a tactic he attributes to his chief protagonists, Wittgenstein, Heidegger and Dewey. In a key passage we quoted from earlier in our Introduction, he depicts these primarily as thinkers who:

> Set aside epistemology and metaphysics as possible disciplines. I say "set aside" rather than "argue against" because their attitude toward the traditional problematic is like the attitude of seventeenth-century philosophers toward the scholastic problematic. They do not devote themselves to discovering false propositions or bad arguments in the works of their predecessors (though they occasionally do that too). Rather they glimpse the possibility of a form of intellectual life in which the vocabulary of philosophical reflection inherited from the seventeenth century would seem as pointless as the thirteenth-century philosophical vocabulary had seemed to the Enlightenment. (PMN: 6)

Arguments are thus invoked only when Rorty assumes they are liable to have the right 'causal effect', when they can ease the process of turning us away from philosophy's established concerns. The other 'techniques' are more innovative, and more directly linked with this 'turning-away process', if only because Rorty has much more personal control over them.

Richard Rorty

Historical recontextualization

> A lack of historical sensibility is the original failing of all philosophers. (Nietzsche 1995: 16)

> Just as the patient needs to relive his past to answer his questions, so philosophy needs to relive its past in order to answer its questions. (PMN: 33)

There are two major aspects to Rorty's use of historical considerations in PMN: the 'all-encompassing picture' and the 'timely sketch'. With regard to the first, he tries to envelop his whole venture in the cloak of history by advancing what his friend and seasoned commentator Richard Bernstein has called "a distinctive (and controversial) interpretation of how the history of philosophy has developed" (Bernstein 1992: 19). As for the second consideration, here Rorty constructs topic-specific, 'vignettes' – ostensibly, or so one might be led to believe, to flesh out the historical details of the broader picture. However, although both 'aspects' lend *context* to Rorty's revisionary accounts of 'mind', 'knowledge' and 'philosophy', they are both still resolutely *ad hoc*. Furthermore, their relationship is not primarily 'evidential'; that is, not one in which the 'vignettes' are supposed to stand mainly as *confirmations* of the larger story. To think otherwise is to underestimate how radical Rorty's approach is. He is not interested in 'setting aside' philosophy only to then replace it with 'the definitive history of philosophy' and the severe external constraints on 'accuracy of portrayal' that usually come with such territory.

Rorty's 'history-of-philosophy' – on both the large and the small scale – is history strictly in the service of his desire to show that the problems traditionally regarded as 'perennial' – the kind of problems that philosophers want us to believe "arise as soon as one reflects" (PMN: 3) – are *optional*, and that engagement with them can now be nothing more than an obstacle to the pursuit of better things. That said, it is worth looking more closely at the 'all-encompassing picture' and the 'timely sketches'. What do they involve? How do they contribute to Rorty's strategy?

The 'big picture' invokes the epistemologized conception of philosophy mentioned above, and endeavours to show how thinkers in various guises have, throughout the history of philosophy, aspired to meet the 'internal demands' of that conception – to figure out the *essential features* of knowledge and, *on that basis*, to codify culture-wide, trans-historical guidelines for distinguishing between genuine and bogus knowledge claims. But that is not the whole story.

Rorty is able to throw the blanket of 'epistemology' over a diverse string of thinkers spanning a very long period of time because he subscribes to a *de-intellectualized* interpretation of how change occurs in the realm of philosophical ideas. It is this interpretation that Bernstein calls 'distinctive'.

The central thought behind this interpretation is that generally speaking intellectual change charts a capricious path. It is not simply a matter of human beings 'reasoning' themselves, collectively or otherwise, from one position to another. Accounts that suggest reason, or something akin to it such as philosophical 'argument' or 'theory', always guides the way, that try to sweep the messy, haphazard details of historical progress conveniently under the carpet, are self-serving *rationalizations*.

Change in philosophy

How Rorty thinks 'change' happens in the case of philosophy itself is perceptively described by Bernstein in the following passage:

> There are moments in history when, because of all sorts of historical accidents – like what is going on in some parts of culture such as science or religion – a new set of metaphors, distinctions, and problems is invented and captures the imagination of followers. For a time, when a particular language game gets entrenched, it sets the direction for "normal" philosophizing. After a while, because of some other historical accidents – like the appearance of a new genius or just plain boredom and sterility – another cluster of metaphors, distinctions, and problems usurps the place of what is now a dying tradition. At first the abnormal talk of some new genius may be dismissed as idiosyncratic, as not being "genuine" or "serious" philosophy but sometimes this abnormal talk will set philosophy in new directions. We must resist the Whiggish temptation to rewrite the history of philosophy in our own image – where we see our predecessors as "really" treating what we now take to be fundamental problems. The crucial point for Rorty is to realize that a philosophical paradigm does *not* displace a former one because it can better formulate the legitimate problems of a prior paradigm; rather, because of a set of historical contingencies, it nudges the former paradigm aside.   (Bernstein 1992: 20)

We can see from this that Rorty's 'interpretation' does not *just* seek to provide an alternative, 'deflationary' account of what happened in the history of philosophy. Even though the 'alternative' offering is important, it is not simply that whereas philosophers have been inclined to view their own intellectual ascendance as an inevitable result of winning out in 'argument' against the less rationally compelling claims of their predecessors, Rorty suggests that we should, instead, see them as having reached the very same place by means of fortuitous circumstances.

No, there is an extra *explanatory* factor involved. Rorty's interpretation purports to show us *why* things were more likely to have gone the way he proposes – why the philosophers' own 'change-by-means-of-rational-argument' account is liable to be, at best, naively 'self-deceiving'.

On Rorty's understanding, phenomena that are not normally regarded as 'intellectual' in any strict sense – like images and metaphors – yield the explanatory key. It is such phenomena – rather than, say, 'propositions' or 'formalized arguments' – that foster, sustain and ultimately undermine intellectual motivation. Thinkers get hooked on particular philosophical methods or positions because, whether they are aware of it or not, they are deeply attracted by the embedding or associated images and metaphors. Hence, for example, some philosophers become passionately devoted to the philosophy of mind because they have succumbed to the "mirror imagery" manifested by various "ocular metaphors" (PMN: 13).

The salient insight here is that philosophers are very unlikely to commit themselves to a particular philosophical position or pursuit *solely* in virtue of what we might call 'its formal intellectual qualities'. What keeps philosophers in the game, so to speak, and what draws them into it in the first place, is something more rich-blooded than bare assent to certain narrowly construed, intellectual claims.

There is a good deal more to be said about how this is supposed to flesh out and about the philosophical pedigree of Rorty's explanatory picture. We shall pick up those threads again shortly. But now, we should continue explicating its *function*. How does the 'de-intellectualized' version of philosophical motivation and commitment serve Rorty's explanatory purposes?

It does so in two main ways. First, it smooths out an apparent tension in his 'all-encompassing' story. Rorty talks of philosophical positions waxing and waning according to the coincidental clustering of contingent influences – the dynamic, effervescent process described by Bernstein – and yet he also, as we earlier put it, 'throws the blanket of epistemology' over a whole range of thinkers, thereby apparently denying that there has been much real change and development from Plato down through Carnap and onwards. He is able to do the latter without detracting from the former because richer-blooded, philosophical motivation based on phenomena such as images and metaphors can manifest itself at the philosophical surface in a great diversity of ways.

Philosophers now working on the notion of 'mental representations' at what they regard to be the cutting edge of the philosophy of mind (though perhaps, to flag their vanguard status, they prefer the nomenclature: 'Cognitive Science') might subscribe to an explicitly anti-Cartesian account of 'representations' (though for trend-setting purposes, they might prefer to see themselves as pitting their wits against the Cartesian demons in Fodor's notion of a language of thought). However, such philosophers could still be enthralled by the kind of images and metaphors which fuelled the imaginations of Descartes and his followers – they could still legitimately belong under the cover of Rorty's epistemological blanket. Though separated on the face of things by chasms of argumentation, philosophers may nevertheless be inextricably linked by their obsession with sub-intellectual phenomena.

For a further, more detailed, illustration as to how all this fleshes out, consider Rorty's own extrapolation from Heidegger's exploration of "the way in which the West has become obsessed with the notion of our primary relation to objects as analogous to visual perception" (PMN: 162–3). First, Rorty sets out the primary thought behind the whole story:

> The historical roots of the Aristotle–Locke analogy of knowledge to perception are beyond the scope of this book, but we can at least take from Heidegger the idea that the desire for an 'epistemology' is simply the most recent product of the dialectical development of an originally chosen set of metaphors.

> (PMN: 163)

Then he outlines the successive stages of the plot. He starts off by admitting that it is too 'simplistic' to couch things in 'linear' terms, but claims it may be helpful to conceive of the originating metaphor as that wherein our beliefs are 'determined' by direct confrontation with the relevant objects (the example Rorty gives is of a geometrical figure proving an appropriate theorem). This is followed by an adherence to the notion that grasping how it is we are able to improve on our knowledge of things has to involve the comprehension of the workings of something like a visual process: 'the Mirror of Nature'. Knowledge itself thus becomes thought of as a bundle of 'accurate representations'. And the next step is to formulate the idea that, to take possession of such assured representations, we have to locate an epistemically elite class of reflections within the Mirror. These are the kinds of representations, the perception of whose nature forces consent. There can be no qualms about their 'accuracy'. As such, they serve as the 'foundations of knowledge'. The discipline that identifies them for us – 'the theory of knowledge' – thereby earns the authority to ground the rest of culture. The theory of knowledge, or 'epistemology', therefore unfolds as the search for representations that have 'built into them' the capacity to compel consent. This line of development purports to show that the general, influential view of philosophy as a discipline engaged in an essentially epistemological task of finding 'immutable structures' that shape 'knowledge, life and culture' according to the corresponding representations (i.e. what Rorty calls 'the neo-Kantian consensus') resulted from "an original wish to substitute *confrontation* for *conversation* as the determinant of our belief" (PMN: 163).

The second task fulfilled by Rorty's de-intellectualized notion of philosophical motivation and commitment is the more direct explanatory task we discussed earlier. If phenomena like images and metaphors, and *only* such phenomena, underpin philosophical pursuits, then it will always take a movement at the level of such phenomena to cause a real change in philosophical direction. To someone captivated by the images and metaphors woven into the fabric of their commitment to a philosophical view, evidence or even formal 'proof' that the view in question is suspect or even untenable will be insufficient to cause the person concerned to stop looking for ways to discount such material or nevertheless shore that view up. By the same token, if, for some reason or other, the appeal of these surrounding images and metaphors wanes, then *whatever* the seemingly intrinsic intellectual merits of the view, whatever the arguments in its favour, some opposing view might suddenly begin to appear more credible as *its* 'motivational baggage' exerts greater appeal.

If Rorty is right about all of this, then philosophers' own, more intellectually exalted, accounts that make their movement from position to position a matter of 'rational judgement' are not just mistaken, but also, to reiterate, 'self-deceiving'.

Now it is appropriate to consider where the timely sketches – the 'vignettes'– fit in.

Timely sketches

Recall that Rorty's aim is to release philosophy from its traditional 'problematic', and from the stranglehold of epistemology – the theory of knowledge – in particular. To do this, he divulges some of the historical sources of the images and metaphors that lock philosophers into their orthodox concerns – something he thinks even some of his co-opted philosophical heroes fail to do: "Wittgenstein's flair for deconstructing captivating pictures needs to be supplemented by historical awareness – awareness of the source of [all this] mirror imagery" (PMN: 12). Once these 'sources' are revealed to be accidental historical trends and unforeseen circumstances rather than anything 'rationally compelling', the veneer of the intellectual inevitability of traditional concerns is going to shatter. Then no thinker need any longer feel they *have to* try to discover answers to questions like: "What are the necessary and sufficient conditions for something to be counted as knowledge?" or "How is it that the mind is able to represent reality correctly?"

The 'vignettes' are employed in a series of 'short, sharp shock' treatments where Rorty quickly unveils the historical basis of concerns that are thought to be of *purely philosophical* interest. So, for example, in the first part of PMN, he uses brief sketches to "try to show that the so-called intuitions which lie behind Cartesian dualism are ones which have a historical origin" (PMN: 10). Notice that the exclusive purpose of these historical forays is to open up the *possibility* of philosophy always being able to take a different route through the realm of ideas. Given this expressed purpose, it is not necessary that Rorty deliver anything over and above piecemeal, historical plausibility. Complete and detailed accuracy is surplus to his requirements.

Appropriation

Rorty has a consistent flair, verging on genius, for appropriating the work of other philosophers. His early papers invoked a host of thinkers such as Aquinas, Descartes, Kant, Peirce, Whitehead,

Blanshard, Austin, Ryle, Strawson and Wittgenstein. But it was not until the appearance of PMN and the works that fed into it (see Chapter 3) that Rorty's aptitude for appropriation began to manifest itself to the full.

In keeping with the flexibility of his overall strategy, Rorty finds various ways to make use of different philosophers throughout PMN. At times, it can look as if major figures such as Hegel and Nietzsche are brought into play simply to lend if not exactly 'credibility' (for, as in this instance, they may be regarded with suspicion, even hostility, by the tradition Rorty is dealing with), then at least some degree of *gravitas* to his own claims – as if Rorty is relying on their intellectual weight to pervade his writing. But this apparently dubious dependence on 'arguments from authority' is just a cosmetic spin-off from Rorty's other, more substantial appropriations – something he may feel entitled to indulge in given that he aims to destabilize traditional philosophical practices and convictions rather than argue readers into rational submission regarding an alternative position.

Rorty's other kinds of appropriation include: adoption of views, lines of argument and themes, judicious selection of quotations (some of which are not always made explicit, a technique for beguiling critics that Rorty shares with Michel Foucault), co-option of philosophers who do not necessarily endorse – and may even seem to oppose – the position he envisages for them, and the extension or development of philosophers' ideas. In due course we will say more about how Rorty's 'ways of appropriation' have evolved. Meanwhile, the last two types just listed deserve a few additional comments.

When Rorty decides to co-opt someone for his PMN project, he usually tries to show that what is 'best', and, when possible, what is the natural 'dialectical outcome', in the relevant work should be expressed in terms of the liberating 'outlook' he wishes to superimpose upon it. The process confers dual philosophical favours. Rorty ostensibly does the thinkers a favour by reformulating their position so that its ends up in better overall shape, and he does himself a favour in thereby creating new allies. Some of Rorty's conferrals of such 'favours' can seem selfishly one-sided at first – as when he rounds up Heidegger and Wittgenstein to further his pragmatist cause. However, *patience* is an integral part of the process. While it may appear that Rorty is merely attempting to make short-term rhetorical gains by being provocative, his later writings confirm that he is in it for the long haul, that he is prepared to spill a considerable amount of ink to make his victims look comfortable in their new philosophical clothes, and to show that his co-options *do* make sense despite initial appearances to the contrary. What we witness in PMN is part of a long public campaign to change our perception of the significance of certain thinkers (and, in the case of those still living, such as Derrida and Davidson, to change *their self-perception*, their sense of their own philosophical significance).

The extension or development of philosophers' ideas is such a commonplace feature of the tradition Rorty is confronting in PMN that it might not seem worth drawing attention to his own contributions in this respect – certainly not as an illustration of his 'unique approach'. But such an assessment overlooks the ingenuity and creativity Rorty brings to the task – qualities that *do* make his contribution exceptional. A good example is Rorty's 'distinctive (and controversial) interpretation of how the history of philosophy has developed', to which we said we would soon return.

This interpretation derives from a number of philosophers. Bernstein maintains, with some shrewd insight, that it "can be seen as a novel blending of themes suggested by Heidegger, Derrida, Foucault, Kuhn and Feyerabend" (Bernstein 1992: 19). However, its *explanatory* dimension is best viewed as a creative extension of the work of the famous American philosopher W. V. Quine.

Quine extended

Quine is just one of Rorty's many co-opted allies, but he is central to Rorty's overall project. Davidson, Quine's ingeniously faithful follower, is equally important in many respects, and often depicted as more so. This is perfectly understandable, given the sustained attention that Davidson elicits from Rorty. But it was Quine who made the initial creative leap, after which Davidson's moves, though insightful and almost always immensely congenial to Rorty's close-watching eyes, were inevitably less groundbreaking.

Quine was someone Rorty urged to abandon the last vestiges of traditional epistemology – such as a distinction between "the given and the postulated" (PMN: 171) – that still infected his thinking. Rorty claims that such 'vestiges' prevented Quine from becoming the fully fledged pragmatist the main thrust of his work otherwise dictated he should be. Quine never signalled any sort of public approval of this particular 'favour', and all the signs are that he was

Richard Rorty

unlikely ever to do so (for some gentle, but firm disavowals of Rorty's views on him, see Quine, 1990). However, 'fully fledged' or not, Quine was responsible for resurrecting at least the possibility of pragmatism when it seemed to have been killed off for good by the dominance of logical positivism in the twenty or so years leading up to the early 1950s.

This revived 'possibility of pragmatism' is, as John Murphy aptly puts it, "what remains of modern empiricism once it is purified of the two dogmas that in large part conditioned it" (Murphy 1990: 81). The dogmas in question are those famously targeted by Quine's 'Two Dogmas of Empiricism', a paper that became, after it was published in 1951, one of the most influential in twentieth-century philosophy. Quine officially defined the dogmas thus:

> One [dogma] is a belief in a fundamental cleavage between truths which are *analytic*, or grounded in meanings independently of matters of fact, and truths which are *synthetic*, or grounded in fact. The other dogma is *reductionism*: the belief that each meaningful statement is equivalent to some logical construct upon terms which refer to experience.
>
> (Quine 1963: 20)

The first dogma contends that there is a sharp division between truths that depend on nothing more than the meaning of the terms used to express them (to apprehend that they are true, we need only understand this 'meaning'), and truths which are based on factual considerations additional to matters concerning only their 'meaning' (to grasp that they are true, we need to investigate the relevant facts). As for the second dogma, this expresses the empiricist's vision of founding knowledge on experience by showing that each sensible statement about the world can, and should, be linked to a corresponding experience.

In Quine's 'purified' picture there is no irrevocable boundary between claims which hold true according to the vicissitudes of experience and those which so hold, as he memorably puts it, "come what may".

This dispenses with the first dogma. Furthermore, the relationship between language use and experience is irredeemably *holistic*: "our statements about the external world face the tribunal of experience not individually but only as a corporate body" (Quine 1963: 41). This leaves no foothold, either, for the second dogma.

However, it is Quine's *naturalistic* conception of what makes the truth of some statements appear forever unchallengeable that Rorty 'extends' in his own interpretation of the history of philosophy. In that conception, truths are not anchored in their place within communicative exchanges by some correspondingly immovable features of 'reality', nor by any logical or conceptual 'glue'. They are instead held fast by a surrounding 'web' of beliefs and a field of contingently associated social forces such as practices, customs, habits and conventions. So the explanation as to why it can appear that a certain claim *must* be true is thoroughly naturalistic. No mysterious or inexplicably stubborn part of the world accounts for 'appearances' here. To have ascertained that it seems a particular statement *has to be true* is not to have thereby latched on to something philosophically special about what it is true of. It is rather to have availed oneself of the truth of a claim that occupies an entrenched position in social discourse, a position where nobody is in the least bit inclined to dispute it because, for example, it serves a useful purpose or "nobody has given us any interesting alternatives which would lead us to question it" (PMN: 175).

Rorty extends this naturalistic explanation of how truths become socially entrenched to the 'mechanics of change' within the history of philosophy itself. Consider the kind of idealized, hygienic explanation of philosophical belief Rorty is trying to supplant:

> When philosophers believe something philosophically significant (say) P they believe it *because it is true* (and for no other reason).
> When, over time, they – or their successors – change their minds and come to believe Q instead (where Q now obviously implies that P is false) it is again *the truth of* Q that does the persuasive work: they come to believe Q because *it* is true (and for no other reason).

Of course few philosophers would spell out the process of historical change in quite such stark terms – all sorts of evidence and argumentation usually enter the picture to facilitate *awareness* of the relevant truths. But these matters are extraneous in the sense that they play no *more* than a facilitative role. When it comes to the philosophical crunch, it is *truth* that does most of the motivational work.

But is it the *bare truth*? Can it be? Suppose P is believed only because it is true? Then there is no rational route to Q if Q clearly implies P is false. It seems the only way to break the grip of P *and keep truth in the frame* is to allow that the truth-related grounds for believing P are weaker than the actual truth of P – thereby invoking something fallible like 'P's appearance of being true'. However, this shifts the motivational burden to 'the appearance and prospect of truth'. And this in turn puts greater emphasis on the contextual features that are needed to help create the appearance and prospect of truth. If the truth of P did all the work by itself in this respect, it would still be very difficult to explain how belief could change from 'belief in P' to 'belief in Q' (how could P, considered only on its own 'truth-appearing' merits, come to appear false after it had once appeared true?).

These difficulties facing a hygienic explanation of how philosophy changes and develops over time seem to confirm Quine's own view that truth cannot be 'isolated out'. They are also indicative of concerns that lead pragmatists to contend it is futile even to speak of notions like 'bare truth', as if truth has some philosophically identifiable essence. Rorty shares these concerns, and they will be explored in Chapter 3.

When Rorty makes the innovative move of applying to philosophy itself a Quinean-type explanation as to how claims become socially entrenched and hence assume an air of intellectual inviolability, he offers an account of the history of philosophy in which the acquisition of philosophical beliefs should not be seen as attempts to zoom in on truths that can then be fixed in time by the sheer force of their own veracity. On Rorty's account, philosophical beliefs are sensitive to all sorts of determining influences outside the realm of narrowly defined truth. They are 'stabilized' and protected from unwanted and uncalled-for intellectual interference by those very same influences. This explains why philosophical change can be so slow and arduous on some occasions and yet so swift and painless on others. To shift a philosophical position, it is necessary to overcome its 'social inertia'. This can be done by engaging with the position 'head on' – bringing to bear the 'counterforce' of (say) a philosophical argument (usually an example of the 'arduous way'). It can also be done by simply abandoning the beliefs involved for reasons unconnected with their truth value – perhaps because, all of a sudden, those beliefs have ceased to generate any interest (which can be an example of the 'swift and painless' way).

Narrative

There are a number of reasons why Rorty regards narrative as such an important tool for achieving his aims – and for expressing philosophical views in any case. He believes narratives can induce the Gestalt-like switches that are needed to view philosophical commitments in a fresh light – one that reveals, for instance, that they are 'optional'. Narratives can do this because they have richer linguistic resources available to them than the arguments and theories philosophers traditionally rely on to instigate change. These resources can be employed in ways that bypass standard theories and arguments, thus avoiding further entanglement in the presuppositions of the positions the narratives are addressing. Furthermore, such resources enable a narrative stroke of the pen or quiver of the vocal chords to engage with, subvert or outflank the kinds of metaphors and images that, in Rorty's eyes, do all the real motivational work behind the scenes of philosophical belief acquisition. Rorty also prefers narratives because they are easier to construct without unwittingly incorporating any of the spurious distinctions which philosophers traditionally introduce to elevate their discourse to a position of repressive, judgemental power over all other areas of discourse.

Rorty's use of narrative is generally intimately connected with his 'historical recontextualizations', but he also 'tells stories' that are completely fictional to lend imaginative plausibility to the kind of philosophical switches of context he feels are needed to free us from orthodox positions. A brilliant example of the latter is his tale of 'The Antipodeans' that takes up a sizeable chunk of Chapter Two, and should be read in full to appreciate its inventive force. It begins in quasi-Nietzschean fashion: "Far away, on the other side of our galaxy there was a planet on which lived beings like ourselves" (PMN: 70). Then, the ensuing fable challenges preconceptions about the nature of mind, about how the mind should be accounted for in philosophy. It does this by building up a picture of these beings as creatures who, on the surface, were very much like us except for the fact that "they did not know they had minds" (*ibid.*). They lived a life very similar to our own, but they never developed a vocabulary that catered for anything like 'consciousness', 'mental states', 'spirit' and 'mind'. Such a vocabulary did not emerge because they made prior breakthroughs in neurology and biochemistry that enabled them to talk instead about the details of their 'neural states'. When an expedition from Earth arrived on the planet in 'the middle of the twenty-first century', the philosophers on board were fascinated by the absence of 'the concept of mind' in the Antipodean culture. This tale may seem to hark back to Rorty's earlier career, to the time when he advocated a form of 'eliminative materialism'. However, the point of the tale is *not* to establish any substantial gains for such a position, but rather to open up the possibility that the whole philosophical problematic associated with the notion of 'mind' may be optional. We return to Rorty's idea that philosophical concepts are 'contingent' later in the book (see pp. 109–15)

The central chapter

> Chapter Four is the central chapter of the book – the one in which the ideas which led to its being written are presented.
>
> (PMN: 10)

The theme of the chapter is the denial of 'privileged representation', a theme that is 'central' not just to PMN, but to the whole of Rorty's subsequent philosophical career. And the ideas, as Rorty himself tells us, "are those of Sellars and Quine" (PMN: 10). They form an important part of an ongoing series of 'internal criticisms' levelled by fully paid-up members of the analytic tradition, but gain their potency in this context when they are pitted directly against "the notion of two sorts of representations – intuitions and concepts" (PMN: 168) and thus, more generally, against what Rorty considers "the Kantian foundations of analytic philosophy" (PMN: 170).

Earlier, in Chapter Three, Rorty claims that Kant "gave us a history of our subject, fixed its problematic, and professionalised it" (PMN: 149). Kant did this "by building into our conception of a 'theory of knowledge'" an 'insight' that has been characterized by C. I. Lewis as follows: "There are in our cognitive experience, two elements; the immediate data, such as those of sense, which are presented or given to the mind, and a form, construction, or interpretation, which represents the activity of thought" (Lewis 1956: 38). Rorty maintains that far from being the product of bare 'insight', the partition described here is the outcome of a long tradition in philosophizing that has been dominated by optional metaphors of 'epistemological confrontation' between the mind and reality or, more precisely perhaps, between mind and the objects of knowledge that reality 'contains'. As we saw above, it was partly his reading of Heidegger that inspired Rorty to put this kind of historical spin on Kant's contribution to 'philosophy-as-theory-of-knowledge' and gave him "the idea that the desire for an 'epistemology' is simply the most recent product of the dialectical development of an originally chosen set of metaphors" (PMN: 163).

In Chapter Four, Rorty uses Sellars and Quine for extra leverage in ejecting two key distinctions spawned by Kant's intuition–concept division:

> The distinction between what is 'given' and what is 'added by the mind'

and

> That between the 'contingent' (because influenced by what is given) and the 'necessary' (because entirely 'within' the mind and under its control). (PMN: 169)

Without some such distinctions, says Rorty, "we will not know what would count as a 'rational reconstruction' of our knowledge", nor will we know "what epistemology's goal or method could be" (*ibid.*). In short, 'philosophy-as-theory-of-knowledge' will cease to be a viable concern.

Sellars attacks the first of the above 'distinctions', and Quine, as we saw earlier, the second. But Rorty discerns two common features in their approach: 'behaviourism' and 'holism'. Their approach is behaviourist in the sense that they both raise behaviourist issues about the 'epistemic privilege' attributed to certain claims on the basis of their being reports of correspondingly privileged 'representations'. Thus Quine poses the question as to whether an anthropologist will ever be able to gather evidence that marks a particular distinction within the actual sentences to which speakers under scrutiny give apparent, complete assent. This is the distinction between contingently empirical and conceptually necessary truths. Sellars questions whether the weight carried by first-person testimony concerning (say) pains we experience or thoughts we notice ourselves thinking is greater than, or somehow significantly different in kind from, that carried by the reports of experts on subjects like 'mental stress' or 'the mating behavior of birds' (PMN: 173). In both cases, the main thrust of the questioning suggests that the distinctions involved outstrip the behavioural evidence for positing their existence. Hence, Rorty says that these issues raised by Quine and Sellars can be subsumed under the following general query: how do our fellow speakers know when they should take us at our word and when they should seek additional confirmation of what we are saying? He contends that the answer to this question need not invoke a philosophically principled way of discriminating modes of 'confirmation':

It would seem enough for natives to know which sentences are unquestionably true without knowing which are true "by virtue of language". It would seem enough for our peers to believe there to be no better way of finding out our inner states than from our reports, without their knowing what "lies behind" our making of them. It would seem enough for *us* to know that our peers have this acquiescent attitude. That alone seems sufficient for that inner certainty about our inner states which the tradition has explained by "immediate presence to consciousness", "sense of evidence", and other expressions of the assumption that reflections in the Mirror of Nature are intrinsically better known than nature itself. (PMN: 173–4)

The behaviourist criteria that Rorty alludes to are not themselves intended to be 'philosophically principled'. They do not involve 'behaviorist analyses' of 'knowledge claims' or 'mental states' (PMN: 176) because:

To be behaviorist in the large sense in which Sellars and Quine are behaviorist is not to offer reductionist analyses, but to refuse to attempt a certain sort of explanation: the sort of explanation which not only interposes such a notion as "acquaintance with meanings" or "acquaintance with sensory appearances" between the impact of the environment on human beings and their reports about it, but uses such notions to explain the reliability of such reports. (PMN: 176)

This 'large behaviorism' is the *holistic* link between the approaches of Quine and Sellars. It holds that epistemic justification or confirmation is 'social', that its tentacles of support reach out into the surrounding community of fellow 'knowers' rather than down into 'foundations', 'reality', or any philosophical surrogates. In this 'horizontal' scheme of things: "Nothing counts as justification unless by reference to what we already accept, and . . . there is no way to get outside our beliefs and our language so as to find some test other than coherence" (PMN: 178). Sellars and Quine are thereby committed to the 'premise' that "we understand knowledge when we understand the social justification of belief and thus have no need to view it as accuracy of representation" (PMN: 170).

Rorty's self-penned gloss on all this is that 'knowledge' is a matter of 'conversation' concerning what the appropriate members of the relevant communities are inclined or prepared to say in that respect: "justification is not a matter of a special relation between ideas (or words) and objects, but of conversation, of social practice" (PMN: 170). The general moral he also draws here is crucial to his whole project:

> Once conversation replaces confrontation, the notion of the Mind as Mirror can be discarded. Then the notion of philosophy as the discipline which looks for privileged representations among those constituting the Mirror becomes unintelligible. A thoroughgoing holism has no place for the notion of philosophy as 'conceptual', as 'apodictic', as picking out the 'foundations' of the rest of culture, as explaining which representations are 'purely given' or 'purely conceptual', as presenting a 'canonical notation' rather than an empirical discovery, or as isolating 'trans-framework heuristic categories'.   (PMN: 170–71)

Whither philosophy?

> Our present notions of what it is to be a philosopher are so tied up with the Kantian attempt to render all knowledge-claims commensurable that it is difficult to imagine what philosophy without epistemology could be.   (PMN: 357)

> Once we have detranscendentalized, contextualized, historicized, genderized the subject of knowledge, the context of inquiry, and even the methods of justification, what remains of philosophy?   (Benhabib)

Imagine that Rorty succeeds in showing that traditional philosophical concerns are both problematic and optional in the senses defined early on in this chapter (recall these were 'problematic' in the sense that they involve 'hopeless and vainglorious representational assumptions' about mind, knowledge, truth and the nature of philosophy, and 'optional' in the sense that they are the product of contingent socio-historical factors rather than the inevitable march of reason). What then? What becomes of philosophy?

In the third, and final, part of PMN, Rorty offers pragmatism, conversation, edification and hermeneutics. But, despite the honorific references to Dewey, and to a lesser extent James, 'pragmatism' is not presented as a substantial, fully developed position, something that might plug the worrying gaps left by the demise of traditional philosophy. It is presented more as a relaxed, insouciant, attitude of mind that refuses to take such worries seriously.

Furthermore, the notion of 'conversation' is introduced as little more than the 'sense of style' that goes along with the pragmatist's relatively unconstrained outlook on philosophy:

> "Philosophy" is not a name for a discipline which confronts permanent issues, and unfortunately keeps misstating them, or attacking them with clumsy dialectical instruments. Rather, it is a cultural genre, a "voice in the conversation of mankind" (to use Michael Oakeshott's phrase) which centres on one topic rather than another at some given time not by dialectical necessity, but as a result of various things happening elsewhere in the conversation. (PMN: 264)

'Edification' stands for the general project of finding better ways of describing ourselves or, to be more dramatic, 'remaking ourselves', "as we read more, talk more and write more" (PMN: 360). But, again, this apparently leaves philosophy with no distinctive role, nothing that prevents it from being swallowed up by those areas of culture, such as literature, where practitioners are more accustomed to letting ambitions and self-depiction follow the lead of the imagination rather than reason. If pragmatism, conversation and edification all seem too vague and flimsy to keep philosophy firmly afloat once it abandons its traditional problematic, does hermeneutics look any more promising?

Rorty takes the term "hermeneutics" from Gadamer, a philosopher he co-opts as someone who also wants "to get rid of the classic picture of man-as-essentially-knower-of-essences" (PMN: 364). The term has a 'technical' ring, and also a weighty historical tradition behind it. Does philosophy therefore have a better chance of surviving if it adopts a pragmatic–conversational–edifying stance for cosmetic purposes, but undergoes a hermeneutic transformation on matters of substance?

All speculation of this pessimistic kind about philosophy's mirrorless future is, in fact, way off the mark. If the thought here is that perhaps such a transformation could yield 'theories of interpretation' and the like, the answer is "Yes, it is conceivable that philosophy *could* so survive, but if it did so, that would mean Rorty's critique had largely failed." What Rorty has to offer in the last sections of PMN has nothing to do with providing a "successor" or a continuation of traditional philosophy by other means. He is quite firm about this:

> I want to make it clear at the outset that I am *not* putting hermeneutics forward as a "successor subject" to epistemology,

as an activity which fills the cultural vacancy once filled by epistemologically centred philosophy . . . "hermeneutics" is not the name for a discipline, nor for a method of achieving the sort of results that epistemology failed to achieve, nor for a program of research. On the contrary, hermeneutics is the expression of hope that the cultural space left by the demise of epistemology will not be filled – that our culture should become one in which the demand for constraint and confrontation is no longer felt.

(PMN: 315)

For those who react to PMN with the above speculative concerns about philosophy surviving its 'hermeneutic transformation', Rorty's clarification on the role of hermeneutics is presumably going to make it look as if the answer to their worrisome query is "No, philosophy will not survive, not as 'a discipline', 'a research program' or anything else that is recognizably *philosophical.*" But for Rorty himself, fretting about whether philosophy can survive if it takes on board his recommendations is as pointless as past cases of anxiety about whether poetry could survive in the free-versifying hands of Ezra Pound, whether music could survive in the avant-gardist hands of Stravinsky or whether art could survive in the anti-retinal hands of Duchamp. This does not mean that Rorty is comparing himself to figures such as these – for he is not yet doing 'post-epistemological' philosophy in PMN. He is preparing the ground for the emergence of those who might produce such philosophy; he is in the position of a literary critic who tried to show that metered verse had already had its 'Nietzschean minute', that before the world 'cooled down' it was time for all good poets to try something new.

The kind of worries that we have just described are also conceptually skewed as regards the nature of philosophy. Someone who thinks that Rorty's recommendations could destroy it is wrong not just in thinking that philosophy-as-epistemology has captured the essence of philosophy (so, when that goes, philosophy goes with it), they are wrong in thinking that philosophy has an essence at all. What decides whether post-epistemological thinking is 'philosophical' will not be its relative proximity to the supposed essence of the subject, but all sorts of contingent factors such as whether it goes on in, and is supported by, the appropriate institutions such as philosophy departments in universities, whether the articles and books which contain that kind of thinking are put on the 'philosophy shelves' in libraries and bookstores, whether the thinkers concerned call themselves 'philosophers' and so on. The 'success' of such thinking will be determined on similarly contingent grounds. So Rorty's answer to "Whither philosophy?" is roughly "Wait and see": "The conversational interest of philosophy as a subject, or of some individual philosophers of genius, has varied and will continue to vary in unpredicable ways depending on contingencies. These contingencies will range from what happens in physics to what happens in politics" (PMN: 392).

Interim assessment

> There is something undeniably attractive about the picture of philosophy as *strenge Wissenschaft* aimed at formulating, analyzing, and once and for all settling questions, in the sense of discovering the right answers to them. When one is actually engaged in philosophical inquiry, the picture is virtually inescapable. It would be hard to philosophize if we did not believe that the problems we were working on might yield to our efforts; if nothing else, belief in the problem-solving picture is what Holmes once called "the trick by which nature keeps us at our job".   (Luban 1998: 282)

Although PMN is a meaty and groundbreaking text, it is also in many ways a transitional work. Rorty's pragmatist cards are not yet on the table. Moreover, for all the plausibility of Rorty's 'anti-essentialist' stand and the upbeat rhetoric about edifying, non-truth seeking, conversational discourse being able "to take us out of our old selves by the power of strangeness, to aid us in becoming new beings" (PMN: 360), there is a disconcerting tentativeness in Rorty's portrayal of post-epistemological philosophy, as if it is not *simply* that Rorty is still finding his own feet in this respect or 'preparing the ground'. In contemplating how the 'edifying philosophy' he favours is inclined to be, and probably *has to be*, reactive against and parasitic upon the 'systematic philosophy' he decries, Rorty seems not yet entirely sure whether the results of getting the tradition off our backs will be entirely beneficial, even in his own case.

For the purposes of an 'interim assessment', we will put this along with other possible reservations on hold for the reader's future reference, and consider instead some ways in which Rorty's approach has often been wrongly assessed at this transitional stage. The kind of 'reservations' we keep on the shelf include:

1. Is Rorty's approach more 'argument-dependent' than he supposes? In particular, does his whole 'anti-representational' stance depend on an argument concerning the impossibility of impartially comparing representations with reality?

2. Do Rorty's 'narratives', such as the tale of 'The Antipodeans', embody their own philosophical assumptions? And if so, does this defeat their main aim? Should they be allowed to 'speak for themselves'? *Can* they do so?

3. Does Rorty's approach run aground on its own *motivational* difficulties? Once *all* traditional philosophical concerns are put aside, it seems that exhortations to produce new and exciting descriptions of ourselves and our world are empty (i.e. because such 'descriptions' are always the by-product of fevered ambitions to achieve something other than just 'more interesting and useful descriptions'). Rorty salutes the "sort of optimistic faith which Russell and Carnap shared with Kant – that philosophy, its essence and right method discovered at last, had finally been placed upon the secure path of a science" (PMN: 173). He reminds us "such optimism is possible only for [those] of high imagination and daring, the heroes of our time" (*ibid.*). But it is difficult to see how such optimism, and such heroes, can emerge on the strength of a stripped down agenda that contains only such neutral injunctions as: "Go forth and produce new and better descriptions." The general worry is captured by Luban's remark above about 'the inescapable picture'; it is that when words like 'Truth' and 'Reality' go, so does the focal point of the philosophical imagination, the motivation for trying to think our way into a better future for humanity.

As later chapters unfold and a fuller picture emerges, the reader will be in a better position to take these reservations back down off the shelf themselves and figure out whether they should carry any great weight.

Although, as we have tried to show, Rorty takes some care to explain exactly what he is up to in PMN, his approach is often misunderstood by critics. Their 'misinterpretations' tend to veer between two extremes. Some critics take Rorty to be moving away from the analytic tradition, but in a fairly 'straight line', as it were, by doing something similar in kind: *arguing a case* against philosophy-as-epistemology. Hence they take him to task for failing to do the expected things – such as identifying flaws in, and counter-examples to, the arguments of philosophy thus conceived (and the arguments for thus conceiving philosophy). Their view is: since Rorty has made nothing like a watertight case against the prospect, philosophy-as-epistemology, if there is such a phenomenon, can – and probably should – just carry on regardless (perhaps this is one of the reasons why 'epistemology' itself is an area of philosophy over which Rorty's work has, as yet, exerted surprisingly little influence).

To be fair, a number of the 'Rorty-is-arguing-a-case' interpretations are more nuanced. Some critics do not just naïvely take Rorty to be doing the kind of things 'analytic-philosophers-who-argue-a-case' ordinarily do. Instead they charitably propose to interpret him as such to make the most sense of his writing. They then tend to conclude that, even on this 'charitably imposed' interpretation, Rorty does not have much worthwhile to say. Others spot that Rorty's approach makes an emphatic 'historicist' break with the analytic tradition and its predecessors, but consider him to be *arguing a historical case*. When they find themselves able to catch him out on matters of historical detail (e.g. concerning Locke's conception of 'ideas'), they cease to take him seriously. Once again, philosophy-as-epistemology supposedly escapes unscathed.

The second category of 'extremist critics' assume precisely what the 'charitable interpreters' thought they could, and should, avoid: that Rorty is not even trying to 'make a case' of *any* kind, that he has completely forsaken philosophy's 'normal discourse' of 'rational argumentation' and is merely indulging in 'rhetoric'. Their verdict is equally complacent: Rorty's rhetoric can be ignored – so it is carry on as usual as far as philosophy-as-epistemology is concerned.

Rorty's approach is open to such misunderstandings because it is so 'multifaceted'. Crudely, as we have already said, he deploys whatever 'technique' he deems necessary to achieve his goals. This can wrongfoot those who do not share, or who fail to recognize, these goals. It can also strike those embroiled in more traditional approaches as disingenuous – as if Rorty has betrayed the very methods he invokes by his lack of sustained commitment to them. For Rorty, this simply misplaces the burden of commitment that should be tied to *ends* rather than methods as such. Rorty is deeply sincere about his 'ends' – this much comes out in "Trotsky and the Wild Orchids":

> I am sometimes told, by critics from both ends of the political spectrum, that my views are so weird as to be merely frivolous.

> They suspect I will say anything to get a gasp, that I am just
> amusing myself by contradicting everyone else. This hurts . . .
> Perhaps this bit of autobiography will make it clear that, even if
> my views about the relation of philosophy and politics are odd,
> they were not adopted for frivolous reasons.   (WO: 5)

However, in pursuing these ends by philosophical means, he seems
to be flying in the face of a traditional 'purist' conception of 'methodology'.

According to this conception, philosophy is the paradigm of pure
and open inquiry – its methods should involve following the line of
argument wherever it leads. The philosophical mind should accordingly engage with its subject matter in this spirit of freedom and not
allow its thoughts to be subverted by antecedent ends, however non-
frivolous, praiseworthy and well intentioned. That Rorty's approach
appears to conflict with this idealized portrait no doubt accounts for
much of the resentment PMN generated among philosophers (he
himself recounts that the book was "disliked by most of my fellow
philosophy professors" (WO: 12)). But it is important to try to see
things from Rorty's own point of view. It is not that he is wilfully
bucking the intellectual principles and practices of an honourable
tradition. He is as enamoured of the spirit of free and unflinching
intellectual inquiry as anyone within that tradition. No, he believes
that the worship of specialized philosophical methodology is the
worship of a false idol, that 'results-wise' the tradition has been, at
best, treading water for a very long time. He thinks he can indicate
the way forward by showing that it is possible, and advisable, to
break new philosophical ground, stimulate new ways of thinking and
thereby generate more productive results. Whether he is right in
thinking this remains to be seen. History will no doubt issue its own
verdict: "In reality, a philosopher's role is acknowledged only after a
certain period of time; it is, in short, a retrospective role" (Foucault
1996: 85).

Chapter 3

Pragmatism

"Pragmatism" is a vague, ambiguous, and overworked word. Nevertheless, it names the chief glory of our country's intellectual tradition.   (CP: 160)

Consolidation?

After *Philosophy and the Mirror of Nature*, Rorty's next book was an important collection of articles gathered together in 1982 under the title *Consequences of Pragmatism* (CP). Since it fleshed out more details of "various topics dealt with sketchily" in PMN (CP: x), the publication of this collection can be seen, in large part, as a consolidating venture. The pragmatism that hovers in the background throughout much of *Philosophy and the Mirror of Nature* is brought out into the open. Moreover, some of Rorty's most significant 'acts of appropriation', involving thinkers such as Heidegger, Dewey, Wittgenstein and Derrida, are put into a clearer context by demonstrations as to how Rorty actually reads their work. The deep disenchantment with the notion of 'philosophical method' that surfaced in PMN is explained in more depth, along with the correlatively deplored 'Kantian' insistence that philosophy is "more than a kind of writing" (CP: 93). And finally, Rorty returns with renewed confidence to the theme of "what a postphilosophical culture might look like" (CP: xxi).

However, *Consequences of Pragmatism* also reconfirms that the all too common conception of Rorty as an 'analytic philosopher suddenly gone bad' is mistaken. It shows that while Rorty's dissatisfaction with the analytic tradition may not have made much of a *public* impact before *Philosophy and the Mirror of Nature* – so a commentator like Bernstein *is* quite right to say that "prior to its publication Rorty was known primarily as a philosophy professor who made important contributions to the discussion of such technical professional issues as 'the mind–body problem', 'incorrigibility' and the epistemological status of 'transcendental arguments'" (Bernstein 1992: 258) – many of the most challenging ideas in PMN had been forming in Rorty's mind at least as far back as 1972 when the paper "The World Well Lost" (reprinted in CP: Ch. 1) was presented to the Eastern Division of the American Philosophical Association. This means that *Consequences* is not so much a consolidation of territory previously stormed in PMN, as additional proof that Rorty's relationship to the analytic tradition has always been much more convoluted and ambivalent than the 'Rorty-turns-rebel-overnight' reactions to PMN suggest.

World without realism or idealism

The route to objectivity has been historically marked by a search for some common ground guaranteeing interpersonal discussion and the settlement of differences. That an explanation of objectivity must pick out this common ground is implicit in the thesis that it is to be found in a world of external realities, but the postulation of common ground outside offered an impersonal basis and failed to be explanatory. The alternative of looking favourably towards agreement or consensus as the fabric of objectiveness opens the gates to conventionalism as an explanation of the fact of consensus itself; it makes access to objectivity dependent upon the things we consensually believe, trapping objectivity in the bias of agreed wisdom. Perhaps the trouble lies in the assumption that there is something to be shared, and the answer is to be found in the radical thought that there is no common ground at all. (Newell 1986: 101)

The "true world", an idea which is no longer good for anything, not even obligating – an idea which has become useless and superfluous – consequently, a refuted idea: let us abolish it!
(Nietzsche 1954: 485)

"The World Well Lost" makes for an excellent opening to *Consequences*. Although it is densely written, elusive and complex, this article single-handedly prepares the path for a revival of pragmatism by trying to show the futility of what have been traditionally seen as the main philosophical alternatives: realism and idealism – these being regarded as such on the understanding that either the world is mind-independent (as required by realism) or whatever is so designated must somehow be part of the mind (as dictated by idealism). Furthermore, although it was written well before the publication of *Philosophy and the Mirror of Nature*, WWL *already* manifests key features of the vintage Rorty approach: acute historical awareness combined with an opportunistic eye on new developments.

The 'new developments' come in the shape of an intriguing *verificationist* line of argument constructed independently by both Davidson and Stroud. Rorty mainly concentrates on Davidson's version as evinced in his unpublished 'John Locke Lectures' and prepublication versions of his seminal article 'On the very idea of a conceptual scheme' (Davidson 1984; Stroud 1969). Like Sellars and Quine, Davidson is a key figure in Rorty's conception of how analytic philosophy has fostered its own internal critique. Stroud, however, turns up in Rorty's *Introduction* as an anti-pragmatist, 'intuitive realist', someone who thinks that the real significance of some philosophical problems outruns the scope of verificationist responses (see pp. 79–82 for further discussion).

Rorty's historical acumen enables him to soften up the reader for the radical conclusions of the Davidson–Stroud argument. He sets the scene by discussing how the now commonplace "notion of alternative conceptual frameworks" (CP: 3) was brought to the fore when 'Hegel's Historicism' "gave us a sense of how there might be genuine novelty in the development of thought and society" (*ibid.*). But he also provocatively points out that Hegel's outlook was only made possible, somewhat paradoxically, by Kant, "himself the least historicist of philosophers" (*ibid.*). For, says Rorty, it was Kant who bequeathed us an enduring conception of the mind as an entity "divided into active and passive faculties, the former using concepts to 'interpret' what 'the world' imposes on the latter" (*ibid.*) – a conception criticized in the core chapters of *Philosophy and the Mirror of Nature*. With such a ruling conception, it is difficult to avoid the further thought that, since the passive faculties, by their inert nature, have to be relatively immutable, all 'change' belongs on the side of the active faculties and their related inputs. But, if we then assign anything of conceptual importance to the passive part of the mind, so that its understanding of the world is to that extent 'fixed' or 'predetermined', we may start to wonder what the world might seem like to a mind that exhibited a different mix of the active and passive or even different primary 'ingredients', and hence whether such minds "might thus be conscious of a different 'world'" (*ibid.*). And this raises the further prospect that *our world*, the world we are currently familiar with, might be just one among many possible worlds – different worlds which would come into 'existence' for us if our 'conceptual framework' were to change in the relevant respect.

Having filled in some of this historical background as to why the notion of 'alternative conceptual frameworks' has become 'a commonplace of our culture', Rorty then suggests that the notion is in fact highly problematic, that it "contains the seeds of doubt about the root notion of a 'conceptual framework', and hence of its own destruction" (CP: 4). This is a precursor of the much grander attempt in PMN to show that the 'dialectic' of analytic philosophy leads, in theory, if not in practice, to the erasure of that whole tradition.

The main problem with the notion of alternative conceptual frameworks is to find some philosophically unbiased and informative way of specifying what it is that these 'frameworks' go to work upon, what it is that they actually 'frame' or 'conceptualize'. Doubts raised by this problem infect the whole idea of distinguishing between anything like "a receptive wax tablet on the one hand and an 'active' interpreter of what nature has imprinted there on the other" (CP: 4).

At this stage, Rorty ups the historical bidding: when Quinean objections to the distinction between necessary and contingent truths (i.e. between truths that *must* hold fast whatever the prevailing situation and those that could turn out to be false in different circumstances) are added to the overall picture, "the Kantian notion of 'conceptual framework' – the notion of 'concepts necessary for the constitution of experience, as opposed to those whose application is necessary to control or predict experience'" (CP: 5) looks ready for dismantling. But, says Rorty, "there is a simpler and more direct objection to the notion of 'alternative conceptual frameworks'". By this he means the Davidson–Stroud verificationist argument that his whole discussion has been leading up to.

A conceptual framework that differed *in kind* from our own, and not just in degree, would render many, if not most or even *all*, of our beliefs about the world false – or, to put things more cautiously: from within that kind of framework, a disconcerting number of such beliefs would *appear to be false*. This plausible thought invokes two awkward options, each of which threatens to destabilize our own worldview:

1. Many of our beliefs about the world we feel familiar with *are* false.
2. When comparing 'conceptual frameworks', there is no way, in principle, of determining which one yields the greater amount of truth about the world (so we have no grounds for confidence in the truth-generating powers of our own framework).

The most significant case here is a conceptual framework that generates a view of the world in which *all* our world-related beliefs turn out to be false. However, this dramatic case is ruled out by the verificationist argument itself. Rorty does not state the argument explicitly, but rather describes the assumptions that lead to its conclusion.

If we share Quine's dim view – as Rorty assumes we must – of "the possibility that 'meaning' can mean something more than what is contextually defined in the process of predicting behaviour" (CP: 6), we will tend to cash it out by identifying appropriate behaviour, or 'speech dispositions', "rather than in terms of mental essences (ideas, concepts, chunks of the crystalline structure of thought)" (CP: 5). Then the idea of a radically different, belief-destroying conceptual framework collapses in on itself.

Why? Because behaviour-related, 'meaning-attributions' can only exert their grip in a truth-saturated context. Wherever truth is missing from the scene, meaning itself has no conceivable reference points. Suppose we conjecture, after some observation of its behaviour, that by the utterance of "XYZ", a certain creature means to say "That object is a tree"? If we further suppose that no supplementary true beliefs regarding what it is for something to be an object, what it is for an object to be a tree, and so on, can be detected in this situation (so the creature does *not* appear to believe things like "Trees have branches", "Trees are a source of timber", etc.), then it seems we can furnish no credible evidence for the initial conjecture, no good reasons for thinking that by "XYZ" the creature in question really *does* mean "That object is a tree" and, moreover, no good reasons for identifying a linguistic act (i.e. of 'utterance') in the first place rather than simply the making of a noise.

When confronted by a 'foreigner's' conceptual framework, our attempts to understand it by translating its 'contents' will never come up against 'the limiting case' where all the relevant beliefs:

must be viewed as false according to a translating scheme that pairs off all or most of his (or her) terms as identical in meaning with some terms of English. We will not reach this case (so the Davidson argument goes) because any such translation scheme would merely show that we had not succeeded in finding a translation at all. (CP: 6)

For according to the embedding line of argument, *truth empirically structures meaning*. It does this in the strong sense that its existence – the existence of truth – is *required* for meaning to be observably demarcated. Absent truth, how could we decide between the hypothesis that what we are confronted by is creatures behaving in some unfathomable way on the basis of an untranslatable conceptual framework and the conjecture that we are witnessing nothing more than the emission of various sounds – meaningless babble? The 'radical conclusion' of the verificationist argument now looms before us:

> Once we imagine different ways of carving up the world, nothing could stop us from attributing "untranslatable languages" to *anything* that emits a variety of signals. But, so this verificationist argument concludes, this degree of open-endedness shows us that the purported notion of an untranslatable language is as fanciful as that of an invisible colour. (CP: 6)

In the light of this kind of conclusion, the distinction between 'conceptual frameworks' and 'the world' that is thus conceptualized seems to collapse. When realists gesture towards "a hard, unyielding, rigid *être-en-soi* which stands aloof, sublimely indifferent to the attentions we lavish upon it" (CP: 13), the gesture is philosophically empty. Such gestures invoke "the notion of something *completely* unspecified and unspecifiable – the thing-in-itself, in fact" (CP: 14). As such, they pick out nothing that can play a meaningful role in the construction of a conceptual framework.

The collapse of the 'framework–world' distinction does not, however, usher in 'idealism' because the truth of all our practical beliefs about 'the world' that assume or imply this world is *not* simply a 'mind-based phenomenon' (for example: "Trees really exist and are not a figment of our imaginations" remains completely untouched): "If one accepts the Davidson–Stroud position, then 'the world will be just the stars, the people, the tables, and the grass' – all those things which nobody except the occasional scientific–realist philosopher thinks might not exist" (CP: 14).

This leaves the field wide open for pragmatism, an approach which considers truth to be something that emerges from social practices as no more than a "compliment paid to sentences that seem to be paying their way and that fit in with other sentences which are doing so" (CP: xxv). Truth is ascribed as a befitting sign of success in the quest for predicting, controlling and 'generally coping with' things for our mutual benefit. Its ascription is thus answerable to those practices and their reality-oriented demands rather than some practice-independent, 'unspecified and unspecifiable', and therefore 'well lost', world.

Pragmatism minus truth

> For the pragmatist, true sentences are not true because they correspond to reality, and so there is no need to worry what sort of reality, if any, a given sentence corresponds to – no need to worry about what "makes" it true.　　　　　　　(CP: xvi)

> As long ago as 1969 I argued that nothing can usefully and intelligibly be said to correspond to a sentence.　　　(Davidson 1987)

Whether we read *Consequences of Pragmatism* as a largely consolidating enterprise or a series of articles which enable us to put the development of Rorty's ideas into proper perspective (or, as seems more sensible, as a bit of both), there is little doubt that the emergence of pragmatism into the daylight is one of its major themes. For although Rorty still, at times, invokes the 'conversational' and 'hermeneutic' transformations described in the final part of *Philosophy and the Mirror of Nature*, it is the idea of 'philosophy-as-pragmatism' that most consistently captures his imagination in his post-PMN writings. The questions as to what Rorty's conception of 'pragmatism' involves and whether that conception is philosophically viable are therefore key issues in this chapter.

The 'emergence of pragmatism' begins straight off when Rorty tackles the thorny problem of 'truth' in his lengthy "Introduction" – the final member of an important trilogy of such inauguratory writings (the others being, as we have noted, the introductions to *The Linguistic Turn* and *Philosophy and the Mirror of Nature*). This problem concerning truth is 'thorny', not least because it is one about which pragmatism has historically had some of its most radical and least immediately palatable things to say, one that, for the very same reason, provokes the most hostile, anti-pragmatist sentiments from its critics and rivals.

By the same token, it makes plenty of strategic sense for Rorty to confront the problem quickly and directly. If pragmatism can win the battle over truth, or even hold its ground, it has a much better chance of winning the overall war against the opposing tradition that has until relatively recently looked certain to overwhelm it.

Classic American pragmatism – the pragmatism of Peirce, James and Dewey – was shunted aside by the Frege–Russell tradition in analytic philosophy and then kept on the fringes of philosophy by the positivists and later developments in the philosophy of language. These days, as Rorty acknowledges, it "is usually regarded as an out-dated philosophical movement – one which flourished in the early years of this century in a rather provincial atmosphere, and which has either been refuted or *aufgehoben*" (CP: xvii; see also Rorty's "Introduction" to Murphy 1990: 1). The tradition was partly re-instated by Quine (e.g. 'Two Dogmas of Empiricism' in Quine 1953), but gained little further ground because:

- pragmatism attracted no suitably influential advocates (Quine's endorsement, while vigorous at times, was characteristically concise and judicious. As such, it never amounted to anything like a full scale 'campaign');
- the original written works of the founders of pragmatism – Peirce, James and Dewey – betrayed concerns that could only appear anachronistic given the way philosophy later developed (for example: an emphasis on the foundational role of 'experience' that tended to look very naïve in the light of philosophy's wholehearted 'linguistic turn').

Furthermore, pragmatism incurred a good deal of philosophical hostility from the outset – the kind of hostility it later found very difficult to shake off – because it appeared to *subordinate truth to human interests*. This was considered tantamount to subverting the hallowed aim of 'objective intellectual inquiry' – inquiry that supposedly yields unbiased insight into things *as they are* irrespective of how the majority of human beings at any particular time would like them to be and/or would benefit from them so being (i.e. the kind of inquiry mentioned at the end of the previous chapter).

Thus early on, Bertrand Russell, who was to become one of pragmatism's most damaging critics, took William James firmly to task for maintaining that "the 'true' is only the expedient in the way of our thinking" (James 1978: 106): "I find great intellectual difficulties in this doctrine. It assumes that a belief is 'true' when its effects are good" (Russell 1945: 817).

This kind of criticism hit home. For James was, as said, a founder of pragmatism. However, the short passage about 'truth and expediency' Russell was responding to is one that, as Hilary Putnam reminds us, "is most often plucked out of context and used as a stick with which to beat James" (Putnam 1995: 8). To redress matters, Putnam first quotes the relevant passage from James in full:

> "The true", to put it very briefly, is only the expedient in the way of our thinking, just as "right" is only the expedient in the way of our behaving. Expedient in almost any fashion; and expedient in the long run and on the whole of course, for what meets expediently all the experience in sight won't necessarily meet all further experiences equally satisfactorily.   (James 1978: 106)

He then shows that Russell's hyper-critical reading of James was a grossly unfair 'misreading' because it contained at least three major flaws:

1. It ignored important explicit, 'on site' qualifications to James's thematic statement (e.g. "to put it very briefly" and "Expedient in almost any fashion").
2. It ignored, even, the very fact that James's statement *was* thematic, treating it instead as a putative, substantive definition of "true".
3. It failed to acknowledge the complexity of James's overall account of 'expediency', a complexity that belies Russell's narrow interpretation wherein "truth" is simply taken to mean "has good effects".

Nevertheless, Russell's heavy-handed hostility concerning pragmatism's treatment of truth undoubtedly set the tone for future philosophical responses. This means that in confronting the issue of 'truth', Rorty has to overcome the lingering suspicion that it is pragmatism's weak spot, the Achilles heel in its otherwise robust, Jamesian 'can-do' approach .

Unlike Putnam, however, Rorty does not even attempt to set the record straight on the finer technical details of time-honoured criticisms of pragmatism's conception of truth, nor does he put forward a radically revised account of truth that is specifically designed to cater for such criticisms. Instead, he boldly restates what he regards to be the fundamental features of a "pragmatist theory about truth" (CP: xiii), extols the virtues of this 'theory' and then gives it a contemporary flavour by situating it on the map of recent quasi-technical debates over 'realism' – "which has come to be synonymous with 'anti-pragmatism'" (CP: xxi).

The term 'theory' is, as we might expect, used wryly – with philo-sophical tongue firmly in cheek. Rorty's approach to truth is reso-lutely anti-theoretical and Davidsonian:

> Correspondence theories, coherence theories, pragmatist theo-ries, theories that identify truth with warranted assertability (perhaps under 'ideal' or 'optimum' conditions), theories that ask truth to explain the success of science or the conversations of some elite, all such theories either add nothing to our under-standing or have obvious counter-examples.
>
> (Davidson 1987: 135–6)

Rorty's pragmatism puts 'truth' squarely in the 'atheoretical' category that 'mind' and 'knowledge' were placed in earlier by PMN. His rhetoric in this respect is quite familiar: "This theory says that truth is not the sort of thing one should expect to have a philosophically interesting theory about" (CP: xiii). Indeed, a more strictly accurate title for this section would be "Pragmatism Minus a *Theory* of Truth".

Rorty does not attempt to produce a *conclusive* argument to seal the fate of theoretical approaches to truth, but he offers three main reasons for believing that it is *highly unlikely* there will ever be a philosophically interesting 'theory of truth' and that the quest for such a theory should therefore be abandoned. These concern:

(i) the *prima facie* status of true statements,
(ii) the longstanding lack of philosophical success in finding some-thing interesting to say about truth in general,
(iii) the impossibility of performing the kind of 'meta-verification' operations required by correspondence accounts of truth.

On the *prima facie* status of true statements, Rorty seems to be saying something like this:

> If we set aside traditional philosophical agendas and actually look afresh at what it is that various true statements like "2 + 2 = 4" and "Bacon did not write Shakespeare" share *solely in virtue of being true* (the examples are Rorty's own), there appear to be no compelling grounds for thinking "there is much to be said about this common feature" (CP: xiii).

To help make this stick, and harking back, perhaps, to James who made a similar move, Rorty offers what he considers to be an obviously insightful comparison with morals. Pragmatists may "see certain acts as good ones to perform, under the circumstances, but doubt that there is anything *general* and useful to say about what makes them *all* good" (CP: xiii, emphasis added).

Furthermore, to add weight to the *prima facie* case, Rorty cites the lack of success philosophers have had, over time, in producing a substantial theory of truth: "Pragmatists think that the history of attempts to isolate the True or the Good, or to define the word 'true' or 'good', supports their suspicion that there is no interesting work to be done in this area" (CP: xiv).

In a sense, this is itself yet another *prima facie* ploy. Rorty seems to be claiming that the conspicuous absence of success in theorizing about truth has to constitute, after concerted efforts to achieve such success over a long period of time, *prima facie* evidence that the whole project is misguided, evidence that 'success' has not been achieved because its achievement is probably impossible.

Rorty's general point about 'lack of success' is reiterated in particular connection with a ubiquitous idea that has done much to make the pragmatist's refusal to dwell on the theoretical aspects of truth's answerability to 'how things really stand' seem to be not just woolly evasion (which is bad enough!), but a philosophically offensive brand of wishful thinking. This is the idea of 'correspondence' itself, the view that all non-trivial, true sentences 'correspond to' or 'match' language-independent 'reality', and that *only* the 'correspondence relation' involved can explain the 'practical utility' of such sentences (e.g. explain how modern science flourishes: it does so by systematically yielding claims that correspond to how things are in the world).

To discredit the idea of correspondence, Rorty observes that: "Several hundred years of effort have failed to make interesting sense of the notion of 'correspondence' (either of thoughts to things or of words to things)" (CP: xvii), and then concludes:

> The pragmatist takes the moral of this discouraging history to be that "true sentences work because they correspond to the way things are" is no more illuminating than "it is right because it fulfills the Moral Law". Both remarks, in the pragmatist's eyes, are empty metaphysical compliments – harmless as rhetorical pats on the back to the successful inquirer or agent, but troublesome if taken seriously and "clarified" philosophically. (CP: xvii)

For those obdurate souls who are inclined, instead, to take this 'discouraging history' as a warrant for inferring only that the workings of 'the correspondence relation' are philosophically elusive and have yet to be discovered, Rorty further indicates there is something incoherent about the very thought that such a 'relation' could ever have explanatory force.

To invoke bare 'correspondence', without being able to explicate the micro-details of how it functions, is an empty gesture – no better, Rorty contends, than invoking '"dormative power' (Molière's doctor's infamous explanation of why opium puts people to sleep)" (CP: xxiv). But, on any imaginable interpretation of how truth matches reality, such details are never going to be available to us.

Suppose we concern ourselves with the truth of individual claims as expressed in particular sentences, and thus with how *language* enters into a correspondence connection with the world referred to by the words in such sentences. Then, says Rorty, we will find ourselves in the impossible position of having to take a 'meta-verificationalist' step *outside* language (for a straightforward verificationalist move would stay within the realms of language) in order to examine how it hooks up to extra-linguistic reality:

> One cannot see language-as-a-whole in relation to something else to which it applies, or for which it is a means to an end . . . The attempt to say "how language relates to the world" by saying what makes certain sentences true, or certain actions or attitudes good or rational, is, on this view, impossible.   (CP: xix)

"Impossible" is a very strong term, strong enough to make it puzzling as to why Rorty does not build on this line of thought to produce a *conclusive* argument – one which renders his appeals to other considerations redundant. We can only speculate that since he is manifestly uninterested in arguments in themselves, he prefers to produce an overall picture, one which is multifaceted enough to liberate us from the trap of trying to theorize about truth – that perhaps he believes a formally compelling argument might, by itself, still leave us hankering after the very thing it purports to demonstrate we cannot achieve.

Thus far, Rorty's pragmatist 'theory of truth' is almost entirely negative: a theory to put an end to theorizing, a blatant piece of 'anti-theory'. Rorty expects to win the battle over truth by showing that the forces of theory marshalled against pragmatism are bogus, and that when 'theory' is set aside, pragmatism has the most useful things to say about truth, however mundane these may sound to traditional philosophical ears.

For those expecting a more substantive account of truth, there is apparently little by way of compensation in Rorty's positive pronouncements. He is careful to stick with banal, virtually sub-philosophical characterizations – those where theorizing about 'correspondence' is replaced by much more informal talk of 'coping': "the activity of uttering sentences is one of the things people do in order to cope with their environment" (CP: xviii).

What are the virtues that Rorty would have us perceive in this downbeat, insouciant approach to truth?

These are largely parasitic on the success of his anti-theoretical stance. If Rorty is right about the gross philosophical folly of trying to theorize about truth, then pragmatism has the advantage of avoiding such folly, of doing nothing to ensnare philosophical views on truth in webs of superfluous speculation. Furthermore, by eschewing would-be theoretical substitutes for notions like 'correspondence', Rorty's pragmatism eludes traditional criticisms (such as Russell's). These tend to home in on anything even remotely within the terminological vicinity of a truth-theoretical concept, anything that might conceivably be attempting to do the kind of work done by terms like 'correspondence' (e.g. James's 'Expediency' and Dewey's 'Warranted Assertibility'). To this extent, it was imprecise of us to claim that Rorty 'does not put forward a revised account of truth that is specifically designed to cater for time-honoured criticisms of pragmatism'. Although Rorty does not explicitly announce any such process of revision, he proceeds, by philosophical stealth, to produce just that – to quietly divest classic pragmatism of its traditional terminological vulnerabilities.

Engaging realism

If pragmatism is to lose its 'air of provincialism', it must engage with current philosophical concerns, especially those deemed to be at the 'cutting edge'. It must do so even if it does not share the prevailing view that these particular concerns *are* important. Rorty overcomes this hurdle by pitting pragmatism directly against 'realism' –"a term which has come to be synonymous with anti-pragmatism" (CP: xxi). He thus enables pragmatism to enter a very influential, ongoing debate about the nature of language and the reality it depicts, one from which pragmatism has generally been excluded on grounds of its 'incompetence' concerning the pertinent linguistic considerations and its historical irrelevance to the main issues at stake.

Rorty distinguishes two kinds of realism: 'technical realism' and 'intuitive realism'. The proponents of technical realism believe that developments in the philosophy of language have left pragmatism stranded with an outmoded, verificationist conception of the connection between language and the world. They believe that Quine and Wittgenstein perpetuated Frege's mistaken conception of the relationship between meaning and reference. In this conception, meaning (generated by the intentions of word users) determines reference (what entities language selects from the world's store of things). But it has been supplanted, or so they claim, by a much improved, non-Fregean account of the links between words and the world. This account derives from 'the new theory of reference' as conceived by Saul Kripke.

Frege took a more or less Kantian line on concepts, regarding them as a means of dividing up an 'undifferentiated manifold' according to 'our interests' (Rorty points out that this line leads to Sellars's 'psychological nominalism' and what he calls a "Goodman-like insouciance about ontology" (CP: xxiii)). Kripke, by contrast, views the world as a place that embodies concept-independent divisions into not just 'particulars' (individual 'bits') but 'natural kinds of particulars' (clusters of 'bits' that, so clustered, manifest a distinct nature such as that of 'gold' or 'water'). Thus questions as to whether X has a certain property are to be tackled by straightforwardly realist means: by first finding out what 'X' actually refers to (irrespective of any intentions relating to 'X') and then checking whether that entity possesses the property in question.

Philosophers who fall into the technical realists' camp tend to be philosophers of language themselves like Saul Kripke and "those who turn Kripke's views on reference to the purposes of a realistic epistemology (e.g. Hartry Field, Richard Boyd, and, sometimes, Hilary Putnam)" (CP: xxiii).

Since these realists believe that questions like "Is it true X has property P?" are to be answered by finding out whether what 'X' refers to *really* has P, they also believe that the pragmatist's 'verificationist philosophy of language' – which goes no further in the direction of something 'really being the case' than 'truth according to our interests, capacities and practices' – is wrong.

Intuitive realists include "less specialised and more broadly ranging writers like Stanley Cavell and Thomas Nagel", as well as "others, such as Thompson Clarke and Barry Stroud" (CP: xxii–xxiii). They are not so much concerned with technical deficiencies in the verificationist account of language, as in the lack of depth displayed by the philosophical results of failing to venture beyond what is dictated by 'our interests and practices': "Pragmatists think our inability to say what would count as confirming or disconfirming a given solution to a problem is a reason for setting the problem aside. To take this view is, Nagel tells us, to fail to recognise that "unsolvable problems are not for that reason unreal" (CP: xxiii). How does Rorty respond to the anti-pragmatist force of the considerations raised by these two kinds of realists?

He puts pressure on the 'micro-structure' on the technical realist's position by trying to show that, under pragmatist scrutiny, it lacks explanatory power. Rorty points out that in any realist 'schema' designed to show how language relates to the world via, say, 'correspondence', the terms and concepts used are bound to assume precisely the kind of things the pragmatist finds questionable (e.g. that there is a relation of 'correspondence' between sentences which are true of the world and the world itself, that mention of the language-independent world makes sense, and that invoking such an *objective* relation *explains* why "science *works*, *succeeds* – enables us to cure diseases, blow up cities and the like" (CP: xxiv)).

In each case, the thrust of Rorty's challenge is: *exactly how* does this kind of assumption give the realist more explanatory leverage than the pragmatist? Why, for instance, is it better, in an *explanatory* sense, to say "P is true because P corresponds to the world" than "P is true because, all things considered, it is more fruitful (in all sorts of specifiable ways) to believe P rather than not-P"? Rorty's general strategy is to try to show that the technical realist has no genuinely informative and non-circular answers to such questions. Then, having exhausted its explanatory options, he concludes that:

> Technical realism collapses into intuitive realism – that the *only* debating point which the realist has is his (or her) conviction that the raising of the good old metaphysical problems (are there *really* universals? are there *really* causally efficacious physical objects, or did we just *posit* them?) served some good purpose, brought something to light, was important.   (CP: xxix)

Intuitive realists stress the importance of the intuitions that keep 'the good old metaphysical problems' in business (examples of such 'intuitions' include: "truth is more than assertibility" (which feeds straight into 'The Problem of Truth') and "there is more to pains than brain states" (which helps keep 'The Mind–Body Problem' in circulation) (CP: xxix)). What Rorty's pragmatism disputes is not the very existence of such intuitions, but their philosophical status:

> *Of course* we have such intuitions. How could we escape having them? We have been educated within an intellectual tradition built around such claims – just as we used to be educated within an intellectual tradition built around such claims as "If God does not exist, everything is permitted", "Man's dignity consists in his link with a supernatural order", and "One must not mock holy things". But it begs the question between pragmatist and realist to say that we must find a philosophical view which "captures" such intuitions. The pragmatist is urging that we do our best to *stop having* such intuitions, that we develop a *new* intellectual tradition. (CP: xxx)

Notice that this sort of discussion suggests how the realist's 'intuitions' might be uprooted. These intuitions are brought into philosophical play as insuperable insights. By making historical comparisons with insights that may well have once appeared to be equally irrevocable, Rorty casts a shadow of doubt over the wisdom of regarding *any* intuitions as ahistorically 'given', as insights that philosophy *must always* answer to. If we want to completely uproot 'intuitions', we must dig up the details of their historical context, but the kind of cautionary doubt Rorty raises here is *already* sufficient to prohibit a dogmatic attitude towards current intuitions. Having invoked the *possibility* that intuitions might be overturned, Rorty supplements this 'cautionary' prospect with a more straight-forwardly pragmatic claim:

> The *only* thing wrong with Nagel's intuitons is that they are being used to legitimate a vocabulary (the Kantian vocabulary in morals, the Cartesian vocabulary in philosophy of mind) which the pragmatists think should be eradicated rather than reinforced. But the pragmatist's *only* argument for thinking that these intuitions and vocabularies should be eradicated is that the intellectual tradition to which they belong has not paid off, is more trouble than it is worth, has become an incubus.
> (CP: xxxvii)

Rorty's pragmatism

> Pragmatists keep trying to find ways of making anti-philosophical points in non-philosophical language. (CP: xiv)

In our discussion, we have occasionally reverted to the phrase 'Rorty's pragmatism'. But what does this phrase mean? Perhaps it will be helpful to first clarify what it does *not* mean.

It does not signify a distinctive new form of pragmatism, one that renders the classic versions of Peirce, James and Dewey superfluous. It picks out no fresh pragmatist 'position', 'line of argument' or 'conjecture', nothing dramatically new that embodies the extraordinarily innovative – no philosophical discovery or conceptual invention. It refers to no methodological phenomenon that is supposed to illuminate pragmatism's way forward through culture and history like a flash of intellectual lightning in the philosophical darkness. To say all of this is not to belittle Rorty's contribution to the pragmatist tradition. He has done more – far more – than any other contemporary philosopher to render his own frankly pessimistic characterization of pragmatism's current fortunes, as quoted earlier, anachronistic, to make pragmatism a live philosophical option again and to stimulate worldwide interest in both its doctrines and the founders of those doctrines. It needs only a cursory survey of the acknowledgements to him in the burgeoning literature on pragmatism to corroborate Rorty's immense influence. But, he has attained this influence by consistently playing to what he sees as the inherent and frequently overlooked strengths of classic pragmatism rather than by instigating any major rebuilding programme. His pragmatism is a stripped-down version. It is 'classic pragmatism' redefined in terms which are intended to avoid the kind of criticisms that have dogged pragmatism in the past.

In "Pragmatism, Relativism, and Irrationalism" (CP: Ch. 9), Rorty characterizes the 'redefined' result in three overlapping and interdependent ways. Pragmatism is:

1. Simply anti-essentialism applied to notions like 'truth', 'knowledge', 'language', 'morality', and similar objects of philosophical theorizing. (CP: 162)
2. [The view that] there is no epistemological difference between truth about what ought to be and truth about what is, nor any metaphysical difference between facts and values, nor any methodological differences between morality and science.
(CP: 163).

3. The doctrine that there are no constraints on inquiry save conversational ones – no wholesale constraints derived from the nature of the objects, or of the mind, or of language, but only those retail constraints provided by the remarks of our fellow inquirers. (CP: 165)

Clearly these plug directly into the main themes of *Philosophy and the Mirror of Nature*. If terms like 'truth' and 'knowledge' do not designate *essences*, then there is no way philosophy can intervene within culture to determine in advance, once and for all time, what they *should* mean. If the 'epistemological', 'metaphysical' and 'methodological' differences referred to in (2) are bogus, then in so far as it trades on the alleged existence of such divides, most traditional philosophical discussion has been beside the point. And, if there are no genuinely 'external' limitations on inquiry, traditional philosophy has been wrong in attempting to identify such restrictions (for example: by anchoring claims about the world in aspects of that world).

From CP onwards, Rorty displays endless patience and imagination in trying to ensure that pragmatism looks like the 'natural successor' to analytic philosophy, the remedy for all its deficiencies. But, though the rhetorical emphasis shifts from time to time, the hub of what he is trying to convey never varies. Rorty's version of pragmatism is a historically self-conscious form of thought derived from the core of classic American pragmatism that substitutes plain conceptions of 'usefulness' (which include: 'what is of interest to us', 'what helps us to cope', 'what assuages our pain', 'what we tend to do in the circumstances' and so on) for the more abstract, high-theoretical constructs that philosophy found itself having to invent when it mistakenly assumed proprietorial rights over certain key areas of discourse and hence over intellectual culture as a whole. This heavy emphasis on 'practical utility' echoes James's own explanation of the pragmatist approach:

> The pragmatic method, as [James] defined it, maintains that in order to develop the meaning of an idea, we need only determine what conduct the idea is fitted to produce; this conduct is the idea's *sole* significance. Every distinction in thought therefore consists in a possible *difference in practice* – and *nothing else*. Ideas are genuinely alternative when – and only when – they lead to unlike consequences; when they produce a difference in concrete fact and in conduct *resulting* from that fact.
>
> (Morris 1950: 26, emphasis added)

Philosophy and writing

> The twentieth-century attempt to purify Kant's general theory
> about the relation between representations and their objects by
> turning it into philosophy of language is, for Derrida, to be
> countered by making philosophy even more impure – more
> unprofessional, funnier, more allusive, sexier, and above all,
> more "written".
> (CP: 93)

There are a number of reasons why Rorty is sympathetic to the kind
of Derridean 'counter moves' depicted in this quotation from
"Philosophy as a Kind of Writing: An Essay on Derrida" (CP: Ch. 6).
In *Philosophy and the Mirror of Nature*, he concludes that 'philosophy of language', the most cherished jewel in the crown of late twentieth-century analytic philosophy, is just a continuation of the old
'Cartesian–Kantian problematic', a further abortive attempt to
construct "a permanent, neutral framework for inquiry, and thus for
all culture" (CP: 8). Rorty regards this 'problematic' as having more
or less collapsed in on itself after a long run of unfruitful results and
a more recent series of internal critiques that undermine the sort of
assumptions and distinctions needed to prop it up.

Furthermore, when that 'problematic' wears itself out, the lofty conception of philosophy that goes with it also erodes. There no longer
seems much point in thinking of philosophy as a special, 'overseeing'
discipline, distinguishable from the rest of culture by its high-minded
themes and superior, more rationally hygienic, methods.

If it has no designated 'techniques' or 'problems', it is hard to see
how philosophy can differentiate itself from other disciplines without becoming 'more written'. For when philosophy crawls out from
under the weight of its self-deceptive, vainglorious past, it needs to
be able to capture the hearts and imaginations of those who participate in the flourishing 'markets' for ideas, especially 'new ideas'. And
it can only do this by saying things that look more interesting than
the things said by those, such as novelists, who are already at home
with the notion that they are primarily engaged in 'a form of writing'. In such company, the kind of transparent, self-effacing prose
that analytic philosophers pride themselves upon, prose that tries to
keep forever out of the way of its subject matter, of what it is 'representing', can be a deadly handicap. Such writing, with, as Jonathan
Rée nicely puts it, a "carefully contrived plain-dealing style" (Rée
1998: 7), can only attract widespread attention when harnessed to

something more exciting like 'useful techniques' and 'interesting problems'. Philosophy that sees itself as a textual venture embraces an equivalent of the latter, but it makes no attempt to define its approach and its themes *independently* of its written status.

Rorty recognizes that the Derridean call for a more writerly approach to philosophy could well be construed as a retrograde 'idealist' step by those who probably most need to heed such a call. Writerly philosophy self-consciously plays up its own 'textual qualities' – the qualities it manifests in virtue of being *written*. This is likely to sound an alarm for those who envisage thereby losing touch with extra-textual reality. Derrida's own, much-flaunted, slogan "There is nothing outside of the text" (Derrida 1976: 158) tends to fuel such fears. Rorty takes a rather lighthearted view of all this:

> There is a deep terror among Kantian philosophers of a certain job-related health hazard: the philosopher, after overstrenuous inquiry into our relation to the world, may lose his nerve, his reason, and the world simultaneously. He does this by withdrawing into a dream world of ideas, of representations – even, God help us, of texts. (CP: 96)

The threat of withdrawal into a purely textual world induces no idealist terror in Rorty, nor need it do so, he thinks, in others. So-called 'extra-textual reality' drops out of his pragmatist picture along with 'The World' as depicted in '"The World Well Lost": "'The world' is either the purely vacuous notion of the ineffable cause of sense and goal of intellect, or else the name for the objects that inquiry at the moment is leaving alone: those planks in the boat which are at the moment not being moved about" (CP: 15). Furthermore, text-based, 'writerly philosophy' has richer resources available for 'keeping in touch with reality' than the traditional philosophy it seeks to replace. It is the latter, with its austere delusions of getting behind language to finally figure out how it hooks on to things, to at last "represent *representing itself*" (CP: 96), that runs the greater risk of losing itself in fantasy.

Writerly philosophy has richer resources not just in the sense of availing itself of a much wider stock of words and linguistic ploys, but also in the sense that it can interact with a broader range of texts. Derrida plays around with Hegel's texts, among many others; the sparks fly and new ideas emerge. Perhaps he, or some other writerly philosopher, will do the same sort of thing some time with Feynmann's *Lectures on Physics* or a proof of *Fermat's Last Theorem*. Nothing is off limits. In this context, the lack of a role for a notion of reality that bears no textual fingerprints seems no great loss. For, as Rorty goes on to sum such matters up later in his career: "There is nothing to be known about an object except what sentences are true of it" (PSH: 55). The tradition that runs from Platonism to analytic philosophy via rationalism, empiricism and Kantianism has become increasingly more selective about its textual partners. It shudders at the thought of 'playing around' with texts outside its increasingly restricted fields of interest. Indeed, the very idea of 'playing around with texts' goes against the more serious-minded, analytic grain. Writing that is not open to careful analysis under certain narrow, mainly epistemological, constraints tends to get ignored. This obliterates much of philosophy's own history, but, ironically, it also deletes those areas of contemporary intellectual culture most closely associated with the notion of 'keeping in touch with reality': science and mathematics. And it also means that important areas of practical philosophical inquiry such as medical ethics and business ethics are looked down on as 'second rate', as minor intellectual vocations for those who cannot compete at the cutting edge of high theory.

For an example of how philosophy has restricted its options in this way, compare Leibniz and Wittgenstein. The writings of the former weave a seamless web of scientific, mathematical and philosophical reflections. As for Wittgenstein, even though his work demonstrates a marked degree of logical precociousness early on in his career, his writings then become increasingly 'isolationist' – and this at a time of major breakthroughs in all areas of culture, but in physics and mathematics in particular. His few scattered remarks in this connection have been inflated by some of his followers into 'profound insights', as if he was able to sit on the sidelines of the relevant 'language games' and yet still set the agenda straight for a discipline such as mathematics and its major thinkers like Gödel.

When it comes to the history of philosophy, the comparison becomes even more invidious. Leibniz's writings reverberate with many key developments in the history of philosophy. Wittgenstein's must be read as if philosophy has no sustained history. For only writings that largely overlook such history, or refuse to take it seriously, can contend, as Wittgenstein's famously do, that philosophical problems are:

- caused by philosophers taking language off 'on holiday' in the midst of their reflections,

- correspondingly cured by bringing the appropriate words back from their 'metaphysical use' abroad to their 'everyday', or 'ordinary, and originally intended', use at home.

All the great words of philosophy, words that individual philosophers of genius have become worked up about over the years, words such as 'substance', 'mode', 'idea', 'essence', 'Being' and 'truth', have evolved as terms of art in debates that have developed in very specific historical circumstances. To regard them as having simply slipped out of their proper place when taken into philosophical captivity is to display incredible naïvety about the history of philosophy. The philosophical line of controversy in which such words developed their significance just *is* their proper home. Words like 'substance' or 'essence' have nowhere else to go back to.

Rorty himself takes a much more positive view of Wittgenstein's 'isolationism'. He sees this as free-wheeling lack of professionalism, an attractive feature that frees Wittgenstein's writings from philosophical trappings, opening them, as we will soon see, to an interpretation that makes previous tradition the brunt of satire. Moreover, the writings of Rorty's Wittgenstein put up no principled barriers to 'textual interaction' – Wittgenstein's own reticence in this connection being idiosyncratic, a mere quirk of character that casts no substantial shadow over the further development of his ideas.

Appropriations revisited

To many readers who came to it cold, *Philosophy and the Mirror of Nature* seemed to run roughshod through the history of philosophy. It advocated a 'historicist approach', and yet lumped together a set of figures that were apparently as historically disjunctive as one would ever be likely to find: Dewey, Heidegger and Wittgenstein. Rorty, however, claims that these three philosophical figures: "Are in agreement that the notion of knowledge as accurate representation, made possible by special mental processes and intelligible through a general theory of representation, needs to be abandoned" (PMN: 6). He regards Dewey, Heidegger and Wittgenstein as radical thinkers who "have brought us into a period of 'revolutionary' philosophy (in the sense of Kuhn's 'revolutionary' science) by introducing new maps of the terrain" (*ibid.*). Since they have 'set aside' the 'traditional problematic', Rorty maintains that they are best depicted "as philosophers whose aim is to edify" (PMN: 11–12). And he provides a typically vivid account of what he thinks they can contribute to his strategy for undermining the epistemology-based, analytic tradition:

> If we have a Deweyan conception of knowledge, as what we are justified in believing, then we will not imagine that there are enduring constraints on what can count as knowledge, since we will see "justification" as a social phenomenon rather than a transaction between "knowing subject" and "reality". If we have a Wittgensteinian notion of language as tool rather than mirror, then we will not look for necessary conditions of the possibility of linguistic representation. If we have a Heideggerian conception of philosophy, we will see the attempt to make the nature of the knowing subject a source of necessary truths as one more self-deceptive attempt to substitute a "technical" and determinate question for that openness to strangeness which initially tempted us to begin thinking. (PMN: 9)

But Rorty does not appear to explain how these three thinkers, whose philosophical interests otherwise seem so inimical, *can* be harnessed together without destroying their historical roots. Dewey was fascinated by the idea of a philosophically ungrounded culture freed from Enlightenment fixations, one "no longer dominated by the ideal of objective cognition but by that of aesthetic enhancement" (PMN: 13), Heidegger was ponderously obsessed with the huge question of 'Being', and Wittgenstein was concerned to rescue analytic philosophy from its preoccupation with 'theories'. Furthermore, each was self-consciously responding to a different socio-historical context.

Consequences puts a much better complexion on this unusual choice of 'appropriations'. And it does so by showing in more detail why Rorty feels he is perfectly entitled to haul such figures onto his pragmatist bandwagon.

Dewey

> Dewey was the philosopher who most clearly and explicitly set aside the goal common to the Greeks and the German Idealists (accurate representation of the intrinsic nature of reality) in favour of the political goal of increasingly free societies and increasingly diverse individuals within them. That is why he

> seems to me the most useful and most significant figure in twen-
> tieth-century philosophy. (PSH: 49)

As a founder of pragmatism, Dewey is, it would seem, the least controversial choice. His selection is still surprising, however, because he appeared to have faded into quiet obscurity well before PMN was published and for that reason alone, looked not to belong up in the 'intellectual heroes' category. Some Dewey scholars – and not just the "self appointed gatekeepers of Deweydom" (Conway 1999: 222) – go further than this. They are concerned that the kind of pragmatism Rorty attributes to Dewey is not Dewey's own, that "the Dewey who emerges from Rorty's various sketches bears a suspicious resemblance to Rorty himself" (*ibid.*).

In the two articles "Overcoming the Tradition: Heidegger and Dewey" and "Dewey's Metaphysics" (CP: Chs 3 & 5), Rorty outlines his interpretation of Dewey and defends the brand of pragmatism he extracts from Dewey's writings. The first article examines the similarities and differences between Dewey and Heidegger. They emerge as sharing "an extraordinary amount of agreement on the need for a 'destruction of the history of Western ontology'", but with an "utterly different notion of what might succeed 'ontology'" (CP: 42). Dewey is depicted as a thinker who "sees the epistemological problems of modern philosophy as the adjustment of old metaphysical assumptions to new conditions" (CP: 44). Along with Heidegger, he is viewed as someone who wanted to break free from those very assumptions and also find "a way of seeing things which would take us far beyond the world of historicist philosophising which succeeded Hegel" (CP: 53). Dewey found what he wanted, Rorty tells us, "In turning away from philosophy as a distinctive activity altogether, and towards the ordinary world – the problems of men and women, freshly seen by discarding the distinctions which the philosophical tradition had developed" (*ibid.*).

The latter description has increasingly come to look like a portrait of Rorty himself, but this does not necessarily mean that Rorty wilfully distorted Dewey's philosophical image into his own rebellious likeness. A more plausible explanation might be that in grappling over time with the tensions discussed in "Trotsky and the Wild Orchids" (i.e. between 'individual bliss' and 'political progess', between 'Philosophy' and 'Social Justice'), Rorty has seen fit to resolve them by *following* what he regards as Dewey's lead. Of course, this begs the question as to whether Rorty is right in so regarding Dewey. Those who dispute Rorty's interpretation of Dewey will object that Dewey never completely turned his back on philosophy – least of all metaphysics – and that "his metaphysical forays, particularly in *Experience and Nature*, constitute a strong source of attraction for many pragmatists" (Conway 1999: 223).

Rorty's second article addresses precisely this kind of objection. He suggests that the most fruitful reading of *Experience and Nature* will take its cue from Dewey's own belated hope to produce a fresh version "changing the title as well as the subject matter . . . to *Nature and Culture*" (CP: 72). Such a reading will assimilate the work to 'the history of ideas' rather than "the genre which includes the central books of Aristotle's *Metaphysics*, Spinoza's *Ethics*, Royce's *The World and the Individual*, and other paradigms" (*ibid.*). For then:

> Given such an assimilation, one can see the book not as an "empirical metaphysics" but as a historico-sociological study of the cultural phenomenon called "metaphysics". It can be seen as one more version of the polemical critique of the tradition offered in *Reconstruction in Philosophy* and *The Quest for Certainty*. (CP: 73)

Rorty openly concedes that "for most of his life, Dewey would not have relished this assimilation" (*ibid.*). But he views such reluctance as a symptom of an unsatisfactory split in Dewey's philosophical personality:

> For better or worse, he *wanted* to write a metaphysical system. Throughout his life, he wavered between a therapeutic stance toward philosophy and another quite different stance – one in which philosophy was to become "scientific" and "empirical" and to do something serious, systematic, important and constructive. Dewey sometimes described philosophy as the criticism of culture, but he was never quite content to think of himself as a kibitzer or a therapist or an intellectual historian.   (CP: 73)

Rorty insists that Dewey's hopes for a 'philosophical metaphysics', for something more elevated, more 'serious, systematic, important and constructive' than 'cultural criticism' were forlorn *even by his own lights*: "It is unlikely that we shall find, in *Experience and Nature*, anything which can be called a 'metaphysics of experience' as opposed to a therapeutic treatment of the tradition – on the ground that Dewey's own view of the nature and function of philosophy precludes it" (CP: 77).

In turning Dewey's pragmatism upon itself, Rorty makes what is, as Conway points out, 'a signature gambit':

> He executes an immanent, peritropaic critique of Dewey's pragmatism. That is, he rejects the metaphysical dimension of Dewey's thought, but only in the name of Dewey's own anti-essentialism. Rorty thus saves Dewey's pragmatism by rehabilitating the supposedly fatal tension between his vibrant experimentalism and his retrograde metaphysical urge. He "heals" this tension by orchestrating a collision between these completing aims, which in turn yields a consistently anti-metaphysical interpretation of Dewey's pragmatism.   (Conway 1999: 226)

In this 'anti-metaphysical interpretation', Dewey's 'metaphysical urges' are subdued by his larger aim "To sketch a culture that would not continually give rise to new versions of the old problems, because it would no longer make the distinctions between Truth, Goodness and Beauty which engender such problems" (CP: 86).

Heidegger

Though long revered within the 'continental tradition' for his great originality and erudition, Heidegger was treated with a good deal of contempt by the analytic tradition before the publication of PMN. Until then, he was generally ignored, seen only as the deserving butt of dismissive critics like Carnap and Ayer. The received image was of a mulishly obscure and self-indulgent thinker whose work was useful only for demonstrating the folly of flouting the exacting standards of linguistic clarity advocated by analytic philosophers. Rorty changed this off-hand attitude. By elevating Heidegger to 'hero status' in PMN, he caused many analytic philosophers to sit up and take another, less jaundiced, look at texts like *Being and Time*. This response was still cautious: "Let us see whether Rorty is on to something, whether there is some substance beneath Heidegger's jargon. After all, didn't Ryle once give *Being and Time* a favourable review?" But the upshot was a partial 'incorporation' of Heideggerian ideas into the analytic tradition. For Heidegger was finally deemed to be saying things (about the irreducible 'contextuality' of the 'knowing subject', and so on) that were, 'after all', of interest to that tradition. Rorty would no doubt relish the thought of more analytic philosophers actually reading Heidegger, but his goal was not 'incorporation'. He turned to Heidegger as someone who showed that it is possible to *escape* "the tradition of 'metaphysics' or 'ontology'" (CP: 37). Heidegger belongs with Dewey and Wittgenstein because, like them, he provides an inspiring example of how to avoid the shackles of 'tradition'.

In "Overcoming the Tradition: Heidegger and Dewey", Rorty portrays Heidegger as a thinker who demonstrated how the standard, so-called 'perennial problems' of 'metaphysics' and 'epistemology' arose out of historical developments, but ultimately failed to heed his own historical lessons when continuing to philosophize:

> Heidegger's attachment to the notion of "philosophy" – the pathetic notion that even after metaphysics goes, something called 'Thought' might remain – is simply the sign of Heidegger's own fatal attachment to the tradition: the last infirmity of the greatest of the German professors. It amounts to saying that even though everybody who previously counted as a paradigm of philosophy – Plato, Thomas, Descartes, Nietzsche – turned out to be a step on a path towards chaos, we must still try to be philosophers. For "philosophy" is a name for that activity which is essential to our humanity. No matter how much Heidegger seems to have overcome our professional urge to compete with the great dead philosophers on their own ground, no matter how much he may try to distance himself from the tradition (not to mention his fellow philosophy professors), he is still insistent that the tradition offered us "words of Being". He still thinks that the place where philosophy was is the place to be. He thinks that to cease thinking about what Plato and Kant were thinking about is to be diminished, to lose hold of what is most important, to sink into darkness. If he were true to his own dictum that we should "cease all overcoming, and leave metaphysics to itself", he would have nothing to say, nowhere to point. *The whole force of Heidegger's thought lies in his account of the history of philosophy.* (CP: 52)

In his "Preface" (CP: ix), Rorty says that, with hindsight, he finds this view of Heidegger "unduly unsympathetic" and hopes to put matters right with "a more balanced and useful interpretation in a book on Heidegger". However, much to the disappointment of those who secretly dreamed that Rorty might save them the trouble of having to actually read *Being and Time*, the 'book' has never materialized.

Richard Rorty

Rorty later published 'the fruits' of his "abortive, abandoned attempt to write a book about" Heidegger as the first four essays that make up Part I of *Essays on Heidegger and Others: Philosophical Papers Volume 2* (EHO). But this and subsequent work on Heidegger reiterate very similar lines of criticism to those already voiced in *Consequences*. Rorty still takes Heidegger to task for his inflated view of philosophy, for his "failure to take a relaxed, naturalistic, Darwinian view of language" (EHO: 3), for being unable to "escape the notion that philosopers' difficulties are more than just philosophers' difficulties – the notion that if philosophy goes down, so will the West" (CP: 54).

Wittgenstein

> All philosophy can do is destroy idols. And that means not creating a new one – for instance as in "absence of an idol".
>
> (Wittgenstein 1993: s. 88)

In "Keeping Philosophy Pure: An Essay on Wittgenstein" (CP: Ch. 2), Rorty reads the 'later Wittgenstein' (i.e. the Wittgenstein of *Philosophical Investigations* as opposed to the Wittgenstein of *Tractatus Logico-Philosophicus*) as a satirist, as someone who pokes fun at traditional philosophical concerns:

> Typically, attempts to overthrow the traditional problems of modern philosophy have come in the form of proposals about how we ought to think so as to avoid those problems. When Wittgenstein is at his best, he resolutely avoids such constructive criticism and sticks to pure satire. He just shows, by examples, how hopeless the traditional problems are – how they are based on a terminology which is as if designed expressly for the purpose of making a solution, how the questions which generate the traditional problems cannot be posed except in this terminology, how pathetic it is to think that the old gaps will be closed by constructing new gimmicks. (CP: 34)

This Wittgenstein has qualities that Rorty would like to see when he looks in the mirror of his own writings. He makes no moves *within* conventional philosophical territory, but rather tries to free us from the desire to make such moves by repeatedly showing their foolishness. Such an interpretation chimes well with Wittgenstein's apparent 'quietism', his refusal to propound 'philosophical theses'. However, unlike Rorty, most commentators take Wittgenstein's 'anti-philosophical' remarks to be voiced in the same spirit of 'high seriousness' as his earlier attempts to resolve all the problems of philosophy in the one brief fell swoop of his *Tractatus*. Their Wittgenstein has a sense of humour, makes jokes, even. But he does not 'poke fun' at philosophy. He is, to be sure, a philosophical counter-puncher, and (*pace* our earlier objection that he avoided close encounters with the great and good) pound for pound, one of the best, but he is no satirist.

Rorty's almost 'Swiftian' reading is not based on textual nuances. He identifies no deep points of ironic humour overlooked by those who want to portray Wittgenstein as having something important to say by means of a fairly straightforward critique of the Frege–Russell–early-Wittgenstein tradition. The 'reading' is more a case study, so to speak, in 'anti-essentialist' reading habits – that is, in pragmatism as applied to texts. For Rorty is suggesting that we will get more out of (say) *Philosophical Investigations* or *On Certainty* if we take it to be making fun of philosophers' theoretical pretensions. And this is an example of Rorty's view, amplified in his later work, that a 'good reading' of a text is *not* necessarily one that accurately extracts its 'intrinsic meaning', its 'intended meaning' or any such thing, but one that puts the author's writing to the best extrinsic *practical use*. Here Rorty is always careful to be consistent. He does not try to define the notion of 'usefulness' independently of our 'interests and practices'. It is a *contextual* notion. If we come to share some of Rorty's pragmatist views on the nature and purpose of philosophy, then we will 'get more out of' Wittgenstein by treating his later work as satire.

Since Rorty's anti-essentialist approach to texts raises the possibility that *all* writing is malleable, that *any* text can reasonably be beaten into *any* shape of *any* extrinsic interpretation if the results are appropriately useful, we should not be surprised that he finds it so natural to appropriate the work of philosophers who might otherwise seem strange bedfellows. If he thinks he can show that more can be achieved by making a pragmatist out of a particular figure who does not on the face of things fit the role, then he will feel obliged to ignore other interpretations. This does not mean, as some critics seem to think, that Rorty is simply licensing 'textual recklessness', the kind of irresponsibility about the works of great philosophers that will eventually destroy our intellectual heritage. Imagine someone who comes to believe that we will 'get more out of' Shakespeare's *Hamlet* if we treat it as a satirical comedy, full of surface ironies, as a play that makes fun of 'father figures', of 'soul searching' and *Angst*. If that person's reading of *Hamlet* is sufficiently engaging and convincing, if it appeals to our predominant 'interests' and squares with our prevailing practices, then we may lose our grip on the idea that *Hamlet* is a deep 'tragedy', we may start to find *Hamlet* 'funny' and thus come to regard it as a 'comedy'. But no mere act of textual vandalism is likely to achieve this. Of course, this means that, in Rorty's case, the onus is on him to show that his Dewey, Heidegger and Wittgenstein have more to offer us than other, less controversial versions. We continue discussion of some of the issues raised here in our final chapter when we consider the nature of the 'constraints' on 'redescriptive philosophy'.

Chapter 4

Contingency

Almost as soon as I began to study philosophy, I was impressed by the way in which philosophical problems appeared, disappeared, or changed shape, as the result of new assumptions or vocabularies. (PMN: xiii)

Past the single vision

Philosophy and the Mirror of Nature established Rorty as a significant, if very controversial, thinker, more highly regarded outside philosophy, perhaps, than within, though not necessarily of less overall intellectual importance on that count. The book's evident "success among nonphilosophers" boosted Rorty's confidence, but he was still troubled by the ghost that had haunted his youth: his inability to find a way of "holding reality and justice in a single vision" (WO: 12):

Philosophy and the Mirror of Nature did not do much for my adolescent ambitions. The topics it treated – the mind–body problem, controversies in the philosophy of language about truth and meaning, Kuhnian philosophy of science – were pretty remote from both Trotsky and the orchids. I had gotten back on good terms with Dewey; I had articulated my historicist anti-Platonism; I had finally figured out what I thought about the direction and value of current movements in analytic philosophy; I had sorted out most of the philosophers I had read. But I had not spoken to any of the questions which got me started

reading philosophers in the first place. I was no closer to the
single vision which 30 years back I had gone to college to get.

(WO: 12)

As Rorty "tried to figure out what had gone wrong", he at last
decided that from a *philosophical standpoint*, the very idea of 'holding reality and justice in a single vision' was completely misguided,
that: "Only religion – only a non-argumentative faith in a surrogate
parent who, unlike any real parent, embodied love, power and
justice in equal measure – could do the trick Plato wanted done"
(WO: 12).

The path towards a religious solution of the 'single vision' problem was definitively sealed off by Rorty's anti-authoritarian streak
and his earlier unsuccessful dabble in Christianity, not to mention
his intellectual sophistication. He therefore resolved to write something that would describe how things could look on the other side of
the fascination with a 'single vision'. The upshot was *Contingency,
irony, and solidarity*, a book in which Rorty attempts to explain why
"There is no need to weave one's personal equivalent of Trotsky and
one's personal equivalent of my wild orchids together" (WO: 13). It is
also a book in which Rorty actually starts to practise something like
the kind of 'post-epistemological philosophy' he preached so
eloquently towards in *Philosophy and the Mirror of Nature*.

Befriending time and chance

The line of thought common to Blumenberg, Nietzsche, Freud
and Davidson suggests that we try to get to the point where we
no longer worship anything, where we treat nothing as a quasi-
divinity, where we treat everything – our language, our
conscience, our community – as a product of time and chance.

(CIS: 22)

The need for a 'single vision' *will* seem compelling as long as we
believe there is, or at least ought to be, in the end, only one big,
fundamental thing – Virtue, Truth, Reality, God, Justice or whatever – that we should measure our lives by, something that *all* of our
beliefs, desires and dispositions should answer to. For then, the
value of both our private obsessions and our public concerns can,
indeed *must*, be marked up on a unitary scale of worth: "Should I
suppress my surreptitious desire to commune with socially frivolous,

exotic species of plants because it does not contribute as much to (say) 'the search for Social Justice' as my public contributions towards projects that seek to alleviate poverty?"

If 'one big, fundamental thing' *is* to underpin our aspirations, it has to be the kind of thing that we can, if we so wish, hold forever steady in our mind's eye. It thus has to have an unchanging, eternally reliable aspect, one that enables us to focus on it at all times and whatever the circumstances. In PMN and related writings, Rorty began to suggest that *nothing* can meet such requirements, that any single unwavering thing which appears to fit the bill – such as Plato's 'the form of the Good' – is itself the product of the kind of historical developments it is supposed to transcend, that, as Hegel showed, "nothing, including an a priori concept, is immune from cultural development" (CP: 16).

Contingency, irony, and solidarity finesses this latter suggestion by showing us how we can make firm friends with the idea that *everything* in our lives is the 'product of time and chance'. The book deploys three main strategies to help create and enliven this new 'friendship'. First, it 'redescribes' key areas of our lives in ways which indicate that, whether we like it or not, they are infected by 'time and chance'. These 'key areas' are: our use of language, our sense of personal identity and our community. Secondly, it shows how recent trends in intellectual culture have fortunately geared us up for just such a 'redescription', that the time is historically ripe for graciously accepting the ubiquitous role of 'time and chance' in human affairs. And finally, it provides some handy terms with which we can begin to talk more easily about ourselves, and to one another, as creatures who, once freed from obsessions with ahistorical myths, are able to live playfully at home on the waves of an ocean of socio-historical contingencies.

Language

Why 'language'? Why does *its* contingency matter? Because of its purported 'special link' with 'Truth'. If 'the one big, fundamental thing' can be caught, or held still, in the net of language, then the language users involved will have also captured 'the Truth'. In this sense, language is Truth's convenient 'social representative'. Successfully targeted, it enables us to occasionally take our mind's eye off the big, fundamental thing itself. We can go about our business safe in the knowledge that we have its linguistic counterpart to hand. Rorty challenges this kind of picture, and on all fronts. He denies that language actually plays a *representational* role, that it functions best by somehow standing in for 'reality'. Still stronger, he denies that language *can* play such a role. Furthermore, the notion of *anything*, let alone 'the one big, fundamental thing', *simply* being 'there' waiting to be captured in the net of language, is, he claims, a chimerical notion, a philosopher's fiction that has long outlived its usefulness.

The thought that language is important to the extent that it embodies 'Truth', or even just 'truths', encourages two opposing attitudes. On the one hand, we may be inclined to worship language in its own right as the great repository of Truth/truths, thereby mystifying its status. And, on the other hand, this kind of conception of language may make us come over all 'scientistic' so that we believe much intellectual time should be devoted (probably by the appropriate philosophical experts) to mapping out the precise technicalities of the relationship between language and the world. This, we believe, will eventually give us a *theory* of truth, something we can employ to increase the quota of truths in our cognitive repertoire. Rorty wants to show us how we can steer a path between these extremes by recognizing *the contingency of language*.

We will shortly discuss in more detail what Rorty means by the notion of 'contingency'. But in this context, it suffices to say that he is shifting our attention towards the ways in which languages are 'constructed' by socio-historical forces – "made rather than found" (CIS: 7) – so that words and sentences are thereby 'tools' naturally evolved for 'coping with the world' rather than 'representing' it. Since languages are apt to change in nature according to social circumstances, we should not look to them for evidence as to what any big, fundamental, unchanging thing is like. Nor should we expect ever to be able to find the theoretical key to locking words on to the world and its contents for the purpose of generating more world-based truths.

Rorty reinforces the idea that language is, through and through, a 'product of time and chance' by reminding us that things could not be otherwise. He does this by restating his pragmatist position on truth in plainer than the usual philosophical terms. He thus engages with the reader who is not familiar with the ins and outs of the traditional debate over truth that runs from Plato and Aristotle through to Tarski and Davidson. At the same time, he challenges those philosophers who *are* cognizant of such details to reconsider whether the debate in question has run its course, whether "our purposes would be best served by ceasing to see truth as a deep matter, as a topic of philosophical interest, or 'true' as a term which repays analysis" (CIS: 8). The 'restatement' brings together, in more commonsensical guise, the views Rorty expressed on "our notion of the world" in "The World Well Lost" (CP) and the explication of "a pragmatist theory of truth" he gave us in his "Introduction" to *Consequences of Pragmatism*:

> We need to make a distinction between the claim that the world is out there and the claim that truth is out there. To say that the world is out there, that it is not our creation, is to say, with common sense, that most things in space and time are the effects of causes which do not include human mental states. To say that truth is not out there is simply to say that where there are no sentences there is no truth, that sentences are elements of human languages, and that human languages are human creations.   (CIS: 5)

This stress on languages as 'human creations' connects with a further reason why linguistic concerns are the focus of Rorty's attention very early on in *Contingency, irony, and solidarity*. He would like to alter our whole philosophical approach to language so that we are much less inclined to worry about the association between it and any extra-linguistic consideration, less inclined to try to use language alone as a quasi-technical means of bootstrapping ourselves out of all our philosophical troubles, and still less concerned to reduce philosophy to an exploration of the micro-theoretical details of word–world relations via the philosophy of language. Instead, Rorty would prefer us to enlarge our linguistic frame of reference, to reflect on the historical fate of whole *vocabularies*. Then we will be able to get a clearer view of the huge role such linguistic schemes play in our lives, and the huge corresponding differences an overall change in vocabulary makes. Furthermore:

> Once we realize that progress, for the community as for the individual, is a matter of using new words as well as of arguing from premises phrased in old words, we realize that a critical vocabulary which revolves around notions like "rational", "criteria", "argument" and "foundation" and "absolute" is badly suited to describe the relation between the old and the new.   (CIS: 48–9)

Rorty's discussion of 'vocabularies' thus expands his earlier 'distinctive' account of philosophical change, where images and metaphors supplant 'arguments' and 'rational deliberation' as the vehicles of transformation. When our linguistic frame of reference is suitably enlarged, questions about how the world issues its own guarantees to claims about its nature lose interest. They fail to make much sense, even:

> When we consider examples of alternative language games – the vocabulary of ancient Athenian politics versus Jefferson's, the moral vocabulary of Saint Paul versus Freud's, the jargon of Newton versus that of Aristotle, the idiom of Blake versus that of Dryden – it is difficult to think of the world as making one of these better than another, of the world as deciding between them. When the notion of "description of the world" is moved from the level of criterion-governed sentences within language games to language games as wholes, games which do not choose between reference to criteria, the idea that the world decides which descriptions are true can no longer be given a clear sense. It becomes hard to think that that vocabulary is somehow already out there in the world, waiting for us to discover it.
>
> (CIS: 5–6)

Changes in vocabularies are never *just* a matter of 'rational choice': "Europe did not *decide* to accept the idiom of Romantic poetry, or of socialist politics, or of Galilean mechanics" (CIS: 3). Such changes are instigated, instead, by all kinds of socio-historical events. A myriad of 'contingent', causal factors can play a part, some of them mundane – like having "gradually lost the habit of using certain words and gradually acquired the habit of using others" (CIS: 6). However, in some cases, these 'causes' may be anything but mundane. For Rorty's account tips the balance of power in favour of 'imagination' over 'reason'. Someone who is able to spin webs of intriguingly shiny, new metaphors, and thus create fresh and imaginative ways of talking about things, has a much better chance of influencing the way speakers at large use language than someone who constructs a cast-iron argument for assenting to certain definite propositions about the nature of reality. Hence Rorty's urgent promotion of the Shelleyean view that poets are, and should be, the principal agents of social change, and his great admiration for philosophers outside the field of analytic philosophy, such as Heidegger and Derrida, who dream up idioms far more tantalizing, exotic and causally potent than the swathes of clean-cut jargon that issue as fallout from the ventures of those analytic philosophers of language who spend most of their time tinkering with the technicalities of 'linguistic structure', 'referential apparatus', and so on. With a strong enough imagination, a thinker can, on this understanding, act like a force of cultural gravity on our linguistic habits, bending them into unheard-of shapes.

Selfhood

> Deafened by the acclaim for the hero of politics, it is sometimes hard to remember the quieter heroism of art. After all, how much does the development of poetic style matter compared to the aspiration of whole nations? (Ravitch 2000: 137)

If we are convinced that the world around us is an unnerving swirl of 'contingencies', that it contains no one, big fundamental thing to hang on to while we get our bearings on how to live our lives, we may turn 'inwards', hoping to drop anchor in 'the self'.

There is a cluster of imagined 'necessities', of possible places for anchorage, associated with our notion of 'the self'. The cluster incorporates claims, or 'theses', such as:

1. There *has to be* a self because to deny its existence would be, in some important sense, incoherent.
2. The self has to have certain features, *essential features* – an 'essence'.
3. What makes the self so *special*, so elevatedly unbrutish, is the fact that it somehow partakes of an aspect of 'the eternal' or 'the transcendentally divine'.
4. At the heart of the self lies the 'conscience', which has the capacity to make the right moral choices – such choices lock on to moral principles or laws that rise above the ravages of time.

In keeping with the picture of philosophical endeavour that follows from his view of language and his account of change in the history of ideas, Rorty does not try to *refute*, or even *argue* against, any particular claims of this sort – though, of course, his pragmatist stance entails that *all* substantive appeals to such phenomena as 'essences', 'the eternal', 'the transcendentally divine' and 'timeless moral choice' are mistaken. Instead, he introduces a roving discussion of fresh issues concerning our sense of 'selfhood', a discussion in which such considerations need play no important part. His expectation is that *these* issues will grab our attention. Then the answers to questions like "*Must* there be a self?" or "Does the self have a non-contingent core?" will no longer seem all that important. Indeed, the sentiments behind such questions will themselves fall by the intellectual wayside and our craving for anchorage in the received 'necessities' of the self will simply die down.

Rorty's discussion starts not with thinkers, like Descartes or Locke, who have helped define the terms of traditional philosophical debate concerning the nature of 'personal identity', but with some reflections on Philip Larkin's poem "Continuing to Live", especially its final sections that Rorty quotes as follows:

> And once you have walked the length of your mind, what
> You command is as clear as a lading-list
> Anything else must not, for you, be thought
> To exist.
>
> And what's the profit? Only that, in time
> We half-identify the blind impress
> All our behavings bear, may trace it home.
> But to confess,
>
> On that green evening when our death begins,
> Just what it was, is hardly satisfying,
> Since it applied only to one man once,
> And that man dying.
>
> ("Continuing to Live", Larkin 1988: 94)

He interprets the poem as an examination of the fear of dying, where the main interest lies in making this fear more explicit by reflecting on "what it is that will not be" (CIS: 23). The poem suggests to Rorty a way of achieving this task that agreeably sidelines conventional philosophical worries about the extinction of selfhood – worries such as whether, at the point of death, some special, soul-like substance, or some 'essence', is about to be erased.

What Larkin fears, Rorty tells us, is the extinction of "his idiosyncratic lading-list, his individual sense of what was possible and important. That is what made his I different from all the other I's" (CIS: 23). This apprehension concerns what is unique in Larkin's work, what is special about the various poems he has *created*. The most feared outcome is that his poems will be absorbed into the anonymous morass of culture, that "nobody will find anything distinctive in them" (CIS: 24). More generally, says Rorty, a creative person may worry that: "The words (or shapes, or theorems, or models of physical nature) marshalled to one's command may seem merely stock items, rearranged in routine ways. One will not have impressed one's mark on language but, rather, will have spent one's life shoving about already coined pieces" (*ibid.*).

These remarks may seem to be leading us into a rather superficial discussion of 'artistic originality' and well away from any deeper issues involving 'death' and 'the self'. But Rorty's very next sentence undercuts this impression: "So one would not really have had an I at all" (*ibid.*). This comment could be construed as the conclusion to an underlying *argument* involving premises that somehow equate personal identity with 'creative output'. But to go down that interpretative road would be a mistake. Rorty is not in the business of making further moves in standard philosophical debates on the notion of 'personal identity'. He raises the point about 'never having had an I' in order to stress the existential importance of anxieties about the 'uniqueness' of one's creative output. But he is not trying to make 'a case' for claiming such 'anxieties' are what is important. He is saying something more like: "Here is an interesting way of thinking about 'the self' inspired by Larkin's poem, let us see where this line of thinking takes us."

To complain that it is all very well for leading creative figures to cash out their worries about 'death', about 'what it is that will not be', in terms of the 'uniqueness of their output', but this leaves most of us (who are bereft of the requisite talent) high and dry, is precipitous. We need to be a bit more patient, to follow Rorty's discussion a bit further.

In fact, he anticipates a stronger interjection at this stage: that the whole story will not wash, even for major creative figures themselves. The cue for this anticipation comes from Larkin's own lines at the end of the poem, where "we are told that it is 'hardly satisfying' to trace home one's own distinctiveness" (CIS: 24). Rorty reads Larkin's professed doubts in these lines as doubts about his vocation and as a reminder of 'the quarrel between poetry and philosophy':

> This seems to mean that it is hardly satisfying to have become an individual – in the strong sense in which the genius is the paradigm of individuality. Larkin is affecting to despise his own vocation on the ground that to succeed in it would merely be to have put down on paper something which "applied only to one man/And that one dying . . .". Larkin is pretending that blind impresses, those particular contingencies which make each of us

"I" rather than a copy or replica of somebody else, do not really matter. He is suggesting that unless one finds something common to all men at all times, not just to one man once, one cannot die satisfied. He is pretending that to be a strong poet is not enough – that he would have attained satisfaction only from being a philosopher, from finding continuities rather than exhibiting a discontinuity. (CIS: 24–5)

Rorty believes Larkin's qualms are dissembling. He doubts that "any poet could seriously think trivial his own success in tracing home the blind impress borne by all his behavings – all his previous poems" (CIS: 24), but he does not try to show that there is some defect of *reasoning* in Larkin's misgivings. Instead, he launches into further discussion in which the poet's enthralment with contingent particulars as opposed to universal necessities begins to look much more like an appealing and adventurous way of finding material for constructing a sense of self and much less like an intellectual failing. At the same time, Rorty heads off the objection that the view of 'selfhood' he is offering cannot be generalized, that it only fits history's chosen few, the creative elite.

To achieve these ends, Rorty weaves the preoccupations of Nietzsche and Freud into his account of 'selfhood'. Nietzsche is brought in for three main reasons:

1. His "identification of the strong poet, the maker, as humanity's hero – rather than the scientist who is traditionally pictured as a finder" (CIS: 26).
2. His congenial "definition of truth as 'a mobile army of metaphors'" which "amounted to saying that the whole idea of 'representing reality' by means of language, and thus the idea of finding a single context for all human lives', should be abandoned" (CIS: 27).
3. His tendency to see "self knowledge as self creation. The process of coming to know oneself, confronting one's contingency, tracking one's causes home, is identical with the process of inventing a new language – that is of thinking up some new metaphors" (*ibid.*).

Freud is invoked as someone who makes it plausible to believe that the details of *each person's* life can be viewed as the raw material for self-knowledge, the stuff of poetry. He is brought in because he 'democratizes' the Nietzschean idea of 'self-creation':

For Freud's account of unconscious fantasy shows us how to see every human life as a poem – or, more exactly, every human life not so racked by pain as to be unable to learn a language nor so immersed in toil as to have no leisure in which to generate a self-description. He sees every life as an attempt to clothe itself in metaphors. (CIS: 35–6)

Again, Rorty is not interested in *proving* the 'correctness' of Freud's attempt to construe the self as a 'product of time and chance', to "substitute a tissue of contingent relations, a web which stretches backward and forward through past and future time, for a formed, unified, present, self-contained substance, something capable of being seen steadily and whole" (CIS: 41). He is much more concerned to canvas Freud's views as useful and interesting ways of talking about the self. These views have the added advantage, in Rorty's eyes, of dispensing with another traditional anchor point, 'the voice of conscience', by detaching its workings from any higher authority and then showing how its strictures form part of a rich *continuum* of moral outlooks, one which embraces 'the strange' and 'the perverse'. The Freud who appealed so often to the 'authority' of science was doing so *only* to lend surface credibility to his stance. He does not *really* want to turn psychoanalysis into an exact science:

He lets us see what moral philosophy describes as extreme, inhuman, and unnatural, as continuous with our own activity But, and this is a crucial point, he does not do so in the traditional philosophical, reductionist way. He does not tell us that art is *really* sublimation or philosophical system-building *merely* paranoia, or religion *merely* a confused memory of a fierce father. He is not saying that human life is *merely* a rechanneling of libidinous energy. He is not interested in invoking a reality–appearance distinction, in saying that anything is "merely" or "really" quite different. He just wants to give us one more redescription of things to be filed alongside all the others, one more vocabulary, one more set of metaphors which he thinks will have a chance of being used and thereby literalised.

(CIS: 39)

As readers digest the ingredients of Rorty's discussion, they may, provided he has made the prospect of doing so seem sufficiently alluring, come to appreciate both the ubiquity of the 'contingent components' of their own lives and "the power of language to make

new and different things possible and important" (CIS: 39). Then, as
their interest in traditional philosophical solutions to the 'problems
of the self' wanes, they may find themselves adopting something
akin to Edward Said's attitude towards 'the idea of a solid self',
though, if Rorty's words have really struck home, they will disregard
Said's reservations about the 'form of freedom' involved:

> I occasionally experience myself as a cluster of flowing currents.
> I prefer this to the idea of a solid self, the identity to which so
> many attach so much significance. These currents, like the
> themes of one's life, flow along during the waking hours, and at
> their best require no reconciling, no harmonising. They are "off"
> and may be out of place, but at least they are always in motion,
> in time, in place, in the form of all kinds of strange combinations
> moving about, not necessarily forwards, sometimes against each
> other, contrapunctually yet without one central theme. A form of
> freedom, I'd like to think, even if I am far from being totally con-
> vinced that it is.   (Said 1999: 415)

Community

Empathy with Said's take on 'the self' is liable to generate a significant shift in interest from the philosophical questions traditionally
raised by the notion of 'a solid self' to the more practical issues
brought up by Rorty's discussion (e.g. can we spin a web of 'redescriptions' which encompasses our *whole* life? How can we arrange
things socially and politically so that *each of us* is able to embark on
our own 'self-defining', redescriptive project?). However, this emphasis on 'self-creation' may seem to leave each individual stranded on
the rough seas of social change with no waterproof materials at hand
to build the foundations of our community. Rorty addresses this kind
of concern in the third chapter of *Contingency, irony, and solidarity*
when he responds to charges that he wants to unleash the turbulent
forces of 'irrationalism' and 'relativism' on Western cultures, charges
that he is resigned to facing once he has said "that truth 'is not out
there'" (CIS: 44).

Rorty starts off by explaining the reasons why his 'response' deliberately bypasses the need to construct 'arguments' against such
charges for purposes of conclusively 'refuting' his critics. He reminds
us that on his own account of intellectual change, time spent devising

formal arguments for such purposes would be time mostly wasted: "The trouble with arguments against the use of a familiar and time-honored vocabulary is that they are expected to be phrased in that very vocabulary" (CIS: 8). On that account – "of intellectual progress as the literalisation of metaphors" – the most effective way of dealing with "objections to one's redescriptions of some things will be largely a matter of redescribing other things, trying to outflank the objections by enlarging the scope of one's metaphors" (CIS: 44).

Rorty sees his main task as one of showing how the very institutions and cultural practices of liberal societies that might appear to be threatened by his recommendation that we embrace 'contingency' will actually be 'better served' by the following of such a recommendation:

> I shall claim that the vocabulary I adumbrated in the first two chapters, one which revolves around notions of metaphor and self-creation rather than around notions of truth, rationality and moral obligation, is better suited for [this purpose] the preservation and progress of democratic societies.   (CIS: 44)

The vocabulary Rorty prefers is thus 'better suited', he tells us, because liberal democratic societies thrive on the 'freedom' it confers: freedom to value different things, freedom to pursue different lines of inquiry and, most importantly, freedom to live one's life outside the constricting shadow of a 'higher authority'.

If we imagine a community in which the shadow of a higher authority eclipses the possibility of the kind of relativism and irrationalism Rorty gets accused of – even an 'authority' draped in an ideal, benign Enlightenment form such as 'Truth' or 'Rationality' – it is difficult to see how these first two 'freedoms' can still be preserved. By the same token, Rorty maintains, the menace of 'relativism' and 'irrationalism' will seem illusory if we imagine a community that operates with *his* preferred vocabulary.

History and radical contingency

In his discussion of 'community', Rorty tries to show that 'liberalism' and 'contingency' are made for one another. He is not so much concerned with the 'conceptual fit' here, since he does not see the 'vocabulary' that makes most sense of his notion of 'contingency' as providing anything like the intellectual foundations, or 'justification', for liberalism. The match is rather a 'pragmatic' one, and to familiarize us with its possibilities, Rorty describes its historical pedigree.

It might seem strange at first to try to live without grounding one's beliefs and dispositions in *some* external consideration, something that serves as an intellectual compass, something that guarantees one is on the right and proper track. But, Rorty tells us, history is there to reassure us, to furnish examples that make the whole prospect look less daunting. He draws analogies with historical movements such as Romanticism, recalling how the poets of that movement made an artistic leap of progress in the dark by elevating 'self-creation' above traditional conformity and 'imitation'. And he calls on figures such as Hegel, Nietzsche, Freud and Berlin to trace out a multi-layered conversation in which they feed us lines from our common intellectual heritage that both reconcile us to the idea of a philosophically ungrounded life and alert us to the creative potential of such a life.

Suppose Rorty succeeds in persuading us that we must face up to 'contingency', and that learning to live with it could be an exciting, liberating enterprise? Is there nothing more to say? Can we not step back and question whether we *ought* to be so persuaded? Rorty apparently leaves us little room for such a reflective manoeuvre.

If we step back far enough to bring traditional worries to bear on Rorty's recommendations – worries such as whether his interpretation of history is correct, whether it is premature to give up on the possibility of a theory of truth, or a criterion of knowledge, which improves or at least regulates our cognitive capabilities, and so on – he will simply retort that we have not yet got into the swing of things, that if we try out the 'vocabulary of contingency' just a bit longer, then the futility of such worries will become obvious. Even so, we can still ask some pointed questions about the notion of 'contingency' itself without needing to step that far back.

This notion carries a great deal of weight in Rorty's overall scheme of things, yet it is never explicitly defined. It is given an implicit, 'contrastive' definition *en passant*: things and events are 'contingent' in the sense that they do not fall under traditional philosophical descriptions which make reference to concepts such as 'necessity', 'essence', 'reality', 'truth' and 'obligation'. Clearly Rorty is reluctant to provide anything more than a contrastive definition because he does not want to risk turning the notion of 'contingency' into a fully fledged *philosophical* notion, something which displaces concepts like 'necessity' but offers philosophers an excuse to carry on working within the same old problematic. We are entitled, however, to question the *implications* of Rorty's notion. In detecting the irredeemably contingent nature of human life, has he detected something that does entail such radical changes in our view of ourselves and the world?

At first blush, there seems to be something fishy about drawing any radical conclusions from the discovery that our lives are inundated with 'contingencies'. Suppose, for example, we take the claim that certain states of affairs are contingent to mean that those states of affairs *need not have* occurred, that they were 'historically optional'? When it appears that a certain state of affairs *just had to come about*, the information that it was 'contingent' in this latter sense – that some other state of affairs *could have occurred* – can lead to a radical revision of our outlook. But it does not have to do so. To learn that things 'could have been otherwise' can be a trivial lesson – even if their taking place had previously seemed inevitable: it looks like the earth had to be the size it is, but we discover that it could have been any number of different sizes.

But what if the discovery of 'contingency' involves not just a small adjustment to our stock of 'matters of fact', but the destruction of something large and intellectually important like the belief that certain longstanding philosophical problems are inevitable, that there is no way of thinking adequately about the human condition without encountering such problems? Then, surely, the realization that such problems are contingent, in the sense of 'historically optional', has radical implications – will we not wish to give up on our attempts to tackle such problems?

In an insightful footnoted aside to a useful discussion of Rorty's treatment of epistemology in *Philosophy and the Mirror of Nature*, Michael Williams calls Rorty's contention that certain philosophical problems are 'optional' "one of Rorty's favourite eye-brow raising claims":

> Problems that seem to arise independently of contentious, theoretical ideas will have an air of being wholly "natural" or "intuitive". This aura of naturalness will make them seem compelling, even if seemingly insoluble. Theoretical diagnosis aims to dispel this aura. This sheds light on one of Rorty's favourite eye-brow raising claims: that concern with this or that problem is "optional". To a philosopher under the spell of the apparent intuitiveness of a particular problem, Rorty's *insouciance* can

only look like intellectual irresponsibility. But if the problem can be revealed as an artifact of theoretical ideas that, once made explicit, are anything but compelling, it is the diagnostician's "irresponsibility" that turns out to be the illusion.

(Williams 2000: 211)

Williams's remarks show how Rorty might be absolved of the charge of irresponsibility, but they take us no nearer the answer as to whether we will, or should, be inclined to give up on problems that are revealed to be optional.

The short answer, for practical purposes, is: "We may or we may not". Whether we *ought* to drop such problems is a more complex issue. What our discussion so far shows is that *by itself* the attribution of 'contingency' has no direct implications. Moreover, we, ourselves, were rash to say that the discovery about the contingency of the earth's size yields only a trivial lesson in factual adjustment. The upshot of such a discovery will always depend on prior historical developments and the surrounding context of beliefs and practices. Imagine, for example, that the very same kind of information is revealed in a society that believes the exact size of the earth was predetermined by the creator of the universe. Against this background, reconsider Rorty's position on 'contingency'. What he has to show is not *just* that what seemed intellectually inevitable is in fact 'optional', but also that, given this fact, it *is* better to pursue another option. Think of someone who compulsively plays chess and believes that, even though she finds it very difficult and painful to go on doing so, she has no choice: she was destined to play *that* game. Suppose we convince her that this belief is wrong, that her chess playing is the chance result of spending too much time hungry and locked alone in a cold, chequered-floored room as a very young child, that in trying so hard to win chess games, she is trying to overcome the negative feelings associated with that early environment? Should she give up playing chess? Should she take up chequers instead, a game that could well satisfy some of her quirky, subconscious needs without requiring so much pain and exertion? Is it not open to her to refuse to take up chequers on grounds that it is too easy and intellectually unsatisfying? Now let us extrapolate the point to philosophers' trademark compulsions.

In asking philosophers to consider giving up their theoretical pretensions – to abandon the search for a 'final account' of truth, an explication of the relationship between mind and body, and so on – is

Rorty asking them to do something equivalent to switching from chess to chequers? Might it not be sensible for some philosophers to continue playing the traditional philosophy game on the strength of its intrinsic intellectual rewards, even if they come to recognize that it is 'optional'?

Of course Rorty is always going to zero in on phrases like "intrinsic intellectual rewards", but perhaps the philosophers in question can use it in a sense that deflects his objections. For they may recall how Leibniz once made a very useful distinction between 'hypothetical' and 'absolute' necessity. If something is 'hypothetically necessary', then it is necessary – *has to be so* – only on a hypothesis that certain other conditions obtain. So, for instance, if it has already been established that there are over one hundred guests at a party, it is (hypothetically) necessary that there are more than forty quests at the party. The distinction does its best work in disambiguating cases where the antecedent conditions are forgotten and the 'necessity' is mistakenly attached in isolation from them: for example there might be slippage from "Given the rules of soccer, it is necessary that the team that scores the most goals wins" to "It is necessary that the team that scores the most goals wins". Someone who slips into believing the latter, may feel *compelled* to argue against reforms of soccer that suggest other considerations, such as the number of fouls, would determine who wins a game. Technically, this involves issues about what is called 'scope'. Hypothetical necessity takes the whole 'conditional combination' of 'hypothesis' and 'consequential claim' under its wing, or 'within its scope':

> Necessarily [If there are over one hundred guest at a party, there are more than forty guests at the party]

To link the necessity involved in this case directly to the 'consequential claim' here (i.e. 'Necessarily [there are more than forty guests at the party]') is to make a mistake about the scope of this brand of necessity, to commit what might be called 'the fallacy of the slipped modal operator' ('necessity' being such an operator). In practice, this 'fallacy' is usually innocuous: it normally does no harm, for example, to take the background conditions concerning the rules of the game for granted and speak as if it is 'necessary' that the team scoring the most goals in a soccer match is the winner of that match. So much for 'hypothetical necessity'.

By contrast, things are 'absolutely necessary' when they *must be so* regardless of any other conditions. Necessity gets no stronger than this. Leibniz used the 'hypothetical–absolute' distinction primarily to try to squeeze some degree of human freedom into his otherwise deterministic account of the world: only 'absolute necessities' preclude such freedom. But our philosophers might use it to fend off Rorty's charge of 'contingency'. 'Sure', they might say, 'the Problem of Free Will is not *inherently* important (i.e. it is not "absolutely necessary" that the problem be so regarded), but given that it has reared its head in our culture, its importance is undeniable (i.e. "hypothetically necessary")'. Such a 'defence' might also try to evade Rorty by elaborating on the way in which the problem 'rears its head': 'Given we are attracted to such concepts as "physical determinism" and "free choice", the Problem of Free Will is bound (again, as a matter of "hypothetical necessity") to seem important', and so on.

This putative line of criticism needed to be given an airing because Rorty is, at times, inclined to write as if the verdict of 'contingency' regarding a philosophical practice will *automatically* provide sufficient motivation for ditching that practice. However, the criticism is in danger of misrepresenting Rorty's whole approach to 'contingency'. In the first place, it is simply wrong to portray him as laying claim to the *discovery* that, despite received appearances, certain phenomena are contingent. This overlooks Rorty's concerted refusal to endorse the 'appearance–reality' distinction presupposed by such a depiction.

Furthermore, he does not want to put forward anything of the order of a 'contingency thesis' – it is not that he wishes to *assert*: "All things that might appear otherwise are, in fact, 'contingent'." He has to be wary of such substantive claims:

> The difficulty faced by a philosopher who, like myself, . . . thinks of himself as auxiliary to the poet rather than to the physicist . . . is to avoid hinting that this suggestion [that a talent for speaking differently, rather than arguing well, is the chief instrument of social change] gets something right, that my sort of philosophy corresponds to the ways things are.   (CIS: 7)

Rorty invokes 'contingency' more in the spirit of intellectual experiment. He suggests that we try out a way of speaking in which terms and phrases for 'non-contingencies' like "essences" and "necessary truths" have no important place.

In *Philosophy and the Mirror of Nature*, Rorty tried to show that the 'internal dialectic' of analytic philosophy had *itself* put intense pressure on the vocabulary that embedded the 'old necessities'. But he did not attempt to *demonstrate* conclusively that the vocabulary in question was thereby rendered unworkable or rationally incoherent. Instead, he took the view that the combination of a lack of historical progress and the internal tensions just referred to provide sufficient reason to take a crack at something else. Then he constructed a narrative to reveal how things might flesh out under an alternative, 'edifying', pragmatist regime.

Irony

> Ironist theorists like Hegel, Nietzsche, Derrida and Foucault seem to me invaluable in our attempt to form a private self-image, but pretty much useless when it comes to politics.
>
> (CIS: 83)

Rorty's 'third strategy' in facilitating our friendship with his leading notion is, we said, to provide us with handy terms for 'redescribing' ourselves as creatures of contingency. His discussion of historical movements and creative figures floats some pregnant possibilities in this connection. But Rorty brings matters both more up to date and more down to earth, as it were, by adding some catchy, contemporary terms – terms that almost *anyone* with a modicum of formal education or reflective awareness can feel at home with.

First and foremost, he offers a convenient label for those who buy into his whole story. Such a person can then call themselves 'a liberal ironist'. Rorty takes his definition of the "liberal" component here from Judith Shklar (1984), who regards liberals as "people who think that cruelty is the worst thing we do" (CIS: xv). As for the "ironist" part, Rorty explains its significance thus:

> I use "ironist" to name the sort of person who faces up to the contingency of his or her own most central beliefs – someone sufficiently historicist and nominalist to have abandoned the idea that those central beliefs and desires refer back to something beyond the reach of time and chance. (*ibid.*)

Suppose we take Rorty's advice and consider ourselves to be 'liberal ironists', how are we to further describe ourselves to those who remain suspicious of such a tag – fearing, perhaps, the subversive force of 'irony' or unable to see why 'cruelty' should be such a big deal?

We could identify with one (or more) of Rorty's emblematic figures, such as Proust, taking inspiration from *their* innovative ways of capturing contingencies in language:

> Proust temporalised and finitised the authority figures he had met by seeing them as creatures of contingent circumstances. Like Nietzsche, he rid himself of the fear that there was an antecedent truth about himself, a real essence which others might have detected. But Proust was able to do so without claiming to know a truth which was hidden from the authority figures of his earlier years. He managed to debunk authority without setting himself up as an authority, to debunk the ambitions of the powerful without sharing them. He finitised authority figures not by detecting what they "really" were but by watching them become different than they had been, and by seeing how they looked when redescribed in terms offered by still other authority figures, whom he played off against the first. The result of all this finitisation was to make Proust unashamed of his own finitude. He mastered contingency by recognising it, and thus freed himself from the fear that the contingencies he had encountered were more than just contingencies. He turned other people from his judges into his fellow sufferers, and thus succeeded in creating the taste by which he judged himself.
>
> (CIS: 103)

But, though this might lend extra verve and colour to our conversation, it could also leave us somewhat isolated, unable to share our central concerns with those who tend to give large books a miss or simply do not warm to Proust, finding him in some way repugnant, perhaps, or even just plain boring.

To solve this kind of problem, to offer us a number of more widely accessible self-reference points, without forcing us to turn our backs on related idiosyncratic interests, Rorty enlarges on his view of 'liberal ironism'. As freshly hatched liberal ironists, we will naturally tend still to worry about being 'put on the spot', about being asked to elucidate or, even worse, *justify*, our new-found position. We cannot turn to Rorty for a ready-made *argument* to employ in such situations, and it would be far too difficult and time-consuming for most of us to recapitulate the twists and turns in his 'narrative account' as to why 'liberal ironism' is supposed to turn out to be such an attractive position. But we can avail ourselves of this 'enlarged view' – Rorty's further redescription of what liberal ironism involves.

Final vocabularies

In the fourth chapter of *Contingency, irony, and solidarity*, Rorty introduces the useful notion of a 'final vocabulary' and then reorientates his definition of what it is to be an 'ironist' in the light of this notion. A final vocabulary is a vocabulary of our highest hopes, but also of 'the last resort':

> All human beings carry about a set of words which they employ to justify their actions, their beliefs, and their lives. These are the words in which we formulate praise of our friends and contempt for our enemies, our long-term projects, our deepest self-doubts and our highest hopes. They are the words in which we tell, sometimes prospectively and sometimes retrospectively, the story of our lives. I shall call these words a person's "final vocabulary". (CIS: 141)

Such a vocabulary is not one that homes in on what its owner considers to be 'the ultimate truth of the matter'. It is 'final' rather in the sense that "if doubt is cast on the worth of these words, their user has no noncircular argumentative recourse" (*ibid.*). Here Rorty is returning to an old theme: the very general problem of 'circularity' that dogged him early on in his career. But he is no longer so perturbed by it. The fact that final vocabularies have no prior justification is not a sign that there is something deeply wrong with such sets of words. Indeed, given their value to their owners, we should not expect them to depend on anything more fundamental (otherwise the chances are *that* would have already been incorporated as a better linguistic terminus).

Having introduced this idea of a final vocabulary, Rorty then uses it to expand on his conception of an 'ironist'. Such a person satisfies the following three conditions:

1. "She has radical and continuing doubts about the final vocabulary she currently uses, because she has been impressed by other vocabularies taken as final by people or books she has encountered".
2. "She realises that argument phrased in her present vocabulary can neither underwrite nor dissolve these doubts".
3. "Insofar as she philosophises about her situation, she does not think that her vocabulary is closer to reality than others, that it is in touch with a power not herself". (CIS: 73)

Richard Rorty

What is liable to irritate Rorty's fellow philosophers most about all this is the paltry role played by *their* discipline. Of course, philosophical terms of art are not banished from final vocabularies – some of us may well find that we can furnish nothing superior to wrap 'the story of our lives' in than references to 'categorical imperatives', 'necessary truths', ' causal conditionals', and the like. But Rorty assumes that in the long run 'words of philosophy' can fare no better than other kinds of words because they will have to compete with those words on more or less equal terms, having only their practical usefulness and metaphoric attractiveness to commend them. That is to say, they will not be able to embody any of the 'self-justifying' properties philosophers have always hoped to find, the sort of properties that force assent from all 'rational beings' across time. The history of philosophy is largely the graveyard of vocabularies that seemed to their creators to wear their complete and compelling philosophical justification on their sleeve. If an ironist's final vocabulary *does* have a philosophical dimension, she will be well aware of the contingent status of its linguistic ingredients. She will not tend to believe that no other set of words *could* offer a better description of 'reality'. And she will not be tempted to try to *infer* anything of universal importance – anything that everyone, everywhere should consider important – solely on the basis of her own philosophical words of last resort.

Having digested Rorty's 'definitions', a would-be liberal ironist can then begin to get the hang of explaining and defending her position by absorbing the entertaining lessons in the art of 'self-redescription' offered in the rest of the book. There she will find a rich menu.

She will be able to learn how to deflect conventional philosophical criticisms by making invidious, pre-emptive comparisons between liberal ironism and its competitors – paradigmatically: 'metaphysics'. The trick in the latter case is to make the metaphysicians come off far worse by ensuring that they look unsophisticated (because they are so enamoured of the thought of getting a final fix on 'reality'), inflexible (because they are hypnotized by a uniform set of techniques, a 'methodology'), over-impressed by passing platitudes (which they try to pass off as deep and enduring 'intuitions'), oblivious to historical developments and reluctant to recognize the fruitful interconnections between different texts and different genres. She will also be able to make the acquaintance, though largely on Rorty's own terms, of thinkers and writers he regards as connoisseurs of his two key themes 'contingency' and 'cruelty'. Here she may be spurred on by the hope of becoming more at home with 'contingencies' than the connoisseurs themselves. For when Rorty discusses such figures as Nietzsche and the early Derrida, for example, he describes them as thinkers who desperately want to assimilate themselves totally to contingency, but never quite succeed, who improve on the performance of their significant predecessors in this respect – the thinkers they are personally most anxious to differentiate themselves from – but remain vulnerable to similar differentiating moves, or 'improvements', on the part of their successors.

As for the 'connoisseurs of cruelty', the budding liberal ironist will be introduced to two types. The first type understands the effects of cruelty on a 'social scale' and writes the books that help us form our 'social conscience', books on such topics as "slavery, poverty and prejudice" (CIS: 141). These "include *The Condition of the Working Class in England* and the reports of muckraking journalists and government commissions, but also novels like *Uncle Tom's Cabin*, *Les Miserables*, *Sister Carrie*, *The Well of Loneliness*, and *The Black Boy*" (*ibid.*). The second type grasps the subtleties of special kinds of cruely – "the ways in which particular sorts of people are cruel to other particular sorts of people" (*ibid.*). Those who belong in this category may write on psychology, but "the most useful books of this sort are works of fiction which exhibit the blindness of a certain person to the pain of another kind of person" (*ibid.*). The blindness to Anna's pain displayed by some of the characters in Tolstoy's *Anna Karenina* is the kind of thing Rorty has in mind. He thinks that in reading what skilful writers have to say about such blindness we will be helped to avoid unwittingly displaying anything like it ourselves.

By invoking this distinction, Rorty is able to push his discussion still further beyond the boundaries of ordinary, or 'normal', philosophy. He does not try to *prove* that 'cruelty' should be high on the philosophical agenda because he accepts that: "For liberal ironists, there is no answer to the question 'Why not be cruel?' – no noncircular theoretical backup for the belief that cruelty is horrible" (CIS: xv).

The prospective liberal ironist who has followed him this far can now draw on the resources of literature in place of 'noncircular theoretical backup'. And she can do so without regret that she has forsaken the rigour of traditional philosophy. Such 'rigour' is out of place in this new territory. It is liable to be more of a hindrance than

Richard Rorty

a help in formulating and resolving the most vital issues at stake. For she will now want to tease out the details of the contingencies that make up her own life and to relate her best story about the value and purpose of those contingencies to the suffering and social hopes of others. She will also be concerned to negotiate the boundaries between her private desires and her public duties. Rorty's liberalism, and his final way of dealing with the tensions within his adolescent ambitions, dictate that 'limited negotiation' is as far as she will get. The public and the private domains can never be completely harmonized at a less than prohibitive price. A single vision is always going to cost far too much.

Chapter 5

Liberalism

When it comes to political deliberation, philosophy is a good servant but a bad master. (PSH: 232)

Privacy and solidarity

Rorty's way of coming to terms with the disturbing conflicts in his adolescent ambitions is to relinquish the thought that they *have to be* brought into harmony, and thus to give up on the idea of a single, self-redeeming vision. The liberal ironist can pursue surreptitious bliss *and* social justice with a clean intellectual bill of health. Neither of these sets of desires, or 'interests', is beholden to the other. Those 'tensions' that Rorty previously experienced as an uncomfortable, perhaps even unbearable, *intellectual* strain are replaced by the messier, but less head-spinning, grind of *practical* strife. There will never be enough time and resources for *each one of us* to both keep well topped up with our preferred, private delights *and* spend time putting the rest of the world right. However, deciding where to draw the line here is a pragmatic affair, not something to get into throes of theoretical agony about.

This practical 'dividing line' separates the private and public facets of the self. These are the two sides of an apparent dichotomy that is central to the main themes of *Contingency, irony, and solidarity*. The latter 'division' is a feature that many of Rorty's critics in analytic philosophy in particular – to whom almost any perceived 'dichotomy' is like a red rag to a bull – try to throw back in his face. But, it is open to Rorty to keep wielding his pragmatist sword of protection. In his book *For The Love of Perfection: Richard Rorty and Liberal Education*, Rene Vincente Arcilla offers an insightful summary of Rorty's conception of the public–private distinction as a 'pragmatic tool':

> He is not interested in separating the public and private realms on the basis of some literal, naturalistic, absolute boundary. He wants only to determine degrees of separation that emerge in certain circumstances, and which can be respected for certain purposes. His critics have misunderstood him if they think that he conceives of the separation in black-and-white terms, for the purposes of making a point of theoretical principle. The public–private distinction is a pragmatic tool that promises to help us mitigate conflict between individuals and society. Even if it proves to be rough and fuzzy when contemplated in abstraction, if in using it we are able to iron out certain conflicts, then we will have all the reason we need to affirm its significance.
>
> (Arcilla 1995: 124)

Moreover, Arcilla could have added that the so-called 'dichotomy' boils down to nothing more than a 'redescription' of the clash of interests within the self that inevitably occurs in 'free societies'.

In such societies, the participants are bound, since relatively free to do so, to hit upon all sorts of different ways of pursuing their lives. Some of these will be dominated by 'private projects' based on the whims of personal satisfaction. They will thus often involve diverting, or simply withholding, considerable amounts of energy and commitment from the public realm. Others will involve a happy convergence of private and social interests, as when, for example, people get their main kicks from charitable deeds or public service. Still others will lead to an abdication of personal goals. But there is no *principled* way to determine where the line *ought to be* drawn here. The relation between the private and public facets of the self is best governed by the sort of 'pluralistic practical economy of creative energy' that tends to emerge spontaneously in liberal societies.

If, on the one hand, too much 'energy and commitment' is side-tracked to the inner recesses of the self, then charismatic propagandists for 'the public realm' tend to spring up – with an appropriately appealing tract, novel, film, piece of journalism or whatever (for example, Bob Geldof and Live Aid) – to entice people into deploying more of those assets for the benefit of others, for 'the social good'. On the other hand, when an inordinate amount of personal enthusiasm becomes tied up in the public realm – imagine a society where each person forgoes most of their personal enjoyment in the pursuit of a grim public ideal (say, keeping the streets and public buildings scrupulously clean at all times and in all weathers) – enticing 'advertisements' for more personalized projects will suddenly appear, the source and form of which can never be predicted (for example, Thomas Merton publishes an autobiography, *The Seven Storey Mountain* (Merton 1948), and applications to enter monasteries and other such places of contemplative refuge soar).

Phrases like "too much" and "inordinate" have close connotations of 'measurement' and 'calculation', but are best left imprecise in Rorty's view. For he believes there is no 'theory' that can strike a 'perfect balance' or 'optimum' here. Judgements about such matters must vary according to existing personal preferences, the creative skills of the 'propagandists' or the 'advertisers', and the prevailing 'social vision', whenever there is such a thing.

Philosophers, and fellow travellers, would very much like an appropriate theory or at least something more precise. Even if they concede to Rorty that they cannot pluck the required overarching principles out of the metaphysical skies, they would like at least a more systematic account that pays its respects to our best 'intuitions'. Rorty thinks his pragmatist approach offers better prospects. Pandering to intuitions for the sake of an all-embracing theory will hinder progress as fractional squabbles break out over their source or 'ownership' ("Whose intuitions? Those of White males? The rich? The politicians? Experts? The impartial observer? The academic elite?") as well as their 'justification' ("What makes *that* intuition central to our requirements?"). But it will also take the power out of the hands of those best suited to making creative, community-wide 'adjustments' to the expenditure of 'energy and commitment': the 'propagandists' and the 'advertisers', the veritable poets of social change.

In Rorty's pragmatist society, nobody keeps looking back over their shoulder to see whether a higher authority *of any kind* is sanctioning their life choices, the ways they spread their energies between self-fulfilment and public duty. How they divide up their time and resources between personal growth and social progress is largely their own affair, influenced only by friends, advisers, mentors and inspirational figures. Instead of looking back, they look *forwards* to the most appealing prospects of happiness offered by the most creative exemplars in their society, letting the 'spread', or 'division' of energies, free fall accordingly. Given their background, their individual character traits and talents, it makes good practical sense for some people to be impressed by socially capricious projects, turning away from the woes of the world to carry them out. For others, it is best to throw themselves into ventures designed to benefit society or even the world at large over the longer term.

This discussion of Rorty's 'public–private' distinction should shed some light on a related theme of *Contingency, irony, and solidarity* that some of his critics have also jibbed at. This is the theme of 'Solidarity'. What seems to bother Rorty's detractors most is what they take to be the *anomalous* status of this theme. They are unable even to see it as a 'related' phenomenon. Rich appreciation of 'contingency' needs not much by way of persuasion to turn into 'irony'; that much is quite clear to them. But they think it takes a strange, unwarranted leap to get from either to 'solidarity'. For *both* contingency and irony appear to cut the ties that bind us to one another. Furthermore, they also fly in the face of "the traditional philosophical way" of explaining 'human solidarity': "To say that there is something within each of us – our essential humanity – which resonates to the presence of this same thing in other human beings" (CIS: 189).

One of Rorty's most provocative philosophical skills is that of being able to bring unexpected elements together in the Gestalt switch of a quick and plausible narrative. These may involve incongruous figures such as Dewey and Heidegger and/or equally discordant themes. His treatment of 'contingency', 'irony', and 'solidarity' is a splendid example of the latter. For, rather than bowing to the conventional line that regards respect for 'contingencies' and 'ironies' as socially corrosive, Rorty contends that proper recognition of their role in life can actually clear the path for greater empathy and understanding between human beings, and hence for 'solidarity'.

Such recognition unshackles us from "ideas like 'essence', 'nature', and 'foundation'" (CIS: 189) – the mainstays of the 'traditional philosophical' conception of what generates human solidarity. But, this then "makes it impossible for us to retain the notion that some actions and attitudes are naturally 'inhuman'" (*ibid.*). Without an 'essentialist criterion' to shackle our emerging sense of who is our neighbour, who we should go out on a limb for – of what kind of person is worth really caring about – we are freed up to be more imaginative, more generous spirited, and hence more expansive, in our affinities. On Rorty's understanding, moral progress actually *requires* such 'expansiveness':

The view I am offering says that there is such a thing as moral progress and that this progress is indeed in the direction of greater human solidarity. But that solidarity is not thought of as recognition of a core self, the human essence, in all human beings. Rather it is thought of as the ability to see more and more traditional differences (of tribe, religion, race, custom, and the like) as unimportant when compared with similarities with respect to pain and humiliation – the ability to think of people wildly different from ourselves as included in the range of "us". That is why [I said in Chapter 4 that] detailed descriptions of particular varieties of pain and humiliation (in, e.g., novels or ethnographies), rather than philosophical or religious treatises, were the modern intellectual's principal contribution to moral progress. (CIS: 192)

New territory

Contingency, irony, and solidarity ushers its readers into new philosophical territory. Enough of the familiar names and topics are there to make the book look as if it belongs on the philosophy shelves in libraries and bookshops. But just about everything has been 'recontextualized', and many of the dominant metaphors have been supplanted. In this territory, a fresh agenda emerges along with a different – much more 'literary' – way of 'doing philosophy'.

The agenda introduces a series of what we might call 'post-pragmatist issues'. After bringing pragmatism centre stage in *Consequences of Pragmatism*, Rorty barely mentions it in *Contingency, irony, and solidarity*. Dewey's name crops up a number of times, as does James's on occasion, but the term "pragmatism" itself does not even figure in the book's index. The classic pragmatists' progress was hindered by their felt need to spend a lot of time in their opponents' backyard trying to gain philosophical credibility. Thus it was hard for them to get beyond the stage of fighting over tradition-worn topics like the 'nature of truth' and so forth with tradition-upholding people like G. E. Moore and Bertrand Russell. In *Philosophy and the Mirror of Nature* and *Consequences of Pragmatism* Rorty was still in there with them, continuing their struggle – if by other, no doubt in his view more 'progressive', means. But, in *Contingency, irony, and solidarity*, he moved on to explore the kind of issues that arise once a pragmatist stance is well established, once it ceases to be merely *reactive*. Then, granted the pragmatist is no longer worried about explaining and justifying her approach to her arch opponents on more or less their terms, and that Rorty has improved diplomatic relations with both 'Continental Philosophy' and the 'Literary World', there is plenty of scope for launching new topics, lightening the methodological load and realigning priorities.

After *Philosophy and the Mirror of Nature* came out, those alarmed readers who thought that Rorty *had* burned his bridges then wondered whether he would carry on doing philosophy at all and whether, if he did, it would involve something weird and wonderful – poetic philosophy, perhaps a novel, or even a philosophical graffiti equivalent of Duchamp's 'bearded Mona Lisa' – something, at any rate, that would help generate philosophy's version of the *avant-garde* revolution in the arts. *Contingency, irony, and solidarity* is 'weird and wonderful', but for vastly different reasons. It is weird because it manages to still *be* philosophy without tackling philosophy's central 'problems' and without using philosophy's primary 'techniques' of argument and analysis. It is 'wonderful' because Rorty achieves this with an erudite elegance and lightness of touch that seem to have virtually no precedent in recent philosophical writing. So many philosophers seem unable to avoid striking a self-dramatizing, pretentious note when they try to break new ground in the subject that Rorty's adroit, good-humoured, low-key, 'conversational' approach should be welcomed, even by those who strongly disagree with the resulting views.

He spins a web of narratives that are designed to make it seem quite 'natural' for us to become interested in the possibilities for self-creation *and* the possibilities for standing shoulder to shoulder with greater and greater numbers of those in pain, those who are suffering and need shelter from the Storm of Being – more natural than being interested in how to pin down in an appropriate theory the 'essence' of our humanity or how to identify the underlying, 'rationally justifiable', 'general principles' of a 'just society'. But Rorty is well aware that this very 'naturalness' is an artifice, the product, itself, of 'time and chance'. He knows that its charm will be lost on some people and may rub others up the wrong way. But he sees his job as that of creating a pragmatist ambience of attractive ideas in which it will exert the maximum appeal, in which others – even the extraordinarily distanced, alienated, 'Others' hypothesized by many continental thinkers – may recognize some worthwhile concerns.

Priorities within the Storm of Being

'Twas in another lifetime, one of toil and blood,
When blackness was a virtue and the road was full of mud,
I came in from the wilderness, a creature void of form.
"Come in," she said,
"I'll give you shelter from the storm."
("Shelter from the Storm", Bob Dylan 1974 © Ram's Horn Music)

Since the self is 'made' rather than 'discovered', there have to be 'forces' and 'materials' for the making thereof. And Rorty's view is that these must be predominantly *social*: "there is nothing to people except what has been socialised into them – their ability to use language, and thereby exchange beliefs and desires with other people" (CIS: 177). He has no romantic attachment to the idea of a pure, pre-social self. A creature that was left to create its entire being in 'the wilderness' *would* be 'a creature void of form'. We do not need to qualify "form" with anything cautionary like "recognizable" because such qualifications drop out of the picture on account of the Davidson–Stroud verificationist line of argument referred to in our discussion of *Consequences of Pragmatism* in Chapter 3. To be a 'self' is to be recognizable as such within a community of selves.

Ideally, the social resources that engage to shape the self should help kindle the kind of spark that inspires it to buck some of the stifling, tradition-bound weight of those very origins, resources that encourage it to deviate from orthodoxy, find undreamed-of causes of pleasure and concoct new-fangled ways of describing things. Such stirring waywardness helps keep the private–public boundaries in good shape. But even blazing powers of self-invention are limited. They cannot insulate the self from the brute contingencies of material reality; they cannot provide permanent shelter from the Storm of Being. They cannot do this because the self's relationship to the world is neither mediated by an all-absorbing, protective cushion of 'Idealism' nor the sort of malleable relationship that can be had with other 'selves':

> For our relation to the world, to brute power and to naked pain is not the sort of relation we have to persons. Faced with the nonhuman, the nonlinguistic, we no longer have an ability to overcome contingency and pain by appropriation and transformation, but only the ability to *recognise* contingency and pain. The final victory of poetry in its ancient quarrel with philosophy

– the final victory of metaphors of self creation over metaphors of discovery – would consist in becoming reconciled to the thought that this is the only sort of power over the world which we can hope to have. For that would be the final adjuration of the notion that truth, and not just power and pain, is to be found "out there".   (CIS: 40)

There is little point in joining the ranks of those small-minded critics who think that if they can just find a 'contradiction' or anomaly in Rorty's writing, his whole pragmatist sky will fall in. But it is worth pausing to examine whether Rorty has pushed things self-consistently far enough in this account of the limitations on self-inventiveness.

Rorty has taken his main cue from "the revolutionaries and poets of two centuries ago". What they 'glimpsed', he thinks, was "that anything could be made to look good or bad, important or unimportant, useful or useless, by being redescribed" (CIS: 7). The 'small-minded' critical response to this is, first, to evince shock and horror at the thought that Rorty has set a relativistic intellectual virus among us that could destroy all that is precious, enduring and good, but then, after he tries to put some restrictions on the powers of redescription, to press him hard on why the "anything" does *not* include things like "brute power" and "naked pain".

In reply, Rorty need not appeal to anything bordering on the 'inconsistent', like an 'essentialist' account of such 'power' and 'pain'. He does not have to say that the 'nonlinguistic' has special properties that cannot be encapsulated in language. Instead, he can simply stick with the view that the vocabularies we tend to use give us, as yet, no 'causal power' over the 'nonlinguistic'. Where he could perhaps be a bit more adventurous is in pausing to reflect on the importance of the 'as yet' clause here.

On his own anti-essentialist view, *nothing*, and hence neither power nor pain, has an unreachable, and hence unshakeable, essence – so perhaps we should be looking for ways to create the redescriptive control over things we presently defer to, for ways of redrawing the boundaries between ourselves and 'the nonlinguistic'. When someone like South Africa's Archbishop Desmond Tutu sincerely describes his cancer as 'a blessing', as something that has greatly increased his appreciation of the value of life, and then other people in similar positions come to share his sentiments, perhaps the otherwise recalcitrant image of this kind of illness as being something that represents the sort of 'brute power' and 'naked pain' over which we have little causal control is thereby undermined. Perhaps there is a radical lesson here about 'human possibilities' that Rorty has failed to encourage us to take to heart.

Meanwhile, lacking such control over the Storm of Being, we need to assess our 'priorities' for living together within it. Rorty suggests an important 'reversal' here. Having advocated that we afford priority to 'imagination' over 'reason', Rorty also champions another *volte-face*: that we give politics priority over philosophy. This can be taken as a straightforwardly *pragmatic* recommendation. When we have put the standard theoretical problems of philosophy to one side, if not behind us, we should turn our attention to practical matters, like politics. But there is more to it than that. Rorty wants us to favour politics over philosophy not just in the sense of spending more of our time on issues concerning social organization and the allocation of scarce resources than on longstanding philosophical problems of unadulterated vintage such as 'the mind–body problem' and 'the problem of free will'. He wants us to do something a bit more subtle: to take an overtly *political* (i.e. rather than philosophical) approach to politics itself.

Staying on the surface with liberalism

> Truth viewed in the Platonic way, as the grasp of what Rawls calls "an order antecedent to and given to us", is simply not relevant to democratic politics. So philosophy, as the explanation of the relation between such an order and human nature, is not relevant either. When the two conflict, democracy takes precedence over philosophy. (ORT: 191–2)

In "The Priority of Democracy to Philosophy", the article from which the above quotation is taken, Rorty explains why he thinks politics should supersede philosophy. This article was prepared for a conference at the University of Virginia in 1984, but it was not published until 1988, just before *Contingency, irony, and solidarity*. Rorty's 'explanation' invokes yet another co-opted ally, the distinguished Harvard political philosopher John Rawls, author of one of the most important books on political theory published in the twentieth century: *A Theory of Justice* (Rawls 1971).

Rorty takes Rawls to be following Dewey's pragmatist lead in showing us "how liberal democracy can get along without philosophical presuppositions" (ORT: 179) and in "putting politics first and

then tailoring philosophy to suit" (ORT: 178). This 'Deweyan' view of
A Theory of Justice springs from Rawls's own further reflections on,
and developments of, his classic work (see especially his seminal
articles 'Kantian Constructivism in Moral Theory' (Rawls 1980) and
'Justice as Fairness: Political not Metaphysical' (Rawls 1985).

A *Theory of Justice* contained passages that encouraged many
readers, including at one time, by his own admission, Rorty himself,
to misread the book by seeing it as yet another attempt to 'legitimize
liberal politics'. On this reading, Rawls's project is continuous with
the Enlightenment's general feeling that moral judgements should
be founded on an account of human nature and, more precisely, with
neo-Kantian views that they should be based on a suitably purified
conception of 'rationality'.

In this respect, perhaps even the book's title, with its focus on
'Theory', was somewhat misleading. However, Rawls's later writings
point to a more faithful interpretation. According to Rorty, they
prompt us to play down the 'Kantian element' that was formerly
'overemphasized' so that we are better able to appreciate its
'Hegelian (i.e. Historical) and Deweyan (i.e. pragmatist) elements'
(ORT: 185). What does most of the prompting is Rawls's more
explicit rendering of his 'metaphilosophical doctrine', his careful explanation of the limits on the role that philosophy plays in the account of liberalism put forward in *A Theory of Justice*:

> What justifies a conception of justice is not its being true to an
> order antecedent to and given to us, but its congruence with our
> deeper understanding of ourselves, and our realisation that,
> *given our history and the traditions embedded in our public life*,
> it is the most reasonable doctrine for us.
>
> (Rawls 1980: 519, emphasis added as in ORT: 185)

Against this background, claims like "the self is prior to the ends
which are affirmed by it" and "we should not attempt to give form to
our life by first looking to the good independently defined" (Rawls
1971: 560) do not commit Rawls to some hefty theorizing by way of a
substantive account of 'the self'. Rorty maintains that a political (as
opposed to 'metaphysical') interpretation of *A Theory of Justice*
enables us to see that the claims Rawls makes do not presuppose the
existence of something socially separate called 'the Self', some
'essence' that can be identified independently of the networks of
beliefs and desires that people manifest in living together. Nor do
they root morality in something either intrinsic to its own nature or

dependent on a necessary feature of the self such as the capacity to make free, rational choices. When Rawls's approach touches philosophical base, it appeals to the contingent historical fact that modern recipients of traditions of religious tolerance and democratic, constitutional ways of governing tend to place liberty ahead of any pre-established conception of 'perfection'. Hence, on Rorty's understanding, "*A Theory of Justice* no longer seems committed to a philosophical account of the human self, but only to a historico-sociological description of the way we live now" (ORT: 185).

Why does any of this matter to Rorty? Why should Rorty be concerned with how Rawls's work is interpreted? Partly the interpretation has to matter to Rorty because *A Theory of Justice* is recognized as such an important contribution to modern political thought. If he can show that it comports with his own pragmatist outlook, this, alone, will add weight to that outlook. But these considerations also carry some authority because the resulting 'reading' illuminates Rorty's own reasons for wanting us to put politics in a position of ascendency over philosophy.

Rawls thinks that the socio-historical development of modern democratic societies precludes the idea that philosophers can theorize an overarching conception of morality into existence that will, in turn, yield a generally acceptable conception of justice:

> The essential point is this: as a practical political matter no general moral conception can provide the basis for a public conception of justice in a modern democratic society. The social and historical conditions of such a society have their origins in the Wars of Religion following the Reformation and the development of the principle of toleration, and in the growth of constitutional government and the institutions of large market economies. These conditions profoundly affect the requirements of a workable conception of political justice: such a conception must allow for a diversity of doctrines and the plurality of existing democratic societies. (Rawls 1985: 225)

More positively, he thinks that the bracketing of conventional philosophical topics required by the acceptance of this 'essential point' will enable us to concentrate on the topics we *can* make some progress with: those concerning the kind of practical political arrangements that best fit our traditions and our considered beliefs. By 'staying on the surface', philosophically speaking, we have a much better chance of both providing an adequate account of such arrangements and leaving room within such an account for a robust notion of personal freedom. In the latter account, the depths that remain unexplored in 'public space' can be explored by individuals, at will, in their personal, or 'private', space.

All this is clearly grist for Rorty's mill. But he does not want to float a pragmatist reading of Rawls just so that he can help himself to Rawls's *arguments*. Much more important is the fact that he can use Rawls's work to add to his stock of 'interesting and appealing' sentences to write about the virtues of liberalism, pragmatically construed. In his reading of Rawls, Rorty treats him as a 'conversational partner', someone who has the knack of saying the kind of things that help make liberalism look like a more attractive proposition.

The strange charm of liberalism

Some alert readers may have found our previous paragraph to be something of a *non-sequitur*. For how do Rawls's arguments 'illuminate Rorty's own reasons' for giving politics priority over philosophy?

It becomes clear that they do this when we pause to reflect on the nature of Rorty's motivation. His 'reasons' are connected with the contingent attractions that politics in the form of liberalism has for him – a charm that can seem strange until we put it in context.

Rorty's own 'final vocabulary' must contain the word "liberalism". But for him this is a word that has been divested of its philosophical trappings. He prefers to use it for its *practical* significations that remain untouched by philosophical interference and for its resonances with other terms in his final vocabulary, like "history", "contingency", "self-creation" and "pragmatism". It speaks to him of the historically hard-won freedom to explore possibilities for self-creation, but also of possibilities for the alleviation of the pain of others. When theoretical preoccupations enter the picture, even to adjudicate on the mix of 'possibilities here', "liberalism" loses practical potency and hence its charm. Rorty is convinced that this negative point about 'theoretical concerns' holds true even across the analytic–continental philosophy divide:

> Deconstruction is marginal to politics – if you want to do some political work, deconstructing texts is not a very efficient way to set about it. Getting rid of phallogocentrism, metaphysics and all that is an admirable long-term cultural goal, but there is still

a difference between such goals and the relatively short-term goals served by political deliberation and decision ... I see politics, at least in democratic countries, as something to be conducted in as plain, blunt, public, easy-to-handle language as possible. I see the enemies of human happiness as just greed, sloth and hypocrisy, and I don't see the need for philosophical depth charges in dealing with them.   (Rorty 1996: 44–5)

Stripped of all but the lightest pragmatist philosophical baggage, "liberalism" designates a political position that searches for the quickest route to practical solutions, taking no detour through theoretical complexities concerning its own 'legitimation' and 'justification'. We should not, then, expect Rorty's 'reasons' to involve detailed arguments in support of liberalism – not even arguments in support of 'liberalism as politics, not philosophy'. Rorty's reasons are linked to his recognition of the contingencies that have shaped his own life – such as being born in a liberal democracy at a time when most socialist states offered grim prospects for those who valued personal and political freedom as well as social wealth. Having abandoned any philosophical attempt to escape those 'contingencies', Rorty found surprisingly fertile means of reweaving them into history and culture and of thus redescribing them in ways that made them look 'more attractive'.

In consequence, though no prophet, he found himself living out a social, rather than a 'single', vision, one in which the institutions and practices of liberal democracies stood out as precious, wondrous phenomena, like veritable orchids in the charred fields of human history. This, he believed, was a vision that many more could live and, indeed, many were already living if they could only see that it was so through the fog of theoretical abstractions and self-recriminations that had been thrown up by misguided intellectuals in the 'rich democracies' of the West. Rorty's various writings on liberalism are not designed to show that it is 'philosophically compelling', 'the rational option, other things being equal', 'the uniquely best political system' or anything like that. They are part of his project to help dispel such intellectual fog and thereby let more of us live better lives.

Utopia and pain

Rorty's liberalism is *utopian*. It looks forward to a time when the main lessons of 'contingency' have been heeded by everyone. However, although at times Rorty seems to waver on this point, he makes it clear that not everyone in utopia *can* be an 'ironist'. For irony is 'reactive'. It needs a stable social target. Moreover it aims to create enough distance between the individual and the customs and practices of her society to open a window on to fresh possibilities for social arrangements. Such 'windows' provide useful safeguards against some of the worst forms of conservatism, complacency and stagnation. But to thrive, a community needs to get on with living the kind of life it has fostered. Not many of its members can stand a bit to one side, always half-gazing through the window of 'alternative options'.

This picture can look 'élitist', as if only the privileged few, the intellectuals, are granted the prospect of a suitably detached perspective. Rorty's intention, however, is to paint a more egalitarian portrait in which any such elitism is, in effect, neutralized. Most participants in liberal utopia will be commonsensical about their own 'contingency'. Their way of life is not something they regard as grounded in 'Truth', 'Reality', 'Rationality' or any other absolute. And they do not see this as a topic for much doubt, debate or further reflection. Their position is not 'inferior', not even intellectually. It resembles that of the majority of atheists in a securely secular society, those for whom controversy over questions concerning the nature and existence of God is a quaint relic of the past. Here 'confidence' in prevailing beliefs and practices is taken for granted, and life is simply to be lived accordingly. For some, however, things can *never* be that simple. They tend to be the intellectuals, the people who cannot stop ironically contemplating the possibility that they have been duped by common sense, that some other, very different, form of life may be more desirable. But they are pretty harmless. Their irony oppresses nobody. They still perform their public duties while waiting in the wings of social life, aware that perhaps one day the visions now unsettling them will become useful tools for shaping more history.

Utopian liberals have their eyes on the prospect of a better future. However, they are also concerned to alleviate immediate pain, especially if it takes the form of cruelty. So strong is this concern that Rorty is even prepared to *define* liberalism in terms of 'the avoidance of cruelty' (CIS: xv). As we noted in the previous chapter, Rorty has no compelling *argument* for so defining liberalism, for giving cruelty priority over other considerations such as 'poverty' or 'equality'. But a closer reading of Judith Shklar (1984), his acknowledged source, reveals how neatly this fits with his naturalistic picture of how human beings make progress by liberating themselves from all 'higher authority':

> To put cruelty first is to disregard the idea of sin as it is understood by revealed religion ... When it is marked as the supreme evil it is judged so in and of itself, and not because it signifies a denial of God or any other higher norm. It is a judgement made within the world in which cruelty occurs as part of our normal private life and our daily public practices.   (Shklar 1984: 8–9)

Postcolonial liberalism

> Your opinion of pragmatism can, and should, be independent of your opinion of either democracy or America.   (PSH: 24)

Rorty puts politics ahead of philosophy because of the 'practical' advantages in doing so, but why does he then restrict himself to *liberal* politics? We have already seen that Rorty's motivation for adopting liberalism is based on its 'contingent attractions'. So, as we said, we can hardly expect him to provide a standard line of philosophical argument that 'justifies' or 'legitimates' his political preferences. However, at the back of our original question is an additional, more precise, query that some critics have voiced concerning not Rorty's actual 'choice' of liberalism, but rather his enthusiastic *advocacy* of its virtues.

The main worry here is that since, as those such as Clifford Geertz have claimed, liberalism is culturally specific to the West, born and perfected there (Geertz forthcoming), Rorty's prolific sponsorship of it smuggles 'imperialist' propaganda in by the back door. Rorty is familiar with this kind of criticism. In a later article, "Pragmatism, Pluralism and Postmodernism" (PSH: 262–77), he acknowledges there are 'postcolonial sceptics', "who suspect that liberalism is an attempt to impose the outcome of a specifically European experience on people who have had no share in this experience" (PSH: 272). And Rorty's 'Deweyan response' to such scepticism is all of a piece with his reply to demands for philosophical validation of his own liberal preferences. It stakes its claims in certain historically contingent practical successes and the corresponding imaginative vision that helped generate those successes:

> We pragmatists are not arguing that modern Europe has any superior insight into eternal, ahistorical realities. We do not

claim any superior rationality. We claim only an experimental success: we have come up with a way of bringing people into some degree of comity, and of increasing human happiness, which looks more promising than any other way which has been proposed so far . . . The utopian social hope which sprang up in nineteenth-century Europe is still the noblest imaginative creation of which we have record. (PSH: 273, 277)

This 'response' is unashamedly 'ethnocentric'. Far from trying to smuggle certain liberal values into political discourse under the cloak of philosophically impartial rhetoric, Rorty *openly* defends such values. Not only that, he openly defends an *ethnocentric defence* of liberalism.

This should come as no surprise. For Rorty's distrust of traditional notions of 'philosophical neutrality' means that he has to keep his feet firmly on local ground not just when choosing a political position, but also when defending that choice. If there is no far-off philosophical place that provides refuge from 'time and chance', Rorty must start his political deliberations from where he is. Notice, however, that a non-relativistic element of normativity enters the picture here. It is *not* that Rorty thinks or wants us to think:

1. There is no philosophically neutral ground
2. Therefore I *might as well* start from where I am (wherever that happens to be).

For there is a suppressed premise in this quick argument that Rorty strongly disputes:

(R) No ground is better than any other ground for purposes of inspiring political deliberation.

This relativistic premise is, itself, supposed to follow from (1). Rorty disputes it because he believes he has particular pragmatic reasons for preferring to stake his political claims on the local ground of American liberalism. These 'reasons' serve two purposes: they block the inference from (1) to (R), the relativistic premise that appears to license (2), and they also introduce 'normativity' by showing why Rorty *ought* to 'start from where he is'.

Rorty's 'particular reasons' may seem to lose the power to serve such purposes when we take a 'bird's-eye view' of them. For then *everyone* who has what they regard as reasons to prefer their own cultural starting point for purposes of political reflection is in the same motivational position as Rorty, and (R) begins to look convincing. But, Rorty wants us to give up the habit of trying to draw conclusions from 'on high'. Of course, the special motivational power of each individual cultural starting point loses its grip at philosophical altitude, but (R) starts to look appealing only for that very same reason: no ground stands out above any other ground because from the overhead view all life looks like a map: *no ground stands out.*

Furthermore, Rorty's particular reasons are not *just* particular reasons. Hence his ethnocentric stance does not slide into the crass provincialism of: "That is the way we liberals do things around here: end of story." For his ethnocentric motivation incorporates a more general account as to why it is usually best to start political deliberations from one's own cultural standpoint. In a paper first published in 1985, a few years before *Contingency, irony, and solidarity*, Rorty calls this account 'anti-anti-ethnocentrism' ("On Ethnocentrism: A Reply to Clifford Geertz", ORT: 203–10). The unwieldy label self-consciously signals Rorty's distance from crude, unreflective ethnocentrism. His version is a piece of philosophically reactive therapy. It is designed to rescue intellectually sophisticated, but insufficiently postmodernist, liberals who "would rather die than be ethnocentric" (ORT: 203) from the quicksand of a correspondingly radical open-mindedness in which all their pride and confidence in liberal values is liable to go under. Such intellectuals "are still using the rationalist rhetoric of the Enlightenment to back up their liberal ideas" (ORT: 207). But this rhetoric steers them straight towards the 'quicksand'. Even as they speak of "something called a common human nature, a metaphysical substrate in which things called 'rights' are embedded" (*ibid.*), they are bound to reflect on its philosophical status: does it take "moral precedence over all merely 'cultural' superstructures" (*ibid.*)? If so, is the belief that it does "itself a cultural bias"? This kind of questioning is as natural as it is problematic for the kind of liberals Rorty has in mind: "Their rationalism commits them to making sense of the distinction between rational judgement and cultural bias. Their liberalism forces them to call any *doubts* about human equality a result of such irrational bias" (*ibid.*).

Rorty's anti-anti-ethnocentric 'solution' to this quandary is to abandon the rhetorical dichotomies such as 'necessary/contingent' or 'natural/cultural' that encourage liberals to both elevate and denigrate their ideals in the same reflective breath, and then to substitute a more pragmatic vocabulary in which the 'limits of liberal tolerance' are figured out sub-philosophically; that is: "case by case, by hunch or by conversational compromise, rather than by reference to stable criteria" (ORT: 208). This process is one of creative 'negotiation' in which, as in any situation where such a 'give-and-take' process is to be worthwhile, the participants come to the table with a strong position *and* the willingness to compromise (without a strong position there is no solid basis for negotiation and without the willingness to compromise, there is no room for progress). For *each* participant, their *own cultural background* is a natural starting point because only that background will furnish them with familiar values, those they are likely to be able both to work with and to manifest historically nurtured, and hence unforced, pride in. A tolerant, historically aware liberal will, on this understanding, stop wallowing in self-recrimination and stand up for much of what her culture regards as valuable while also making sincere attempts to build imaginary bridges into alien territory where those things she cares most about may be viewed with disdain or even hostility.

Rorty's anti-anti-ethnocentrism is, in the end, a remonstration against Enlightenment rhetoric. But it is *not* voiced against the liberal institutions and practices that are still mistakenly associated with such rhetoric. It is, to repeat, a makeshift therapeutic intervention, an attempt to divest those who have access to such institutions and practices from the futile, unnerving, philosophical thought that unless they can appeal to appropriate 'neutral criteria of justification', their belief in the efficacy of these institutions and practices is somehow 'irrational' and it would therefore be wrong to stand up for that belief.

Chapter 6

Some critics

> The notion of an edifying philosopher is, however, a paradox. For Plato defined the philosopher by opposition to the poet. The philosopher could give reasons, argue for his views, justify himself. (PMN: 370)

We have made frequent references to 'Rorty's critics' throughout this book. Now, it is time to say a bit more about them, about who they actually are and what it is they object to in Rorty's work. Because of his broad influence, Rorty has elicited responses from members of a variety of intellectual disciplines, but for brevity's sake we will focus on those of philosophers. It is in their area, in any case, that Rorty's views have stirred up a hornets' nest. In philosophy, those views receive the roughest treatment, accompanied by the least satisfactory attempts to tease out their full implications or even accurately portray them. Presumably these lapses occur because it is in philosophy, rather than, say, literary or political theory, that Rorty is perceived to be the biggest threat, and hence a great deal rides on the possibility of seeing such a threat as 'bogus'. But this invokes the puzzle we mentioned in the Preface. Why, if Rorty's views are so *clearly* wrong, are his philosophical critics so quick to reach for their rhetorical guns? Why are they so inclined to foist false claims on Rorty? Why do they so often content themselves with simply *reasserting* claims that he has long questioned, instead of showing what is right about those claims? One of the most disconcerting features of the hostile critical literature on Rorty is its sheer complacency, its self-satisfied failure to rise to his challenge. In his practical shrewdness of thought, avoidance of metaphysical trappings and straightforward 'no-frills' prose, Rorty has much in common with Hume. But unfortunately, since his analytic critics seem all too reluctant to be stirred from their 'dogmatic slumbers', he has yet to meet his Kant.

Rorty's philosophical critics tend now to fall into two broad categories: those who have been commissioned to engage with Rorty in orchestrated critical responses to his work, and those who feel obliged to attack him while engaged in their own projects. Those in the first category are more often than not involved in a process of 'critical appreciation', and hence usually put at least some degree of *constructive* spin on their 'objections'. We will return to briefly review the state of play with them in the closing chapter. In this section, however, we will concentrate on those more negatively inclined critics who seem unable to pursue their own ventures without pausing to fire some fierce warning shots at Rorty and all who would presume to take him seriously. Sometimes these are simply shots in passing, where Rorty is abruptly dismissed on the kind of stereotypical grounds that this book has tried to demolish: he is a wild relativist, he has cynically substituted rhetoric for philosophy, his overall position is blatantly self-defeating, and so on. There are many such 'passing shots', for Rorty's name comes up in citations and references a great deal more than most other philosophers these days, and within philosophy the balance of opinion probably still swings against him on the majority of traditional issues. But these 'criticisms of the moment' do not usually add up to much more than an unfortunate indictment of the shallow reading and thinking habits of those concerned.

More significant are those cases where thinkers of some stature raise their heads from pet projects or 'work in progress' to voice more carefully crafted, if no less mistaken, protests against what they perceive to be the absurdity of the philosophical threat that Rorty poses. There is an air of irony about such protests that adds a layer of complexity to our original puzzle. If Rorty's views are so absurd, then how can they pose a 'threat'? Why bother with them at all? But the critics in question see no irony in their overheated responses. They see themselves as primarily concerned that *other* readers may have been duped by intellectual fashion, that the obvious 'absurdity' of Rorty's views has been temporarily obscured by his media-friendliness and 'high profile'. On this, rather patronizing, understanding, Rorty's 'arguments' are supposedly so weak that he could not possibly be a proper 'intellectual threat'. Nevertheless, because of his seductive image, he might lead the 'philosophically untutored' astray and thereby divert attention from more serious ventures like the critics' own. Hence they feel moved to speak out, to set the record straight, to forestall the threat that Rorty poses to the masses. Let us look at some cases that fall in this broad category, but are worth more serious consideration: Blackburn, MacIntyre, Nagel, Searle and Williams.

Blackburn: postmodernist relativism

In his book *Spreading the Word* (Blackburn 1984), Simon Blackburn does not spend any time discussing details of Rorty's work, but nevertheless fires a typical passing shot by accusing him, in a trenchant explanatory footnote, of seeing "the *rejection* of questions as the distinctive theme of what he calls pragmatism" (1984: 259–60). This is a silly accusation. Rorty is singularly unimpressed by *certain* questions clustered around assumptions about what is traditionally considered to be philosophically important. He wants us to set aside such questions, not to avoid the activity of questioning as such, but to break free from the assumptions involved and to encourage fresh questions, ones that may lead to more fruitful results than a tradition gone stale has so far produced. There is no scope for a general complaint about rejection of 'questions' here. At the very least, we have to admit that Rorty is obsessed by the big question as to whether the time-worn questions transmitted down through the Western philosophical tradition that begins more or less with Plato and culminates in analytic philosophy are still worth worrying about.

However, in a subsequent book *Ruling Passions: A Theory of Practical Reasoning* (1998), Blackburn takes, on the face of it, a more circumspect approach when he considers the practical upshot of what he regards as Rorty's 'relativistic theory about ethics'.

Although he makes some polite, if rather redundant, gestures (Rorty is: "a more than usually well-informed and articulate opponent of normal, or mainstream, or analytical philosophy" (1998: 287), "not a monster" (1998: 288), and so forth) and has an interesting background agenda (he wants to see what implications relativistic points *about* ethics have for conduct *within* it), Blackburn cannot resist imposing a traditional straitjacket on Rorty's thought. He does so by first shoe-horning Rorty's views back into the kind of rhetorical context they were designed to break free of, a context in which

141

Richard Rorty

designations like "the rational mind" (1998: 287) retain the kind of importance and high seriousness Rorty has for many years decried. Then Blackburn draws some unwelcome consequences that are supposed to undermine Rorty's whole position.

In general, Rorty's ironic brand of 'relativism' is said to be likely to engender a bogus form of 'cognitive instability' in the philosophically unsuspecting. More specifically, his overall approach to 'truth' is supposed to leave him bereft of the capacity to make important distinctions that need to be made.

Blackburn's charges will only stick if he is allowed to get away with the very first move just mentioned: that of forcing Rorty's views back into a rhetorical context where they no longer belong. In *this* context, 'relativism' assumes a structure and significance that Rorty wants nothing to do with: "Insofar as 'postmodern' philosophical thinking is identified with a mindless and stupid cultural relativism – with the idea that any fool thing that calls itself culture is worthy of respect – then I have no use for such thinking" (PSH: 276).

It is not clear just how much of Blackburn's picture of relativism is merely hypothetical exposition or straw person sketching, but he certainly endorses this picture to the extent that he finds its details worth discussing. At any rate, relativism so depicted has a particular inferential structure. *From claims about the inescapable relativity of our moral judgements, we can infer the limits of the rational authority of those same judgements: they do not extend beyond the boundaries of the culture they are relativistically related to.*

The salient problematic 'inference', the one that makes something of a philosophical spectre out of relativism, is that the authority involved here travels no further than its home-grown, cultural recognition or, as Blackburn puts it, "our judgements . . . have no authority beyond that which we give them" (1998: 286). Such an inference is liable to induce philosophical nightmares of 'lost authority' and, more generally, 'unseat confidence' (1998: 287). Furthermore, as the relevant authority shrinks away from remote, external territories where it cannot reasonably demand acknowledgement, the whole process threatens to implode: why should the retreat stop at the boundaries of cultural recognition? If our judgements have no widespread authority, why should they have *any* authority, why should the mere fact that *we* happen to take something to be authoritative mean that it *really is authoritative*? Even *for us*?

From Rorty's perspective, this is a spurious scenario. He feels no temptation to believe in any kind of authority that surpasses cultural authority. The idea of such an authority, of anything like 'universal transcultural rationality' (ORT: 26), is a philosophical pipe dream. In Rorty's worldview, such a phenomenon is impossible. Moreover, even if it *were* possible, it would not be a desirable requirement for having confidence in the kind of 'judgements' we make. Here, local cultural criteria are not just sufficient, but 'best'. Questions as to how far their 'authority' can, or *should*, extend into other territories are to be settled pragmatically: by inter-cultural 'negotiations' and the contingencies of history. On 'alien soil', moral judgements should carry all and only the weight they can pragmatically bear. There is no higher court of appeal.

Blackburn describes the relativist's predicament in terms of a peculiarly pernicious form of 'instability': "The relativist becomes someone who stands ready to disown his or her convictions, and eventually, becomes unstable, incapable of conviction at all" (1998: 287). When he discusses Rorty against this background, Blackburn tries to fend off the kind of 'instability' he sees Rorty as peddling by way of his notion of 'irony'. But the 'background' is unsuitable and the attempt to neutralize 'instability' unsuccessful.

Far from being someone who 'stands ready to disown his convictions', Rorty is ready to stand up for his convictions. What he is ready to disown is the illusion that his convictions can be 'philosophically grounded' in the (traditional!) 'culture-transcending' sense that such grounding is supposed to involve. In disowning the 'illusion', he feels he can also throw off the shackles of the realist assumptions that tend to fuel anti-relativistic rhetoric:

> 'Relativism' . . . is merely a red herring. The realist is, once again, projecting his own habits of thought upon the pragmatist when he charges him with relativism. For the realist thinks that the whole point of philosophical thought is to detach oneself from any particular community and look down at it from a more universal standpoint. When he hears the pragmatist repudiating the desire for such a standpoint, he cannot quite believe it. He thinks that everyone, deep down inside, *must* want such detachment. So he attributes to the pragmatist a perverse form of his own attempted detachment, and sees him as an ironic, sneering, aesthete who refuses to take the choice between communities seriously, a mere 'relativist'. (ORT: 30)

Rorty is not 'unstable' in the relativistic sense Blackburn describes, because his 'convictions', the basis for his 'judgements', are planted in the firm soil of local practical advantages. When wobbling with 'doubt', there is a pragmatic story he can tell himself about why *those* convictions are worth having. Nevertheless, as an 'ironist', Rorty is presumably *meta-unstable*. Do Blackburn's points about the inadvisability of 'instability' tell against *that* condition?

Blackburn makes much of the 'association' between the instability of Rorty's ironists – "never quite able to take themselves seriously because always aware that the terms in which they describe themselves are subject to change" (CIS: 73–4) – and "their realisation that anything can be made to look good or bad by being redescribed" (CIS: 74). On Blackburn's understanding, the ironists "are impressed by the thoughts that lead people to relativism" (1998: 288), but they have made a bad mistake if such thoughts include the 'realisation' about the unlimited scope of redescription. For, far from impressive, the subject of that realisation is a sham: there is no genuine sense of "open to being made to look better/worse by means of redescription" that applies in the case of the things we most care about when making moral judgements. Of course, such things are 'open' to trivial, or other philosophically uninteresting, redescriptions where, for example, the facts are distorted or some weird-minded audience is all too willing to see things from a distorted perspective. But where our current judgement-creating descriptions look obviously correct, then there seems to be no coherent way in which the judgements involved can be overturned, or even destabilized, by a redescription that purports to make things look better or worse as the case may be. To show this, Blackburn, not unnaturally, picks a hard example: the Holocaust. Setting aside the above frivolous options that Blackburn, in his professed puzzlement as to what Rorty is actually up to, feels obliged to run by us, two possibilities emerge. Neither is supposed to be congenial to Rorty's position:

1. That the limits of our moral imagination ("How can I imagine that a truer, fuller, and better description of [the Holocaust] might represent it as anything other than abhorrent?" (Blackburn 1998: 289)) limit the actual moral contours of the case: the Holocaust is a counter-example to the idea that 'anything can be made to look good or bad by being redescribed'.
2. There may be "a way of looking at practical life that is different from ours, root and branch" (*ibid.*) and perhaps someone engrossed in that view on life could produce a correspondingly different way of describing the Holocaust. Blackburn suggests that the *general* possibility raised here (of uncovering a radically

different take on 'practical life') has no immediately destabilizing implications. Such a possibility simply presents us with further "opportunities for moral thought" (*ibid.*), the results of which vary and only 'sometimes cause instability'. As for the Holocaust as a particular 'instantiation' of the general possibility, here "we can dismiss the rival attitudes as the unfortunate or even evil product of various defects" (*ibid.*). The Holocaust is still a 'counter-example'.

With regard to (1), Rorty might well simply reply that of course the Holocaust is always going to seem abhorrent to those of us who know what its perpetrators did. Moreover, this very example provides as good a place as any for digging our moral heels in and resisting views to the contrary, as in (2) above. The fact that a dissenting judgement even tries to make the Holocaust look morally good is *prima facie* evidence that there is something gravely wrong with that 'judgement'. However, all this is consistent with a *Quinean* meta-appreciation (see our previous discussion of Quine in Chapter 2, pp. 51–4) of the reasons why abhorrence of the Holocaust is so resistant to redescriptive incursions. Such reasons do not, and in Rorty's view *cannot*, involve our relation to a culture-transcending core of moral truth (e.g. our 'abhorrence' is fixed in place by its cognitive grip on *the* (i.e. culture-independent) truth about the moral horrors of the Holocaust). They concern, instead, the intricate mesh of cultural forces (customs, beliefs, practices, conventions, and so on) that insulate heartfelt moral disapproval of the Holocaust from radical redescriptive revision. Someone whose meta-philosophical account of moral judgements holds that the matter of their 'entrenchment' is always ultimately a social matter is in roughly the same position as a Quinean who refuses to explain the stubborn nature of mathematical truths such as '2 + 2 = 4' in terms of a corresponding 'transcultural necessity'. The Quinean is seriously meta-unstable about such truths to the extent that, even though they are unable to *imagine* how it could happen, they countenance the bare possibility, the possibility *in principle*, of those truths being overturned by a dramatic reweaving of the wider web of beliefs they inhabit:

> Any statement can be held true come what may, if we make drastic enough adjustments elsewhere in the system. Even a statement very close to the periphery can be held true in the face of recalcitrant experience by pleading hallucination or by amending certain

145

statements of the kind called logical laws. Conversely, by the same token, no statement is immune to revision.   (Quine 1953: 43)

But this kind of intellectual 'instability' need have little short-term *practical* or 'existential' effect. Quineans do not have to hesitate in making daily calculations because the mathematics involved *could* be undermined by some future intellectual earthquake. Rorty can treat the Holocaust with due moral seriousness without making it a lynchpin of a realist conception of moral truth.

The mathematical example is apt because, to fix ideas and make things more "concrete", Blackburn moves on to discuss Rorty's reading of George Orwell's *1984*, a novel in which the manipulation of beliefs about truths like '2 + 2 = 4' plays a vital part.

Rorty's reading concentrates on Part Three. His main theme is 'cruelty' and its connections with human identity. He discusses the ways in which Winston, the hero, is cruelly deprived of any capacity to be the kind of person he aspires to be. In this discussion, Rorty tries to break away from crude 'realist readings' in which this 'primal deprivation' involves detaching Winston's beliefs from *the truth* – so that Winston has no control over who he is *because* he cannot anchor his beliefs in 'objective truth' or 'reality'. Rorty wants to follow a different track from those commentators who "conclude that Orwell teaches us to set our faces against all those sneaky intellectuals who try to tell us that truth is 'not out there', that what counts as a truth is a function of the rest of your beliefs" (CIS: 172).

Hence, Rorty suggests that Orwell's use of emblematic realist truths such as '2 + 2 = 4' is indicative of something more general, and in the end more devastating, than the enforced alienation from reality that the realist fears:

> Getting somebody to deny a belief for no reason is a first step toward making her incapable of having a self because she becomes incapable of weaving a coherent web of belief and desire. It makes her irrational, in a quite precise sense: She is unable to give a reason for her belief that fits together with her other beliefs. She becomes irrational not in the sense that she has lost contact with reality but in the sense that she can no longer rationalise – no longer justify herself to herself.
>
> (CIS: 178)

The example of '2 + 2 = 4' is invoked, says Rorty, because it is "symbolic" for Winston. It plays such an important part in his own ongoing sense of who he is, and who he should be, that to break

Winston's belief in it is to break Winston himself, and *for good*. In other cases, a very different kind of truth, say a deeply religious one, could serve the same purpose.

Blackburn does not urge a blunt realist reading of Orwell, but he pitches an interpretation against Rorty that, in the end, seems to be much the same thing. Rorty's emphasis is on the implications of being deprived of the capacity to weave one's own web of identity-building beliefs, to rationalize in painless peace. Web-independent truth/reality drops out of that picture. But Blackburn sees this as a mistake. He sees Winston's "nightmare" as "that of having one's beliefs manipulated, and so formed in the wrong way" (1998: 292). This 'wrong way' need not be crudely cashed out in terms of offence against "some Platonic, Kantian myth about truth" (*ibid.*), terms that play into Rorty's truth-debunking hands. The 'commitment' that Winston wants to hold on to can be stated "without using *any* concept of truth at all"; it can be presented thus:

(i) He wants it to be the case that he believes p only if p.
(ii) He wants to form beliefs only in areas in which, when he does believe p, then p. (1998: 293)

Without some explanation of the verificationist microstructure here, something that clearly elevates 'believing p only if p' above some pragmatic variant such as 'believing p if all the best social indicators of justification strongly suggest belief in p is preferable to believing "not-p"' (and similarly for (ii) above), Rorty is just going to regard this as one more piece of nostalgic hand-waving.

Blackburn gestures towards some 'microstructural' response here when he talks about the 'norms' that govern the sense of propositions:

> They are *enabling* norms, like the rules of chess. The rules of chess enable people to play the game; similarly the rules surrounding a proposition are what enable people to think in terms of it. To depart from these norms, whether through self-deception, wishful thinking, political control, or anything else, is to begin to lose your right to be regarded as believing that p, and to depart enough is to lose your right to be regarded as thinking about the topic at all. These norms are not 'social' or 'historical' 'conditionings' that a suitably light ironist or suitably acute social theorist can somehow fly away from. They are the structures that enable thought to take place.
> (Blackburn 1998: 293)

But, from Rorty's point of view, this looks just like the desperate pleadings of someone who wants to hang on to an outmoded conception of art: "What you propose cannot be accepted as 'verse' ('painting', or whatever) because it departs from the very norms that constitute the form of art in question." Rorty has two main problems with this kind of 'reactionary' stance in philosophy itself.

First, he cannot see how its incipient 'essentialism' makes much practical sense. Take Blackburn's 'chess' example, an old favourite of analytic philosophers, and one we have already deployed ourselves. Suppose a chess-playing genius begins to take an ironic stance towards traditional chess (making fun of it, perhaps, because it can be so very well played by computers, mere machines), and then introduces a new, more 'serious', way of playing what she still calls 'chess'. Further suppose that in this new way of playing, the 'rules' involved cannot be directly derived from the traditional game. What will determine whether this innovation is accepted as 'chess'? Surely it will be socially contingent factors like whether the 'new game' catches on with former players of the traditional version, whether *they* regard it as 'chess', whether the appropriate organizations concur, whether a 'new-wave chess culture' emerges, and so on. In the face of the former social changes, what would be the point of hand-wringing objections concerning the breaking of the 'enabling norms' of chess?

Rorty also, quite rightly, has difficulty in making sense of 'norms' that are not rooted in society and history. He can accept what Blackburn says about the ongoing *role* of norms, but finds the additional idea of bare 'structures', things that *extra-socially* conspire to make certain kinds of thought possible, incoherent.

In conclusion, it seems Rorty is unlikely to find anything in Blackburn's discussion that should deflect his reading of Orwell as someone who sensitized "an audience to cases of cruelty and humiliation which they had not noticed" and then interpreting this not "as a matter of stripping away appearance and revealing reality", but rather as "a redescription of what may happen or has been happening – to be compared, not with reality, but with alternative descriptions of the same events" (CIS: 173).

MacIntyre: truthfulness

Alasdiar MacIntyre's approach to philosophy is much closer to Rorty's than Blackburn's in the sense that it pays more attention to general historical considerations and less to the distinctive problems and methods inherited from analytic philosophy. But in his book *Dependent Rational Animals* (1999), MacIntyre also takes great exception to Rorty's taste for 'ironic redescription'. He holds that Rorty's version of 'irony' and the redescriptive maxim that goes with it ("Anything can be made to look good or bad by being redescribed") involve a transgression of 'norms of virtue', "an offence against the kind of truthfulness in accountability that is required by the virtues of acknowledged dependence" (i.e. the virtues that must be practised by a society to enable its members to emerge from the processes of cultural nurturing and education as 'independent practical reasoners') (1999: 151–2). The 'norms' MacIntyre refers to are a sort of moral increment to Blackburn's 'enabling norms of sense': "Ironic detachment involves a withdrawal from our common language and our shared judgements and thereby from the social relationships which presuppose the use of that language in making those judgements" (1999: 152).

But MacIntyre's criticism seems to distort the nature of irony. In the first place, it ignores the fact that, although irony can be cultivated, its first steps are involuntary. It is not as if, after first 'seeing through' the philosophical pretensions of absolutist vocabularies, Rorty could then *decide* whether to view such pretensions with irony or just make more effort to step back in social line. This kind of 'insight' brings a degree of ironic detachment with it. The second problem with MacIntyre's complaint is that it overlooks the further fact that irony does come in degrees. A 'refined', 'sympathetic' or 'light' form of irony may involve a very subtle form of 'social reserve' – a 'distancing' that far from threatening 'truthfulness in accountability', enhances it. MacIntyre appears to have forgotten that such irony is closer to 'impartiality' than cynical withdrawal. There is no inferential route from "She views X with irony" to "She is not to be regarded as a reliable truth-teller when she talks about X". A still further problem with MacIntyre's complaint is that it overlooks the limited role that irony plays in Rorty's scheme of things. The role is 'limited' because, as we pointed out in the last chapter, not *everyone* will be an ironist in Rorty's envisaged utopian society. And those who are will tend to conform to current standards of truthfulness. Their eyes are on future possibilities, times when it is right to diverge from the norm, rather than on the chances of undermining the integrity of what they see taken for granted all around them.

The imperative of wholehearted, morally responsible, 'truthfulness' that MacIntyre invokes is convergent with a broader line of criticism that Rorty is all too familiar with:

Pragmatists are often said not to recognise the political and moral importance of truth-telling. I do not think this charge is even remotely plausible. Truthfulness, in the relevant sense, is saying publicly what you believe, even when it is disadvantageous to do so. This is a moral virtue whose exercise is punished by totalitarian societies. This virtue has nothing to do with any controversy between Realists and non-Realists, both of whom pay it equal honour. My claim that if we take care of freedom truth will take care of itself implies that if people can say what they believe without fear then the task of justifying themselves to others and the task of getting things right coincide. My argument is that since we can test whether we have performed the first task, and have no further test to apply to determine whether we have performed the second, Truth as end-in-itself drops out. (Brandom 2000: 347)

As with 'Truth', so, we might add, with the goal of 'Truthfulness-without-irony'.

Nagel: subjectivism and consensus

Neither Blackburn nor MacIntyre are 'Realists' in Rorty's derogatory sense. Thomas Nagel and John Searle are. Both are very critical of Rorty's rejection of the whole *philosophical* apparatus of realist discourse. Both write with an air of intense high seriousness that they seem to feel only realists can aspire to – though Nagel's stance is subtler and Searle's more robust. But, in writing in this way, both unwittingly render their views all the more vulnerable to Rorty's irony.

In *The Last Word* (1997), Nagel tries to defend a 'rationalist' answer "for certain domains of thought" to a question "that runs through practically every area of inquiry and that has even invaded the general culture" (1997: 3). The question concerns the point at which "understanding and justification come to an end" (*ibid.*). And the issue at stake is:

Do they come to an end with objective principles whose validity is independent of our point of view, or do they come to an end within our point of view – individual or shared – so that ultimately, even the apparently most objective and universal principles derive their validity or authority from the perspective of those who follow them? (*ibid.*)

Nagel's rhetorical strategy is to denigrate what he calls 'subjectivist' answers to this question (answers that somehow terminate 'within our point of view'), even though his rationalist alternative is highly problematic. Of course, Nagel does not regard himself as dabbling in mere 'rhetoric'. He takes himself to be 'arguing a case', as befits such a high-minded exponent of realist rationalism.

As we saw earlier in Chapter 2, Rorty started to pull the philosophical plug on Nagel's approach as far back as 1982 when, in the "Introduction" to *Consequences of Pragmatism*, he discussed the intuitive realists' attempt to 'safeguard' the Western philosophical tradition by *universalizing* its concerns (CP: xxxi). In that discussion, Rorty raised two very awkward questions. First, he queried whether the kind of 'problems' tackled by the intuitive realists in general, and subsumed by Nagel's subjective/objective "rubric" in particular, are deeply embedded in the 'human situation' (i.e. as opposed to being historically entrenched in certain cultures at certain times). In raising this issue, Rorty wanted to:

> Illustrate the difference between taking a standard philosophical problem (or cluster of interrelated problems such as free will, selfhood, agency and responsibility) and asking, on the one hand, "What is its essence? To what ineffable depths, what limit of language, does it lead us? What does it show us about *being human?*" and asking, on the other hand, "What sort of people would see these problems? What vocabulary, what image of man, would produce such *problems*? Why, insofar as we are gripped by these problems, do we see them as deep rather than as *reductiônes ad absurdum* of a vocabulary? What does the persistence of such problems show us about *being twentieth century Europeans?*" (CP: xxxiii)

Rorty's second awkward question concerned the 'intuitions' that Nagel appeals to, intuitions that keep traditional problems in play (and, indeed, give them a new lease of life). Are they compelling? Here, Rorty suggested that what is at stake is not whether such intuitions can be rationally grounded, argued out of existence or replaced by even deeper ones, but rather which of two kinds of vocabularies is preferable: one that enshrines such intuitions or one that circumvents them on pragmatic grounds? And this issue, Rorty further suggested, comes down to "one about whether philosophy should try to find natural starting-points which are distinct from cultural traditions, or whether all philosophy should do is compare and contrast cultural traditions" (CP: xxxvii).

In *The Last Word*, Nagel does not address Rorty's awkward questions. Instead, he writes as if they can be discounted because they raise nothing of any philosophical importance, and then he lambasts an "interpretation of reason as consensus" that he rashly attributes to Rorty. This 'interpretation' is extraordinary. First, it is supposed to be an 'easy target', but Nagel makes quite heavy going of its disposal. Secondly, it seems to have little connection with Rorty's actual views. Rorty *never* claims or implies that 'coherence' reduces to the head-counting banality of anything like 'consensus' (cf. "I do not recall that I have ever, even at my worst, spoken of either warrant or truth being determined by *majority vote*", 'Hilary Putnam and the Relativist Menace', in *Truth and Progress* (TP): 55).

From Rorty's vast number of words on his pragmatist conception of notions like 'reason', 'truth' and 'reality', Nagel selects just two quotations, neither of which reveals its proper context or, even as it stands in isolation, remotely justifies the 'reason reduces to consensus' interpretation. After citing an extract from Sabina Lovibond (which at least contains the term "consensus"), Nagel brings in a passage from Rorty that he says "puts the point the same way" (Nagel 1997: 28). The Lovibond extract provides a quasi-Wittgensteinian gloss on her view (which Nagel also quotes) that "the objective validity of an assertion or an argument is always at the same time something of which human beings (those human beings who call it 'objectively valid') are subjectively persuaded" (Lovibond 1983: 37):

> Thus Wittgenstein's conception of language incorporates a non-foundational epistemology which displays the notions of objectivity (sound judgements) and rationality (valid reasoning) as grounded in consensus – theoretical in the first place, but ultimately practical. (Lovibond 1983: 40)

To impose on such a passage a crude 'consensus' thesis of the 'intellectually lazy' kind that Nagel fears will filter up from the already contaminated "lower reaches of the humanities and social sciences" (1997: 6) is odd, to say the least. But things get worse when Nagel ropes in the supposedly analogous remarks from Rorty:

> We cannot find a skyhook which lifts us out of mere coherence – mere agreement – to something like "correspondence with reality as it is in itself" ... Pragmatists would like to replace the desire for objectivity – the desire to be in touch with a reality

which is more than some community with which we identify our-selves – with the desire for solidarity with that community.

(ORT: 38–9)

Here, we are immediately prompted to ask: what is the *same point* that Rorty is supposed to be putting forward here? When Rorty uses the terms 'mere coherence' and 'mere agreement' he is mimicking, and not necessarily endorsing, the language of his opponents. Rorty believes 'coherence' encompasses "a Deweyan conception of knowledge, as what we are justified in believing" (PMN: 9), that covers everything needed to *rationally* guide inquiry. Those philosophers who want to substitute notions such as 'matching reality' or 'universal standards' are living on false philosophical credit. When the time comes for them to cash these notions in, they will – if history is anything to go by – get nothing much for them. Likewise, 'solidarity with a community we identify ourselves with' is a rich metaphor. It is not even the remotest gesture towards the crude idea of cognitively ingratiating ourselves with the people we want to hang out with for the foreseeable future.

When Nagel subjects 'consensus' views to criticism, he suggests they will "turn out to be inconsistent with the very consensus on which they propose to 'ground objectivity'" (1997: 29). Then to give an example of "the standard response of a subjectivist to such argu-ments" (*ibid.*), he quotes from Rorty again, while rather condescend-ingly assuring us he is 'not making this up':

> What people like Kuhn, Derrida and I believe is that it is point-less to ask whether there are really mountains or whether it is merely convenient for us to talk about mountains.
>
> We also think it is pointless to ask, for example, whether neutrinos are real entities or merely useful heuristic fictions. This is the sort of thing we mean by saying that it is pointless to ask whether reality is independent of our ways of talking about it. Given that it pays to talk about mountains, as it certainly does, one of the obvious truths about mountains is that they were there before we talked about them. If you do not know that, you probably do not know how to play the usual language-games which employ the word "mountain". But the utility of those lan-guage-games has nothing to do with the question whether Real-ity as It Is In Itself, apart from the way it is handy for human beings to describe it, has mountains in it. (TP: 72)

The thrust of 'the standard response' instantiated here is that the 'subjectivist' is "not saying anything that conflicts with the contents of ordinary mathematical, or scientific, or ethical judgements and arguments" (Nagel 1997: 29). But this claim to 'speak with the vulgar', while offering an explanation of that way of speaking that does not embody the philosophical assumptions of Realism, will not wash, says Nagel, because:

> The claim that there is nothing more to objectivity than solidarity with your speech community, even if it is extended to the things your speech community says would be true whether they said so or not, directly contradicts the categorical statements it purports to be about – that there are infinitely many prime numbers, that water is a compound, that Napoleon was less than six feet tall. (Nagel 1997: 30)

Again, this is odd. If there is simply a 'direct contradiction' between the kind of claims mentioned here and Rorty's deflationary account of their philosophical status, this ought to have been apparent, and the issues at stake settled in the rationalist's (or realist's, or whatever) favour, long ago, even, perhaps, in an intellectual community that has become as slovenly in its habits as Nagel intimates. But Nagel should recognize, in any case, that to push this line is to beg the key issues at stake. For Rorty would say that there is nothing in 'the content' of *any* ordinary claims that links them inextricably to notions like 'Reality as It Is' or 'inquiry-independent truth'. Nor *could* there be. Such notions may have stirred up a lot of rhetorical froth among some thinkers, but, as Davidson points out, they circle an empty philosophical space:

> It is futile to either reject or to accept the idea that the real and the true are "independent of our beliefs". The only evident positive sense we can make of this phrase, the only use that derives from the intentions of those who prize it, derives from the idea of correspondence, and this is an idea without content. (Davidson 1990: 305)

Searle: robust realism

John Searle resolutely defends two realist claims about knowledge that Rorty, equally resolutely, denies:

1. "Knowledge is typically of a mind-independent reality".

2. Knowledge is expressed in "propositions which are true because they accurately represent reality". (Searle 1992: 46)

Imagine a meeting of Madhyamika philosophers who have gathered together to discuss Searle's *The Social Construction of Reality* (1995). These are the radical philosophers we briefly compared with Rorty towards the end of our Introduction. And they would probably have the same reaction to some of Searle's central remarks on 'realism' as Nagel had to Rorty's remarks on 'mountains' and 'neutrinos'. No doubt they would, for example, feel the need to preface the following quotation with the assurance "Please believe us, we are not making this up":

> As a preliminary formulation, I have defined realism as the view that the world exists independently of our representations of it. This has the consequence that if we had never existed, if there had never been any representations – any statements, beliefs, perceptions, thoughts, etc. – most of the world would have remained unaffected. (Searle 1995: 151)

Why would they treat such remarks with incredulousness? Because they do not believe that the idea of 'independent existence' (or, as they usually prefer to call it, 'inherent existence') is coherent. In their picture of the world, much like Rorty's, *nothing* has an 'intrinsic essence' and, correlatively, *everything* is 'dependently originated': brought into being, and held there for however long, by a complex web of causal factors including linguistic considerations such as 'designation'. Consider Searle's own happy (given our recent discussion) example, Mount Everest:

> Let us assume that there is a mountain in the Himalayas that I represent to myself as "Mount Everest". Mount Everest exists independently of how or whether I or anyone else ever represented it or anything else. Furthermore, there are many features of Mount Everest, for example the sort of features that I represent if I make a statement such as "Mt. Everest has snow and ice near its summit", which would have remained totally unaffected if no one had ever represented them in any fashion and will not be affected by the demise of these or any other representations. (Searle 1995: 153)

Now further consider a simple thought experiment. Imagine the earth evolved in just the way it has done except that:

1. No sentient creatures emerged from the primal chemical soup.
2. Of all the earthly planet's resources, only the lump of matter that would have been called "Mount Everest" if human beings had evolved in the way they in fact have done, eluded a catastrophic cosmic collision (picture this Everest-shaped lump floating on its own in space, snow and ice preserved by the ambient temperatures if it helps).

Now the question is: if the universe at large was nevertheless populated in regions remote from earth by enormously huge creatures, creatures for whom the earth while it survived would have been an incredibly small blip on their equivalent of electron microscopes should they have ever got close enough to view it face to face, would Mount Everest have existed in that world? After the catastrophe, would the floating lump of rock still have been Mount Everest? Would it still have been a floating lump of rock? On the above account, Searle would say "yes". But our imaginative grip on just *what* would have been sitting there in its 'representation-free state' is stretched to breaking point. "Yes" begins to look less robust, however firmly Searle himself might still be prepared to state it. And Rorty's own remarks on 'mountains' begin to look less incredible than Nagel implies they are. The Madhyamikas would not find this surprising. For on their view, if we analyse our conception of 'Mount Everest' rigorously enough, and strip away *all* the mountain's seamless web of multifarious 'causally contextualizing' properties, we will never find a natural breaking point between the mountain and our representational projections on to it, and thus we will never end up with its representation-free core – the mountain-in-itself. Instead, we will end up with nothing. This is the reason that the Madhyamikas claim all things are 'empty' – a term that has often been mistranslated to mean something like 'an ontological vacuum' or 'the void', when it actually means 'empty of *inherent* existence' – the kind of existence Searle's realism naïvely asserts.

The Madhyamikas' views are worth referring to here not just to usher in the possibility of an interesting, even more radical, historical precedent for Rorty's 'anti-essentialism', but also to highlight the parochial nature of the way philosophers like Nagel and Searle approach the debate over 'truth' and 'realism'. An added bonus is that these views show how the 'metaphysics' of realism might be challenged by an alternative metaphysics, a dialectical metaphysics that, in the hands of the great early Indian thinker Nagarjuna or his later Tibetan counterpart Tsongkhapa, thrives on teasing out the unwelcome implications of its rivals. For Rorty himself is not inter-ested in *that* kind of challenge. He does not want us to drop realist metaphysics so that we can turn to a non-realist version with a better 'rational foundation'. He wants to move the discussion on to territory where the metaphysical issues at stake in the debate over realism (issues about the true nature of 'reality', and so on) no longer capture our interest. But to do this Rorty cannot simply 'change the subject', he has to counter Searle's *practical* objections concerning what he regards to be the disastrous social consequences of abandon-ing realism.

In his characteristically forthright and engaging article "Ration-alism and Realism: What is at Stake?" (1992), Searle argues that the kind of realist principles referred to in (1) and (2) above are an important part of 'the Western Rationalistic Tradition', and that to reject the latter: "Makes possible an abandonment of traditional standards of objectivity, truth and rationality, and opens the way for an educational agenda one of whose primary purposes is to achieve social and political transformations" (1992: 72).

Although Rorty is prepared to engage with a few of the "more technical aspects" of Searle's position, and we will come to these shortly, his prior concern is to show that in such passages as the above one, Searle is being unnecessarily alarmist. Rorty thinks that the causal connections between the kind of core principles of realism Searle advocates and our wider social practices are far too weak to make it likely that a rejection of the former will cause an unwelcome upheaval in the latter. This claim against Searle encapsulates a number of Rorty's views. Indeed, on his terms, its truth is over-determined. First, as a matter of empirical fact, the vast majority of people responsible for keeping our culture's methods of inquiry respectable do not know, or care, enough about the truth of 'philo-sophical positions' such as 'realism' to change their ways of going about things when such positions are overturned. "Correspondence is dead. Is all permissible?" Hardly. Nobody cares *that* much about such 'positions' except philosophers themselves, and then only those holed up in a very small, reactionary cave in the ongoing history of ideas. Secondly, Searle's account clashes with Rorty's overall picture of intellectual change that we discussed earlier in Chapter 2 of this book. Realist principles do not provide an intellectual foundation for social practices, and when change occurs, it occurs because the meta-phors that help hold those practices in place have outlived their usefulness or have been supplanted by some unexpectedly sparkling new ones. And, finally, realist principles could *never* be hooked up to methods of inquiry in the ways Searle presupposes because such principles incorporate concepts (of 'independent reality', 'correspondence' and so on) that are vacuous. Beliefs like:

> P is true because it corresponds to reality

> We should only believe P if it corresponds to reality

> Just because P corresponds to reality, we ought to believe it

contain a component ("corresponds to reality") that either has no substantive content (so it cannot motivate belief) or is entirely explicable in terms of some related social procedures and their practical upshot (in which case it is redundant). Rorty's view is that explanation in terms of 'social procedures' is sufficient to preserve the intellectual virtues of objectivity and so forth that Searle is so concerned about:

> Philosophers on my side of the argument think that we can explain what we mean when we say that academic research should be disinterested and objective *only* by pointing to the ways in which free universities actually function. We can defend such universities *only* by pointing to the good these universities do, their role in keeping democratic government and liberal institutions alive and functioning.   (TP: 69, emphasis added)

On a more technical footing, Rorty suggests that Searle's account suffers from mischievous ambiguities in his dominant realist notions of 'independence' and 'accurate representation'. With regard to 'independence', Rorty points out that Searle's usage sometimes implies that to deny 'independence' is to deny that things like mountains existed before people were able linguistically to express the fact that such things exist (note that these remarks provide a bit more context for Nagel's selected quotation):

> But nobody denies that. Nobody thinks there is a chain of causes that makes mountains an effect of thoughts or words. What people like Kuhn, Derrida and I believe is that it is pointless to ask whether there really are mountains or whether it is merely convenient for us to talk about mountains.   (TP: 72)

There is a sense of talking about 'independence' *within* social practices that allows, indeed encourages, us to explore answers to questions like "Is there *really* a golden mountain in Tibet even

though it has never been seen by anyone so far?" But when the resources of the social practices that sustain our ways of approaching
such questions are exhausted, nothing is to be gained by invoking a
further, *philosophical* sense of 'independent existence', a sense that
refers to what Rorty calls 'Reality as It Is In Itself': "nothing could
possibly turn on the answers to questions of independence in *that*
sense" (TP: 72).

Rorty finds similar problems of ambiguity with Searle's notion of
'accurate representation'. It fails to distinguish between two senses
of 'represent accurately'. The first sense is practical and non-philosophical. Here we ask (and usually have criteria for evaluating the
'accuracy' of the answers) whether someone, say a witness (Rorty's
own example) has faithfully represented the facts. This practical
sense of accuracy of representation can go a long way, even in the
more exacting environment of the academy. Consider Rorty's revealing remarks on historians:

> When we say that good historians accurately represent what
> they find in the archives, we mean that they look hard for the
> relevant documents, do not discard documents tending to
> discredit the historical thesis they are propounding, do not
> misleadingly quote passages out of context, tell the same his-
> torical story among themselves that they tell us, and so on. To
> assume that a historian accurately represents the facts is to
> assume that she behaves in the way in which good, honest his-
> torians behave. It is not to assume anything about the reality of
> past events, or about the truth conditions of statements concern-
> ing such events, or about the necessarily hermeneutical charac-
> ter of the *Geisteswissenschaften*, or about any other philosophi-
> cal topic.   (TP: 73)

Here, the sting is in the tail. It is *this* sense of 'accuracy of representation' that has moral and social significance, not the second, philosophically attenuated sense that Searle runs together with it. The
second sense is concerned with issues like "Can parts of language be
paired off with parts of the world?" and "If so, can the referential
relations involved be made transparent?" Rorty's position is that
answers to these latter questions can have little bearing on the social
practices that shore up academic inquiry. More generally again:

> Honesty, care, truthfulness, and other moral and social virtues are
> just not that closely connected to what we philosophy professors
> eventually decide to be the least problematic way of describing

the relationship between human inquiry and the rest of the universe. (TP: 75)

Williams's compelling picture

Bernard Williams is one of Rorty's most incisive and insightful critics. Fortunately, given the rather grim-faced responses Rorty's writing so often receives, Williams is also invariably witty. Furthermore, unlike many of his more dismissive colleagues, Williams takes the trouble to try to get inside Rorty's philosophical skin, an effort that may have been facilitated by the apparent Nietzschean streak in Williams's innovative approach to morality (Williams 1985, 1995; Clark 2001). From that attempted vantage point, he is able to voice complaints that engage with the spirit of Rorty's enterprise rather than passing smugly by on the other side. Consider for example this provocative, and wonderfully evocative, outline of the kind of 'motivational problem' we highlighted, but also shelved, at the end of Chapter 2:

> There is a problem about how this activity [i.e. philosophy in a post-PMN vein] is supposed to co-exist with a consciousness of its own nature. It is hard to see how these new forms of intellectual life can thrive for long, when they are at the same time so professedly second order, derivative and parasitic on the activities of those in the past who have taken themselves to be doing Philosophy in its own right . . . It is not very realistic to suppose that we could for long sustain much of a culture, or indeed keep away boredom, by playfully abusing the texts of writers who believed in an activity which we now know to be hopeless.
>
> (Williams 1983: 33)

Important though such shrewd and provocative observations may be, there is an even more important central area of disagreement between Williams and Rorty. This concerns Rorty's rejection of realism, and of realist accounts of the success of the scientific enterprise in particular.

The disagreement comes to a head in Williams's book *Ethics and the Limits of Philosophy* (1985). There, Williams finds two "notable faults" in Rorty's "description of scientific success and what that success means" (1985: 137). The main textual target is the following passage from *Philosophy and the Mirror of Nature*:

Physics is the paradigm of "finding" because it is hard (at least in the West) to tell a story of changing universes against the background of an unchanging Moral Law or poetic canon, but very easy to tell the reverse sort of story.   (PMN: 344–5)

The first 'fault' concerns Rorty's "attitude to the fact that it is easy to tell one kind of story and hard to tell another" (Williams 1985: 137). Here, Williams bemoans Rorty's failure to explain why "the picture of the world 'already there', helping to control our descriptions of it, [is] so compelling" (*ibid.*). And the second fault is that "Rorty's account is self defeating":

If the story he tells were true, then there would be no perspective from which he could express it in this way. If it is overwhelmingly convenient to say that science describes what is already there, and if there are no deep metaphysical or epistemological issues here, but only a question of what is convenient (it is "simply because" of this that we speak as we do), then what everyone should be saying, is that science describes a world already there. But, Rorty urges us not to say that, and in doing so, in insisting, as *opposed to that*, on our talking of what it is convenient to say, he is trying to reoccupy the transcendental standpoint outside human speech and activity, which is precisely what he wants us to renounce.   (Williams 1985: 138)

Both these allegations are far more problematic than Williams allows. While it is true to say that Rorty provides no quick and easy explanation as to why 'the compelling picture' is so compelling, it is wrong to imply that he provides *no* explanation.

From Rorty's point of view, "compelling" is not a term that makes much sense in grand *philosophical isolation*. That is, there can be no philosophically interesting, non-trivial explanation of a 'picture' being compelling to *everyone*. Why is that? Well, if everyone buys into the same picture, this means that the opposing intellectual options have been shut down, that the streams of social practices capable of opening up such options have converged into a stagnant pool: everyone believes the earth is round and there is no cultural incentive or social will to believe otherwise. What keeps such stagnancy at bay is the diversity of human social practices and the variegated contingencies of history. For the main factor that 'compels' intellectual pictures is not something itself *purely intellectual* like 'rationality' or 'truth', but rather a nest of cultural forces woven together by historically ripened images and metaphors. When the weave is tight and nobody has flown, or fallen out of, the nest, the view from inside is unchallenged and unchallengeable: everything seems to be as it *should* or *must* be. Williams's remarks about the compelling nature of 'the picture of the world already out there' will tend to be endorsed only by those who have not yet ventured very far beyond 'the nest of realism'. They will not be endorsed, and need not be endorsed, as Williams seems to think they should, by *everyone* who encounters them when competent enough to grasp their significance. *Philosophy and the Mirror of Nature* is a long, complex explanation of why the nest of realism provided the kind of comfort to philosophers that, in the end, sapped their creative powers and left them lagging behind those, such as Heidegger, Dewey and Wittgenstein, who fled to help weave other, more intellectually inspiring, nests.

These latter comments also cast a dark shadow over Williams's second allegation: that Rorty's account is strongly self-defeating because even to voice it he has to occupy transcendental ground it expressly repudiates. Rorty has to occupy no such ground to make sensible objections to Williams's 'compelling picture'. He can say that the pragmatic idea of 'convenience' best explains the adoption of such pictures without having to call upon 'transcendental criteria' for the application of that idea. Furthermore, Williams's use of the phrase "overwhelmingly convenient" is ambiguous. Of course, when a certain kind of convenience is 'overwhelming', it will appear totally misguided to speak in ways that buck the trend. But Rorty detects a 'crisis of convenience' in modern intellectual culture, a situation in which 'the picture of a world out there' is no longer so convenient that it provides both a useful way of talking in general terms about the relationship between science and the world *and* answers to deeply puzzling philosophical questions about the nature of this 'relationship'. Hence, contrary to Williams, Rorty can still allow, and, indeed, participate in, the kind of general talk that describes scientists as finding things out about the world while, at the same time, denying that such talk has any additional philosophical currency. The onus is on those who deny this latter point to show that the cluster of notions associated with 'the compelling picture' – notions like 'mind-independent reality' or 'correspondence' – still have some philosophical cash value outside the nest of realism.

Further reflections on Rorty's critics

These discussions of some of Rorty's critics are not intended to be *conclusive*. They do not purport to show that Rorty is 'right' and his critics are 'wrong' about particular substantive issues. What they do try to show is that given the degree of 'incommensurability' or 'mismatch' between Rorty's writing and the responses of his critics, this kind of 'conclusiveness' is impossible – that very often, just when the critics think they have pinned him down, Rorty is off somewhere else introducing yet another take on his main ideas. More generally, this 'communications gap' perhaps explains why many of Rorty's loudest critics in philosophy so often miss the mark. They simply fail to understand what he is attempting to do. Those who are convinced that a certain way of doing philosophy is *the way*, do not seem to notice this. In complaining, for example, that Rorty's arguments are weak, and perhaps assuming also, as Nagel seems to in *The Last Word*, that philosophy cannot travel very far beyond its standard methods of argumentation without succumbing to a fatal form of intellectual dehydration, they are like those reactionary artists, schooled in Florentine draughtsmanship, who denigrated Caravaggio for daring to paint things without the 'foundation' of first drawing them, or those solid, soulless critics of progressive music who kept asking where the melody or compositional structure had gone. Rorty's critics continue vilifying their own empty, enraged hands, not realizing he has long since slipped their grasp. Lest this rhetoric seem too intemperate, let us round off the discussion with a specific example.

Nagel again: naïve resistance to pragmatism

In a critical review of *Truth and Progress*, the third volume of Rorty's collected philosophical papers, Thomas Nagel fails to acknowledge, if he even notices it, that the very distance signalled by his haughty, judgemental tone probably explains why he so often misses Rorty's point. He is puzzled by Rorty's apparent capacity to 'set aside' the traditional problems of philosophy "like tiresome acquaintances who are cluttering up his social life" (Nagel 1998: 3). However, Nagel's discussion of this alleged flaw in Rorty's philosophical character is both blinkered and complacent. Furthermore, it betrays a complete lack of understanding of Rorty's relationship to these so-called 'problems'. When Nagel first brings up this vexed subject, he claims that at least two of the problems in question – "the problem of the external world and the problem of other minds" (*ibid.*) – are often encountered independently of philosophy, that "they arise naturally" (*ibid.*). But this last, swift claim is a strange one to make in the context of reviewing Rorty of all people. Throughout his career Rorty has been highly attuned to the plausible idea that philosophical problems are not 'natural' and do not "arise as soon as one reflects" (*ibid.*) because they have *historical* roots. Problems on the horizon of the philosophical landscape change as social circumstances dictate. Recall, for instance, the candid opening sentence of the preface in *Philosophy and the Mirror of Nature*: "Almost as soon as I began to study philosophy, I was impressed by the way in which philosophical problems appeared, disappeared, or changed shape as a result of new assumptions or vocabularies" (PMN: xiii). It begs all the interesting questions against Rorty here simply to *assert* that such problems are somehow inherent to the human situation, and are thus liable to occur without any philosophical or cultural scene-setting.

When Nagel's discussion returns to what he regards as Rorty's irresponsibly insouciant ways with problems that are dear to just about every analytic philosopher's heart, things rapidly go downhill. For Nagel then ventures into some embarrassing psychological speculation that tells us more about his own limitations as a reader of philosophical texts than about the strangeness of Rorty's 'mental experience':

> I always feel when reading Rorty that his philosophical position must reflect his own mental experience, which is very different from the norm. He seems genuinely to find it possible to change his beliefs at will, not in response to the irresistible force of evidence or argument, but because it might make life more amusing, less tedious, less cluttered with annoying problems. It is more like moving the living-room furniture around. The policy of tailoring your beliefs and truth-claims to suit your interests is the source of well-known horrors. Rorty has no use for any orthodoxies of that kind – his values are impeccably liberal – but he really doesn't feel the force of reason as a barrier to accepting a belief which would make life easier. And I think that without some feeling for the way in which conclusions can be forced on us by the weight of evidence and reasons, it is impossible to make sense of many of the linguistic and reflective practices that Rorty tries to capture in his pragmatist net.   (Nagel 1998: 3)

To this, an obvious retort is: What evidence *forces* Nagel to believe such claims? The empirical evidence suggests that in practice those in possession of beliefs are very resistant to counter-evidence, especially in circumstances where it threatens beliefs that are interest-bolstering. So what is the 'norm' that Nagel refers to? Perhaps he means 'the norm for philosophers'. But again, where is the evidence that they are a special case? Perhaps his use of "norm" involves a pun on 'normative': Rorty's 'mental experience' flies in the face of how such things *should* go. But then, where is the non-circular argument that shows Nagel is right about this?

Let us grant that Nagel *is* right about the norm (and in both senses: happily what people do when they tend to form beliefs by following the guiding lights of evidence and reason is exactly what they ought to do). What makes him think that Rorty's belief-forming 'experience' is abnormal enough to: (1) allow him to change beliefs willy-nilly, and (2) make evidence and reason subservient to his interests? Unless Nagel has some privileged knowledge of Rorty's personal life (where he has seen him regularly moving his beliefs around like 'furniture', discarding the conclusions of arguments he otherwise finds compelling merely because that makes life easier), the answer must be: a superficial and confused reading of Rorty's work. For in his writings, Rorty is not light-heartedly immune to evidence and reason as such, but rather to certain kinds of elevated philosophical explanations as to what they involve (e.g. the kind of explanations that purport to pin evidential adequacy on to evidence-independent reality or invoke transhistorical jurisdiction for the notion of reason). If Nagel is simply taking Rorty's capacity to sideline some of philosophy's traditional problems as a symptom of his 'abnormality', then once more this begs all the interesting issues that Rorty has raised concerning the status of these very 'problems'. It also overlooks the possibility that the *therapeutic* effects of Rorty's overall approach to philosophy may have freed him from the grip of the sort of philosophical issues that Nagel still finds compelling. Rorty's approach includes looking at traditional philosophical problems in the historical round, but it also involves reading what lots of different kinds of thinkers have to say on very different philosophical themes. It should not be surprising that someone who is always making interesting moves on these broad fronts finds it relatively easy to ignore the problems perceived to be so pressing by those burrowed away in small pockets of analytic philosophy. Rorty inhabits a fertile, blossoming space outside the analytic tradition where abnormal philosophical discourse looms large. From this vantage point, it looks as if the analytic tradition is losing its ascendancy, and issues concerning how such a tradition changes and gets replaced or supplanted look far more interesting than how particular moves can still be made within it.

When Nagel turns to more substantive objections, his tendency to misread Rorty does not abate. The review closes with two glaring examples. First, when Nagel responds to Rorty's general line of argument against realism (roughly: we cannot make the required realist step outside our beliefs to determine whether they represent reality, all we can do is make more holistic 'internal' moves such as examining how those beliefs comport with other relevant beliefs), he reverts to a question-begging realist explanation wherein, for example, a claim about the nature of the hydrogen atom "is an assertion about how the world is, independent of our representation of it" (Nagel 1998: 4). And, he then insists that Rorty's own attempt to accommodate the practical upshot of this kind of explanation (e.g. that the hydrogen atom would have had that kind of nature even if human beings had never evolved) is "just mirrors and smoke" (*ibid.*). This overlooks Rorty's concerted attempts to place the burden of proof back on realists like Nagel because *their* explanations are ephemeral. Time and time again, Rorty has asked questions like: what extra-pragmatic substance can be given to the assertion that something is true *because it captures how things really are* (Nagel: "because it correctly describes a non-linguistic fact")?

Nagel bows out with what seems on the surface to be a neatly formulated charge that Rorty's pragmatism is:

> apparently disabled by its own character from offering arguments that might show its superiority to the common sense it seeks to displace . . . we can't try it, unless we are persuaded to believe it, and for that kind of belief – a belief which has truth rather than comfort as its object – pragmatism has no room.
>
> (1998: 4)

But why, if one has read Rorty carefully, and correctly, should one ever think that he would *want* to offer such arguments? On Rorty's account of intellectual change on the larger scale, the shift from position to position is *not* a matter of just following the appropriate line of argument. Metaphors, images and all sorts of historical contingencies do the necessary deeds. While entrenched in the analytic problematic, Nagel is never going to be 'persuaded' to turn pragmatist by external argument alone. His attitude in the review amply demonstrates this: he is unable to consider pragmatist arguments on their own terms, he has to filter them through a network of beliefs and intuitions that distort those arguments into shapes that automatically make them unpalatable. But here is another, Rorty-inspired, account of how Nagel *might* still turn pragmatist. He starts to feel some dissatisfaction with the lack of tangible results in analytic philosophy, but instead of drawing the orthodox conclusion that this only shows how deep and difficult the corresponding problems are, he ponders whether there might be something wrong with the assumptions that (a) generate the difficulties in the first place and (b) keep those difficulties in play despite their intransigence. At the same time, Nagel also notices that a great many of his gifted students and most respected colleagues are no longer reading the literature that perpetuates the discourse of analytic philosophy. For whatever reason, they have moved on to different territory where different methods and themes dominate research and discussion. Perhaps he decides to see what they are up to, and finds himself mostly reading the kind of things *they* read, discussing with *them* what *they* are interested in. Perhaps he finds all this very difficult at first. The books send him to sleep, and in discussion, he cannot help raising what seem to him to be obvious analytical points of objection. However, when, in the latter case, he is continually ignored, he learns to discuss philosophy *without* always falling straight back into his customary analytical ways of thinking. And then, by some strange coincidence, as he begins to get into the swing of things, the sleep-inducing books become more interesting. One night, out of curiosity, he plucks a volume off his old, and now dusty, shelves where the books he previously preferred to consult are kept. It is called *The View From Nowhere*. He flicks through it and wonders why the author made such high drama out of a series of problems that were so obviously contrived. This is the turning point. He resolves to call Rorty in the morning, to ask him whether Derrida's *The Post Card* makes for a good read in the English translation.

Finally, before we leave him, it is worth exposing Nagel's disingenuous use of the notion of 'comfort' or, as he put it earlier, of 'making life easier', where Rorty's pragmatism is casually reduced to an apparently absurd, sofa-lounging criterion of belief, something like:

> For any belief p: if p is true, but its denial q lets us put our feet up and cease worrying about p, then believe q.

When 'making life easier' is interpreted in more seriously practical terms – the kind of terms that echo Jamesian accounts of belief –

Richard Rorty

the idea of believing something on such grounds rather than on the grounds of pure, interest-independent, truth is not so easy to dismiss. And, for those who are pragmatically inclined to want to believe the things that make life non-trivially better for human beings and other relevant parties, the 'mental experience' of the person who is able to resist *that* inclination in favour of a more hygienic, philosophical conception of 'truth' is going to look 'abnormal'.

Back to the puzzle

Our puzzle remains. Rorty's sternest philosophical critics deny his main claims. They think he is wrong on just about every front. But they seem unable to state their denial in terms that do not beg the question or tacitly assume what Rorty himself denies. Time and time again, we find hostile commentators throwing pieces of philosophical vocabulary at Rorty that he has explicitly challenged or even disowned, as if they only need to shout louder to make him hear that he is wrong. But what Rorty's historically attuned ears pick up is something very different from what they think they are saying. Thus when Blackburn defiantly shouts "Justifying something to your peers is not the same thing as getting it right" (Blackburn 2001: 6), what Rorty hears is either a platitude that his own position endorses without comment or a piece of philosophical hand-waving that helps itself to a bogus notion of 'getting things right' (i.e. one that rashly promises to deliver more than his 'Deweyan conception' of knowledge as justified belief). "Suppose", Rorty might ask in such a case, "I have exhausted all the resources of justification available to my peers, and suppose those resources are themselves 'justified' in the sense that they meet other reliable criteria among my peers' peers, and so on, should I still wait for 'truth' to 'get things right'?" His critics seem committed to saying "yes", but unable to tell him what it is he would actually be waiting for, unable to say anything that ought to prevent him from taking the next obvious pragmatist step to dispense with 'truth' as a philosophical prop. Perhaps the conclusion we should draw from Rorty's critics' proven inability to articulate the clear and conclusive refutation of his views that should be so easily forthcoming if he is so obviously wrong is that *they* are wrong. Perhaps that is the solution to our puzzle. Perhaps our earlier talk of a 'mismatch' that prevents a conclusive verdict on the state of play regarding Rorty and his critics was just too kind.

Chapter 7

Rorty's legacy

A turn away from narration and utopian dreams toward philosophy seems to me a gesture of despair.   (Rorty 1999: 232)

The trajectory of Rorty's own philosophical career may seem to have
followed much the reverse direction. His first three books have been
supplemented by a plethora of essays – most of them, it seems, now
reprinted in four substantial volumes. To date, there are three
consecutive collections of academic papers published by Cambridge
University Press (ORT, EHO, TP) and an additional collection of
more 'occasional pieces' published by Penguin under the title
Philosophy and Social Hope (PSH; 1999). In these wide-ranging
essays, Rorty elaborates on the kind of 'post-pragmatist' themes that
emerged from *Contingency, irony, and solidarity* and continues to
develop his interpretations – or 'readings' – of co-opted allies such as
Davidson, Heidegger, Wittgenstein and Derrida. More often than
not, he weaves the various results of these interpretations into
further discussions of liberalism, where the emphasis usually shifts
from its philosophical credentials to its *utopian* prospects: the various ways in which human beings might succeed in working together
to build a better future. The essays also display an increased confidence in 'literary' ploys, especially in the forms of 'strong textualism'
and narratives of 'imaginative possibilities'.

The strong textualist's approach was first explicitly outlined in
Rorty's paper "Nineteenth-Century Idealism and Twentieth-
Century Textualism" (CP: Ch. 8):

> The strong textualist simply asks himself the same question
> about a text which the engineer or the physicist asks himself

about a puzzling physical object: how shall I describe this in order to get it to do what I want? Occasionally a great physicist or a great critic comes along and gives us a new vocabulary which enables us to do a lot of new and marvellous things. Then we may exclaim that we have now found out the true nature of matter, or poetry, or whatever. But Hegel's ghost, embodied in Kuhn's romantic philosophy of science or Bloom's philosophy of romantic poetry, reminds us that vocabularies are as mortal as men. The pragmatist reminds us that a new and useful vocabulary is just *that*, not a sudden unmediated vision of things or texts as they are. (CP: 153)

Rorty's own spirited instantiation of this approach leads to a greater stress in his readings of various authors on what their texts 'can do' for him or, by extension, 'us' (in terms of private satisfaction) and what he, or we, can 'get them to do' (usually, in his case, in terms of furthering the pragmatist cause).

The 'narrative ploys' involve fabricated tales in which Rorty tries to dislodge received philosophical wisdom and preconceptions, as the reader may recall he earlier tried to do in *Philosophy and the Mirror of Nature* with his Antipodean story of 'persons without minds'. Rorty normally proceeds by discussing how things might have turned out in 'a slightly different possible world'.

Thus in one such world, "Heidegger suddenly finds himself deeply in love with a beautiful, intense, adoring philosophy student named Sarah Mandelbaum". She is Jewish and he ends up 'preaching resistance to Hitler'. This imaginary narrative challenges any preconceived notion that there must be 'essential links' between Heidegger's philosophy, his rectorial address and Nazi politics. In another possible world, Nietzsche was "much more central to the rhetoric of Nazism than he actually was" and the all-conquering Third Reich lasted until 1989. The defeated Europeans ended up feeling as disenchanted with Nietzsche, after having him constantly rammed down their throats, as most of those in the real world's Eastern bloc finally did with Marx for similar reasons. This story – entertainingly sketched in a sparkling short review of Derrida's *Specters of Marx* – deftly punctures over-inflated views of Marx's *theoretical* importance (PSH: 193–4 & 210, respectively).

Hope without knowledge: pragmatism revisted

> If there is anything distinctive about pragmatism it is that it substitutes the notion of a better human future for the notions of 'reality', 'reason' and 'nature'. One may say of pragmatism what Novalis said of Romanticism, that it is 'the apotheosis of the future'. (PSH: 27)

Philosophy and Social Hope has the advantage, especially for those unacquainted with very much of Rorty's other writing, of containing an admirably clear and forthright outline of his 'version' of pragmatism. This manifests itself in three consecutive essays that comprise a sort of 'mini-monograph' in the second of the book's five main sections. This part is entitled 'Hope in Place of Knowledge: A Version of Pragmatism' (PSH: 21–90). And the three component essays deal in turn with themes that Rorty explains in his "Preface":

> My choice of themes, and my ways of rephrasing them, results from my conviction that James's and Dewey's main accomplishments were negative, in that they explain how to slough off a lot of intellectual baggage which we inherited from the Platonic tradition. Each of the three essays, therefore, has a title of the form ' – without – ', where the first blank is filled by something we want to keep and the second something which James and Dewey enabled us, if not exactly to throw away, at least to understand in a radically un-Platonic way. (PSH: xiii)

The 'blanks' Rorty refers to are filled in by 'Truth/Correspondence to Reality', 'World/Substances or Essences' and 'Ethics/Principles' respectively, but it is the Truth/Correspondence combination tackled in the first essay that holds the most interest for our present purposes.

"Truth without Correspondence to Reality", begins with some historical scene-setting that ties pragmatism to a Whitmanesque 'future-orientated perspective' in which hope "for results to come" (Whitman 1982: 929) is substituted "for the sort of knowledge which philosophers have usually tried to attain" (PSH: 24). The discussion then returns to the 'thorny problem of truth' and tries to show how the pragmatist response – i.e. 'the pragmatist theory of truth' – blends in with its focus on the future: "This doctrine fits into a more general programme: that of replacing Greek and Kantian dualisms between permanent structure and transitory content with the distinction between the past and the future" (PSH: 31).

The 'future' that Rorty's version of pragmatism looks toward is not one in which 'truth' is ever supposed to emerge triumphant, not even as the natural outcome of 'ideal conditions of inquiry' – an outcome backslidingly envisaged by some within the fold (e.g. Peirce, James and, at one time, Putnam). This cuts out one of pragmatism's two most historically favoured replies to the common charge that it conflates truth and justification (the reply in question being: there is no such 'conflation' because pragmatists will get to 'truth' in the end, and by means of 'justification'). Rorty prefers the other response that sticks solely with 'justification' on its own terms and thereby obviates the need for compensatory talk of 'truth'. Pragmatism's hopes for the future are invested in better and better forms of 'justification'. These are not to be judged as 'better' by their propensity to yield 'truth', but rather according to whether they make for 'better human lives' in the most general and varied senses that can be compared with 'the present':

> To sum up, my reply to the claim that pragmatists confuse truth and justification is to turn this charge against those who make it. They are the ones who are confused, because they think of truth as something towards which we are moving, something we get closer to the more justification we have. By contrast, pragmatists think that there are a lot of detailed things to be said about justification to any given audience, but nothing to be said about justification in general. That is why there is nothing general to be said about the nature or limits of human knowledge, nor anything to be said about a connection between justification and truth. There is nothing to be said on the latter subject not because truth is atemporal and justification temporal, but because *the only point in contrasting the true with the merely justified is to contrast a possible future with the actual present*.
>
> (PSH: 39)

A political romance

At the time of writing, a substantial volume of critical essays on Rorty in the prestigious *Library of Living Philosophers* is under way. This, alone, belies the lowly status attributed to his work by many of his critics in the analytic camp. Meanwhile, in keeping with his emphasis on 'hope' rather then 'knowledge', Rorty's most recent book, *Achieving Our Country: Leftist Thought in Twentieth-Century America* (AOC), invokes a political "romance of endless diversity" in which "the future will widen endlessly" and "experiments with new forms of individual and social life will interact and reinforce one another" (AOC: 24). He contrasts this dynamic, pride-filled ideal of the "Deweyan, pragmatic, participatory Left as it existed before the Vietnam war" (AOC: 38) with the more conservative, 'live-and-let-live' goals of 'multiculturalism' and the "principled, theorised, philosophical hopelessness" (AOC: 37) of the 'spectatorial Left', a political faction that prefers to wallow in its passive, dismal, anti-humanist, theoretical 'knowledge' rather than indulge in the kind of 'hopes' for a better life that can – in true pragmatist spirit – spark off practical, social experimentation.

Much of this busy activity in publishing appears to take us far away from philosophy's traditional methods and concerns, but we would be wrong to view these writings *en masse* as conclusive evidence that Rorty has turned his back on philosophy itself. As in the case of his early relationship to the analytic tradition, Rorty's relationship to philosophy is too complex to sum up in simple terms like that. Moreover, in this instance, the issues extend beyond whether he should be dubbed this or that kind of philosopher. They concern the nature of philosophy and much of the point and purpose of Rorty's writings in connection with it.

Philosophy without a real ending

For Rorty, a phrase like "the nature of philosophy" has too many deceptive associations to be any longer very useful. It has, for example, a strong Socratic affiliation with the question "What is philosophy?" This is the sort of query that dupes us into trying to discover the 'essential constituents' of philosophy or pin down the 'necessary and sufficient conditions' for a mode of thought or an idea to be designated "philosophical". In *Philosophy and the Mirror of Nature* and closely related papers such as "Keeping Philosophy Pure: An Essay on Wittgenstein" (CP: Ch. 2), Rorty kick-started a concerted campaign to persuade us that we should stop thinking of philosophy in essentialist terms, cease regarding it as an autonomous discipline, characterized by a dependence on special texts, methods and problems.

It can sharpen and focus the mind to think that a certain way of proceeding in philosophy is the *only* way of so proceeding (recall how much the very same attitude can push things forwards in the Arts). But history shows that the benefits of this blinkered approach tend to be relatively short-lived. Rorty believes it is time to be more open-hearted and relaxed about what 'doing philosophy' can involve, that the more narrow-minded, uptight approaches he has consistently opposed over the years ran out of steam a long time ago. We beg the question against him on the important issues here, if we claim that Rorty has 'turned away from philosophy' simply because we feel that his writings 'no longer contain enough arguments', 'fail to tackle proper problems' and so on. Whether what he writes is 'philosophy' is a question Rorty is no doubt intellectually untroubled by and perfectly happy to see settled by 'contingent considerations', the kind mentioned in our related discussion at the end of Chapter 2 – such as whether his name is included in the appropriate reference works, whether his books turn up on the 'philosophy shelves' in shops and libraries and whether his views stimulate further discussion within philosophical circles. It would be foolish to try to head off the verdict that will emerge from these quarters on the sole grounds that Rorty has offended against some strict, prior definition of "philosophy". And not just foolish, but uninformatively so. Rather than saying something empty like (as I heard one professional philosopher remark at a meeting of one of philosophy's premier forums, the American Philosophical Association – and I have unfortunately overheard, or been subjected to, many similar remarks since): "Of course, there's no *real* philosophy in *Contingency, irony, and solidarity*" (compare *"The Waste Land* does not contain any *real poetry"* or *"The Large Glass* is not *real art"*), it would be better to describe what specific philosophical purposes the book fails to serve, in what particular respects it so fails and why it ought to have at least tried to serve *those* purposes.

Rorty is often also described as someone who forecasts, and tries his hardest to contribute to, the end of philosophy or, more dramatically, its 'death'. It should be clear by now that this, too, is ill conceived. One of the biggest philosophical ego-trips is the fantasy of writing 'the last philosophical work', the one that somehow brings philosophy to an end or kills it off. But it is very rash to even consider single-handedly terminating something that has no essential nature, that depends for its continued existence on all sorts of contingent factors outside any individual thinker's predictive power and control. Rorty is brave, but not rash – certainly not *that* rash. In any case, his open-minded conception of philosophy as part of 'cultural conversation' precludes even the prophecy of its demise. Recall this quotation, also from our previous discussion in Chapter 2: "The conversational interest of philosophy as a subject, or of some individual philosopher of genius, has varied and will continue to vary in unpredictable ways depending on contingencies" (PMN: 392). Regrettably, even well-informed and sympathetic commentators have slipped up on this last point. Thus, for example, in his "Introduction" to *Rorty and His Critics*, Robert Brandom claims that: "In his classic work *Philosophy and the Mirror of Nature*, Rorty notoriously prophesized approvingly the 'death of philosophy'" (Brandom 2000: x).

Brandom tells us that Rorty "now regrets this rhetoric". He then goes on to 'clarify' Rorty's position in a way that, unfortunately, despite its insight in other respects, muddies the waters a bit on the 'death of philosophy' issue:

> Although he now regrets this rhetoric – he certainly never meant to deny that we would always need professors to help students read the great books that make up the philosophical tradition, for instance – he has never relinquished his commitment to the dissolution of a certain sort of philosophy: philosophy as a discipline with epistemology at its heart, a sort of super-science, limning the limits of the knowable, explaining the nature of the relationship between reality and our representations of it. Philosophy so conceived he presents as a literary genre that arose in response to particular historical demands and conditions, and which has outlived its usefulness. His subsequent willingness to engage and converse with post-modern literary theorists gave some (I would say: those who were not paying close attention to what he was actually saying in those conversations) the impression that he considered philosophy itself *vieux jeux.* . . . this impression is about as far from the truth as it well could be. In fact Rorty sees philosophy as having an absolutely crucial cultural role to play in the current situation – a role far more significant than that envisaged by most analytic philosophers.   (Brandom 2000: x)

There are two problems with this. First, if we return to *Philosophy and the Mirror of Nature* itself, it is difficult to find any intemperate 'death of philosophy' rhetoric that Rorty might have much cause to later regret. He is quite clear that a certain kind of philosophy – the epistemology-based philosophy Brandom refers to – has had its day. Such philosophy is no longer useful and has, in the hands of its internal critics like Sellars, Quine and Wittgenstein, generated a self-undermining dialectic that is fatal once the relevant implications are made overt. Its enthusiastically self-defensive continuation is therefore something of an act of bad philosophical faith. But, even here, Rorty is circumspect, sounding a very proper note of caution:

> The neo-Kantian image of philosophy as a profession, then, is involved with the image of the "mind" or "language" as mirroring nature. So it might seem that epistemological behaviourism and the consequent rejection of mirror-imagery entail the claim that there can or should be no such profession. But this does not follow. Professions can survive the paradigms which gave them birth. (PMN: 393)

And, when reflecting on the "actual result of a widespread loss of faith in mirror-imagery" – one of the best results he could expect from the publication of *Philosophy and the Mirror of Nature* and his later anti-representationalist writings – Rorty still refuses to lay down any firm bets:

> I do not know whether we are in fact at the end of an era. This will depend, I suspect, on whether Dewey, Wittgenstein and Heidegger are taken to heart. It may be that mirror-imagery and "mainstream" systematic philosophy will be revitalised once again by some revolutionary genius. Or it may be that the image of the philosopher which Kant offered is about to go the way of the medieval priest. If that happens, even philosophers themselves will no longer take seriously the notion of philosophy as providing "foundations" or "justification" for the rest of culture, or adjudicating *quaestiones juris* about the proper domains of other disciplines. Whichever happens, however, there is no danger of philosophy's "coming to an end". (PMN: 394)

"I do not know whether we are in fact at the end of an era", "There is no danger of philosophy's 'coming to an end'" – this is hardly the immoderate 'rhetoric' of someone prophesying, "approvingly", the "death of philosophy".

The other problem with Brandom's commentary is *his* rhetoric: the upbeat reassurance he gives us that Rorty sees "philosophy as having an absolutely crucial cultural role to play in the current situation". This rhetoric is ill judged in at least two senses. First, the 'reassurance' it purports to gives us – that Rorty *does* regard philosophy as important – is unnecessary if we understand Rorty's position and misleading if we do not.

Since Rorty does not see philosophy as being under any great threat, there is no need to apply a bicycle pump to reports of the image of its current state of health in his eyes, no need to drum up the reassuring idea that he does after all see it playing a big role 'in the current situation'. I suspect that Rorty would cringe at the latter phrase, in any case. He is acutely sensitive to human distress and returns time and time again in his writings to the various social and economic problems causing this distress. But, just as he thought that what was most important about Larkin's poem was its capacity to help us make the fears associated with dying more *explicit*, Rorty likes to identify the causes of human misery in more concrete terms. Talk of applying something big and vague called "philosophy" to something flabbily entitled "the current situation" is just not his style.

Perhaps Brandom is giving Rorty a dose of his own 'redescriptive treatment' in:

1. calling Rorty's view that 'cognitive assessment' need appeal to no authority "apart from that manifested in social practices" his "master idea"; and

2. saying that Rorty's pragmatist work on making a vocabulary based on 'solidarity-without-a-higher-authority' look more attractive than the traditional philosophical discourse founded on notions of 'truth', 'reality' and 'objectivity' constitutes a "world-historical task" (Brandom 2000: xi–xii).

But this 'treatment' flies in the face of Rorty's own much preferred, philosophically downbeat ways of talking (he even resorts to the wry self-characterization: "weak thought" (EHO: 6)).

The most recent substantial addition to Rorty's body of written work has been an extensive series of detailed replies to critics that includes those published in Brandom's collection (see Guide to further reading for details of other such collections). These replies show that Rorty needs no reassignment of a 'master idea' or a 'great task', world-historical or otherwise, to keep him in the forefront of the philosophy game – even when that game is defined in terms that are far too narrow for his tastes. He responds to each of his interlocutors with great, no-nonsense, candour, willingness to change his mind and a seemingly effortless combination of erudition, patience, generosity and deflationary wit – further proof against the doubters of his commitment to 'genuine inquiry'. The reader invariably emerges from such encounters with the feeling that Rorty has somehow gently turned the tables on his critics, often putting the burden of proof on *them*, but still more often just leaving *them* to explain what all the fuss was about. Here, to cite just one example among many, are some typical nuggets as extracted from Rorty's way of dealing with Richard Shusterman's rather heavy-handed critique in his article "Reason and Aesthetics between Modernity and Postmodernity: Habermas and Rorty" (retractions and points of agreement have been ignored):

> I doubt that I have ever put forward, nor that Derrida would affirm, the view which Shusterman attributes to us both: that language is "more fundamentally aesthetic . . . more a matter of disseminating creativity, persuasive rhetoric and world-making tropes than of logical validity". Language has lots of functions – two of which are problem-solving and world-disclosing – but I doubt that there is any need to debate which of its functions is "fundamental". That would be like asking whether liberal politics is more fundamental than conservative politics, or whether spending money is more fundamental than saving it, or up more fundamental than down . . . I am a bit at a loss about how to deal with Shusterman's claim that I neglect the fact that beautiful flowers, birds, poems, music and other things "make us forget for a moment about language and reason, allowing us to revel, however briefly, in nondiscursive sensual joy". They do indeed. But in what exactly does my "neglect" consist? . . . Shusterman goes on to say that because I am a product of a "puritan America" my "aesthetic program" is one-sidedly driven by the relentless production of new vocabularies and narrative identities". What aesthetic program? I do not know of any fruitful way to bring nondiscursive sensual joy (of the sort birdwatchers like myself get when kingfishers flash fire) together with the sort of non-somatic thrills I enjoy as a person who, as Shusterman puts it, "just likes to read books". But neither do I know any interesting descriptions of the relationship between the somatic pleasures of food and those of sex, or between the non-somatic delight of reading Wodehouse and that of reading Hegel. Do we need an aesthetic theory or an aesthetic "program" to exhibit such relationships? . . . Talking about things is one of the things we do. Experiencing moments of sensual joy is another. The two do not stand in a dialectical relationship, get in each others' way, or need synthesis in a program or theory. We can agree with

Gadamer that "being that can be understood is language" while remaining aware that there is more to life than understanding. Inventing others to reason and then purporting to provide a better discursive understanding of these non-discursive others (a project which stretches from British empiricism through Bergson to existential phenomenology) seems to me a beautiful example of kicking up dust and then complaining that we cannot see.

(Festenstein and Thompson 2001: 154–7)

Rorty is able to respond in similar fashion to criticisms directed at his politics, his pragmatism and his conception of philosophy. This ability to 'carry on the conversation' with philosophers of different persuasions makes a mockery of claims that he has 'turned away' from philosophy and is waiting on the sidelines for its downfall. To a certain extent, this is true even of the narrow, epistemologized brand of philosophy he attacked in *Philosophy and the Mirror of Nature*.

The "primary focus" of *Rorty and His Critics* is, Brandom tells us, "a set of core arguments concerning the notions of truth, objectivity and reality" (Brandom 2000: x). Asking Rorty to speak to such an agenda is more than a bit like asking Ezra Pound to talk about the pros and cons of strictly metered verse, John Cage about classical harmony or Marcel Duchamp about pictorial composition – each can do so, and with an interesting, knowledgeable slant, but this backwards-looking task cannot bring out the best in them. Nonetheless, most of Rorty's critics, even those who profess to agree with him on key issues, are inclined to try to wrestle him back on to *their* philosophical territory before engaging with him. In Brandom's collection, even James Conant, who, in his contribution "Freedom, Cruelty, and Truth: Rorty versus Orwell", *does* make the effort to tackle Rorty on his own post-pragmatist ground by challenging the reading of Orwell presented in *Contingency, irony, and solidarity*, tries to foist specific *theses* on him, as in 'The thesis of Rortian Liberalism':

A moral status is not something one possesses simply in virtue of possessing certain "objective properties". A moral community is something that is *forged* rather than found, something which is *produced within historically created evolved practices*, not something which exists simply as a function of brute historical fact. Moral status is thus conferred and moral concern acquired *through a cultural process* – through participation in certain kinds of communities: communities which have evolved vocabularies which enable one (a) to engage in the activity of moral reflection and deliberation, (b) to express one's solidarity with fellow members of one's community (for instance, by using expressions such as "we" and "us" for insiders and "them" for outsiders), and (c) to view those with whom one expresses solidarity as appropriate subjects of moral concern. One such vocabulary our community has evolved is *the vocabulary of liberalism*. A liberal is someone who thinks *cruelty is the worst thing we can do* and that 'morality' should not be taken to denote anything other than our abilities to notice, identify with, and alleviate pain and humiliation. Someone who is committed to the vocabulary of liberalism thinks that there is *no noncircular theoretical justification* for his belief that cruelty is a horrible thing. He thinks and talks within the midst of certain historically and culturally local practices. He does not take the validity of those practices to rest on an ahistorical or transcultural foundation. He takes his commitment to liberalism to be nothing more than a function of his commitment to his community.

(Brandom 2000: 277)

Philosophers usually have two, not always separate, grounds for turning the work of others into definite theses, as Spinoza famously did with Descartes's *Discourse on the Method*. First, to 'set them up' for criticism – ideally a 'refutation' – and secondly, to sharpen, and hence clarify, their claims. Conant's 'Rortian Theses' appear to serve neither of these purposes well. Their 'internal structure' is too intricate to play them off against one another, or further 'theses', thereby highlighting any contradictions or additional anomalies (in this respect, the 'Liberalism' example above, which embeds many 'subtheses', is typical, and not even the worst case). Furthermore, they consist mainly of complex, interpretative descriptions of Rorty's views, and no 'clarification' seems to emerge from bundling such descriptions up into 'theses'. Rorty's response on this issue is as apt as it is brief: "I think of all of the 'Rortian' theses he lists as suggestions about how to redescribe familiar situations in order to achieve various practical goals" (Brandom 2000: 344).

The redescriptive legacy

Strictly, by his own anti-essentialist, strong textualist, lights, it seems, it is the prerogative of commentators like Brandom and Conant to bend Rorty's writings to their own philosophical will. But such efforts can still be 'judged' – as useful or otherwise. And, in this case, I have been suggesting nothing very useful gets done. Rorty's consummate 'ease of appropriation' has probably encouraged an 'anything-goes', 'relativistic' interpretation of his relationship to individual authors and texts. This interpretation encourages the reciprocal thought that, if Rorty's own words are turned into shapes he does not like, he cannot complain. But he can, and he frequently does – and with perfect entitlement on the pragmatic grounds just mentioned.

Furthermore, the 'ease' is very deceptive. Rorty's 'flair for redescripition' can make it look as if there are *no* constraints in this area, as if 'redescriptive philosophy' is 'philosophy made far too easy'. But believing that Rorty has made philosophy too easy on the grounds of such deceptive appearances is like believing it is easy to sing popular melodies because Dean Martin made it look so easy. There are 'constraints' on redescriptive philosophy, but they involve 'conversational norms' internal to communities of inquiry (e.g."Is the redescription interesting?" or "Does it serve any good purpose to put things like that?") rather than any supposed connection with 'reality' that exists 'outside' those norms and those communities. To help drive this important point home, let us consider an example.

In *Contingency, irony, and solidarity*, Rorty enlists Hegel as a fellow 'ironist'. Here are some of the key passages in which he does this:

> I have defined "dialectic" as the attempt to play off vocabularies against one another, rather than merely to infer propositions from one another, and thus as the partial substitution of redescription for inference. I used Hegel's word because I think of Hegel's *Phenomenology* both as the beginning of the end of the Plato–Kant tradition and as a paradigm of the ironist's ability to exploit the possibility of massive redescription. In this view, Hegel's so-called dialectical method is not an argumentative procedure or a way of unifying subject and object, but simply a literary skill – skill at producing surprising gestalt switches by making smooth, rapid transitions from one terminology to another . . .
>
> Instead of keeping the old platitudes and making distinctions to help them cohere, Hegel constantly changed the vocabulary in which the old platitudes had been stated; instead of constructing philosophical theories and arguing them, he avoided argument by constantly shifting vocabularies, thereby changing the subject. In practice, though not in theory, he dropped the idea of

getting at the truth in favour of making things new. His criticism of his predecessors was not that their propositions were
false but that their languages were obsolete. By inventing this
sort of criticism, the younger Hegel broke away from the Plato–
Kant sequence and began a tradition of ironist philosophy which
is continued in Nietzsche, Heidegger and Derrida. These are the
philosophers who define their achievement by relation to their
predecessors rather than by their relation to the truth . . .

A more up-to-date word for what I have been calling "dialectic" would be "literary criticism". In Hegel's time it was still
possible to think of plays, poems, and novels as making vivid
something already known, of literature as ancillary to cognition,
beauty to truth. The older Hegel thought of "philosophy" as a
discipline which, because cognitive in a way that art was not,
took precedence over art. Indeed, he thought that this discipline,
now that it had attained maturity in the form of his own Absolute idealism, could and would make art as obsolete as it made
religion. But, ironically and dialectically enough, what Hegel
actually did by founding an ironist tradition within philosophy,
was help de-cognitivise, de-metaphysise philosophy. He helped
turn it into a literary genre. The young Hegel's practice undermined the possibility of the sort of convergence to truth about
which the older Hegel theorised.   (CIS: 78–9)

In a relatively short space, Rorty manages to invoke many of his
favourite themes. Indeed, it would not be too 'difficult' to rewrite this
passage as a description of Rorty's *own* legacy. Thus the kind of
worry that surfaced earlier in Chapter 3 with regard to Rorty's interpretation of Dewey (i.e. that on this interpretation, Dewey 'bears a
suspicious resemblance to Rorty himself') may seem apposite here.
And this in turn may fuel further suspicion that Rorty is too easily
able to refashion philosophers in his own image, that he must therefore be operating without proper 'constraints'. But closer inspection
of actual cases should make "ease" a complimentary epithet rather
than a badge of suspicion. For the refashioning of Hegel as 'ironist'
evinced here is far from 'easy'. The impression of effortlessness is a
function of Rorty's unique skills – a sort of philosophical 'Dean Martin effect'. Think of the background historical and philosophical
knowledge that is required to make the passages in question even
remotely plausible. And think of the cultural interconnections that
have to be woven to make it 'interesting'. Imagine a redescriptive

philosopher who wants to do for 'empiricism' exactly the kind of thing Rorty has done for pragmatism. Her first step will probably be to extract a 'purified' version from the classic empiricists like Locke, Berkeley and Hume. But what if she wants to go on to appropriate someone surprising, one of the 'rationalists', perhaps, such as Descartes? Will this be an easy task? Easier than more conventional ploys such as fine-tuning one of Descartes's key 'arguments' or discovering a subtle contradiction in his account of the qualities of the soul?

On Rorty's picture of philosophy, the 'picture' that will no doubt be his main legacy, successful completion of such a task – of virtually *any* such task – is not ruled out in advance. But the 'success factor' is contingent on the appropriate skills. This offends against the view that redescription should answer to 'reality' – in the present case, something like the real, or intended, 'meaning' of Descartes's texts (which would presumably render the task impossible). But, it does not leave philosophy especially vulnerable to indiscriminate redescription at the hands of its main enemies: the know-nothings or the wilfully ignorant. Successful 'redescription' requires considerable knowledge, insight and skill. Rorty has already bequeathed us a batch of writings that encourages readers to set about acquiring such skills – primarily by getting intimately acquainted with more and more texts and authors, with their socio-historical contexts, as well as their possible thematic interconnections.

Rorty has helped do for philosophy what he contends Freud did for the Nietzschean conception of self-creation: democratize it – allowing more views to be heard. Thanks in large part to Rorty, philosophy is no longer dominated by a single voice espousing the application of analytic rigour to the perennial problems handed down by the Platonic tradition. It is teeming with a wide variety of voices and thus brimming with fresh themes. Ghostly figures from philosophy's past and its margins are returning to shake things up, but also offer wise counsel – such figures, of whom Dewey is a good example, look a great deal more interesting and less like mere 'perpetrators of linguistic confusion and error' when the analytic agenda is 'set aside' as Rorty suggests. Furthermore, when the traditional barriers to entry are lifted, voices from different backgrounds, such as African, Native American and Tibetan cultures, are finding a platform for explaining what their heritage can contribute to the ever-enlarging philosophical conversation of the world. Even though Rorty usually writes from a resolutely 'ethnocentric point of view', his contention that it is far better, when putting forward philosophical ideas, to stake out some ground one is historically familiar with and currently happy to occupy (in his case: pragmatism and American Liberalism) than continue the long, fruitless search for some higher, 'neutral ground', is encouraging others to do likewise. Tolerance, persuasion and moral imagination are the practical palliatives he suggests for inevitable 'conflicts of ethnocentric interests'. Meanwhile, the old guard still remains in its ivory tower, and dreams of discovering universally acceptable theoretical solutions.

Tangential influences

Although Rorty is still extremely active in philosophy, and in that sense it is too soon to be speaking of his 'legacy', his considerable body of work has by now clocked up some noteworthy achievements. His writings have provoked wider interest in a variety of authors and texts, and in the possible relationships between them. They have brought new themes to the fore and suggested practical ways that philosophers can hook themselves up to social progress without carrying any excessive theoretical baggage. However, despite the changes described above, the skills required to actually practise 'redescriptive philosophy' are still relatively rare in philosophy itself. As yet, thinkers from other disciplines seem to have been keener to acquire them, and apparently more capable of doing so, than philosophers themselves. Perhaps this is a momentary historical accident; perhaps their need is presently perceived to be greater. But it is also likely that thinkers in these disciplines can see greater potential for progress in Rorty's work because they are not blinkered by the hostile preconceptions of the analytic tradition.

The deaf ear of the analytic tradition is compensated for to some extent by the increasing number of philosophers who commute back and forth across the analytic–continental border, and for whom Rorty's humorous, theory-light reading of figures such as Heidegger and Derrida has helped set a new, more co-operative agenda. At any rate, Rorty's work is hotly debated in tangential disciplines such as legal studies, international relations, feminist studies, literary theory and even business ethics. In legal studies, it stimulates debates over such topics as whether laws should be interpreted 'realistically', whether 'legal pragmatism' should have anything to do with pragmatist philosophy and whether adjudication should be pragmatic through and through (i.e. should it be pragmatic in practice *and* intellectually justified as such?).

Rorty's anti-essentialist conception of human nature has stirred things up in the field of international relations by adding weight to the Argentinean philosopher Eduardo Rabossi's contention that human rights should be treated as *historically* explicable phenomena that require no prior philosophical grounding in a transcultural account of what is distinctively 'rights-demanding' about human beings: "My basic point [is that] the world has changed, that the human rights phenomenon renders human rights foundationalism outmoded and irrelevant" (Rabossi 1990).

In feminist studies, Rorty has provoked much discussion as to whether his critique of epistemology cuts deep enough, whether it still leaves the whole domain contaminated by gender-biased assumptions. More generally, there has been considerable critical interest in Rorty's suggestion that feminists should eschew the false aid of 'realism' and 'universalism' by speaking at all times with the kind of pragmatist tongue that says things like:

> We are *not* appealing from phallist appearance to nonphallist reality. We are *not* saying that the voice in which women will some day speak will be better at representing reality than present-day masculist discourse. We are not attempting the impossible task of developing a nonhegemonic discourse, one in which truth is no longer connected with power. We are not trying to do away with social constructs in order to find something that is not a social construct. We are just trying to help women out of the traps men have constructed for them, help them get the power they do not presently have, and help them create a moral identity as women. (TP: 210)

Rorty's influence on literary theory has been partly vitiated by the mistaken interpretation we discussed at the outset of this book – the interpretation of Rorty as someone who can be called upon to help add philosophical weight to the methods and achievements of literary theorists. But the realization is starting to dawn, as Richard Fyffe points out, that Rorty is offering precisely the opposite kind of help by *freeing* literary studies from the concerns of philosophy:

> Rorty's philosophical work is not concerned with providing a method for literary studies – in the way, for example, Husserl's transcendental phenomenology has been used, or Derrida's deconstruction, or Saussure's signifier and signified. Indeed,

Rorty argues against the notion that literary studies should seek a method in either science or philosophy. Instead, a major thrust of his work has been to argue against the traditional distinction between science and literature. Rorty sees Western culture as moving away from the scientific world-view and toward a more literary form of life in which we understand that the constraints on our knowledge or interpretations are not objective or imposed by the world but instead are conversational. Literature, for Rorty, is an important practice in the enlargement of our cultural conversation. (Fyffe 1996: 2)

In business ethics, this 'enlargement of our cultural conversation' continues. Rorty is an emerging presence that comports well with parallel developments in management thinking. Again, his 'anti-essentialism' provides the main impetus for fruitful discussion, challenging fixed views of the amoral nature of business organizations (e.g. as being primarily 'wealth-generating machines'), views that preclude more flexible accounts in which ethical considerations can play an important role (Malachowski 2001).

The creative fallout from all these discussions that Rorty has worked so hard and so creatively to provoke may yet descend on those still clinging to the thread-worn coat-tails of philosophy's traditional image as the master discipline, those who believe the ideal of 'objective cognition' always trumps that of 'aesthetic enhancement'. This book has tried to show that if anything of the kind does happen, it will probably be to the greater good of everyone concerned.

Guide to further reading

Chapter 1: Platonic yearnings

Jürgen Habermas provides perceptive commentary on both Rorty's account of his 'anti-Platonic turn' in WO and the significance of *The Linguistic Turn* in his article "Richard Rorty's Pragmatic Turn" (in Robert Brandom (ed.), *Rorty and His Critics* (Oxford: Blackwell, 2000), pp. 31–55). Some interesting details of the political aspects of Rorty's upbringing are revealed by his autobiographical comments in *Achieving Our Country: Leftist Thought in Twentieth-Century America* (Cambridge, MA: Harvard University Press, 1998; see pp. 58–64).

Our first chapter could well have been called "From Plato to Hegel" in recognition of the main sea-change in Rorty's way of thinking about philosophy. With Plato, there is no substitute for tackling the main dialogues head on. These are readily available in serviceable translations. For those who nevertheless feel in need of a compass, Bernard Williams's *Plato* (London: Phoenix, 1998) is as admirable as it is brief. Hegel's prose is a formidable obstacle to those not already comfortably immersed in his work and the wider continental tradition that has engaged with that work. But it may well seem worth surmounting after reading Michael Forster's *Hegel's Idea of a Phenomenology of Spirit* (Chicago, IL: University of Chicago Press, 1998) and Terry Pinkard's intriguing biography: *Hegel* (Cambridge: Cambridge University Press, 2000).

To get an authentic sense of how the analytic movement's self-image was constructed, of what exactly it was that Rorty stands accused of turning his back on, it is probably necessary to return to a time when philosophers were freshly inspired by the idea that most, if not all, their 'problems' could be solved by attending to the meaning of the words involved. Rorty's own anthology *The Linguistic Turn* (Chicago: University of Chicago Press, 1967; second, enlarged edition, 1992) is an excellent, and comprehensive, reference point. Otherwise, 1963 was a vintage year, and either Gilbert Ryle's *The Revolution in Philosophy* (London: Macmillan, 1963) or Anthony Flew's *Logic and Language: First Series* (Oxford: Blackwell, 1963) should do the trick.

Chapter 2: Conversation

Philosophy and the Mirror of Nature reacts strongly against the central ideas of some of Western philosophy's key historical figures such as Plato, Descartes, Locke and Kant. It thus presumes some familiarity with those ideas. Readers who lack this should perhaps try N. Scott Arnold, Theodore M. Benditt and George Graham (eds), *Philosophy Then and Now* (Oxford: Blackwell, 1998) or John Cottingham (ed.), *Western Philosophy: An Anthology* (Oxford: Blackwell, 1997). There are plenty of other useful introductory texts that span the tradition Rorty strikes out against, but it is more important in many ways to get to grips with the views of two relatively recent philosophers: W. V. Quine and Wilfrid Sellars. Rorty regards them as the conduits of some of analytic philosophy's most important developments in self-criticism. These are the developments that he thinks have undermined the kind of philosophizing started by Plato and, at the same time, ripened the classic arguments for pragmatism.

In Quine's case, the seminal text is "Two Dogmas of Empiricism", in W. V. Quine, *From A Logical Point of View* (Cambridge, MA: Harvard University Press, 1953). An excellent introduction to Quine's work is Alex Orenstein's *W. V. Quine* (Chesham: Acumen, 2002). More detailed discussion of how Rorty leans on Quine to show how 'imagination' should take priority over 'truth' in philosophy can be found in the editorial introduction to Alan Malachowski (ed.), *Rorty: Sage Masters of Modern Social Thought* (4 vols) (London: Sage Publications, 2002) and Alan Malachowski, "Truth over Imagination: Rorty and Quine" (2002, forthcoming). As for Sellars, the best place to start is his *Empiricism and the Philosophy of Mind*. This is now available in an edition that has the advantages of both an introduction by Rorty and commentary from Robert Brandom (Cambridge, MA: Harvard University Press, 1997). Detailed critical responses to the central themes of *Philosophy and the Mirror of Nature* can be found in three key sources: Malachowski (ed.), *Reading Rorty* (Oxford: Blackwell, 1990) and *Rorty: Sage Masters of Modern Social Thought* (4 vols) (London: Sage Publications, 2002) and Robert B. Brandom (ed.), *Rorty and His Critics* (Oxford: Blackwell, 2000). For a useful discussion of Rorty's narrative concerning the 'Antipodeans', see Kenneth T. Gallagher, "Rorty's Antipodeans: An Impossible Illustration", in Malachowski (ed.), *Rorty*.

Chapter 3: Pragmatism

As its title suggests, Michael Lynch's *Truth in Context* (Cambridge, MA: MIT Press, 1998) provides some useful background to debates on the nature of truth and to Rorty's place within them. The literature on pragmatism has burgeoned since Rorty's first robust interventions on its behalf. This is also true of the three main subjects of 'appropriation' discussed in this chapter (Dewey, Heidegger and Wittgenstein), though evidence of a direct causal link is less clearcut. To date, the most comprehensive discussions of Rorty's approach to pragmatism can be found in Herman J. Saatkamp (ed.), *Rorty and Pragmatism: The Philosopher Responds to His Critics* (Nashville, TN: Vanderbilt University Press, 1995), John Pettegrew (ed.), *A Pragmatist's Progress? Richard Rorty and American Intellectual History* (Lanham, MD: Rowman and Littlefield, 2000), and Malachowski (ed.), *Rorty: Sage Masters of Modern Social Thought* (4 vols) (London: Sage Publications, 2002), especially volume 2. See also C. G. Prado, *The Limits of Pragmatism* (Atlantic Highlands, NJ: Humanities Press, 1987); Hilary Putnam, *Pragmatism* (Oxford: Blackwell, 1995), and Russell B. Goodman (ed.) *Pragmatism: A Contemporary Reader* (London: Routledge, 1995).

Though unsympathetic to Rorty, Jim Tiles's *Dewey* (London: Routledge, 1992) is a good introduction. Rorty's pragmatist take on Heidegger may make more sense after reading Mark Okrent, *Heidegger's Pragmatism* (Ithaca, NY: Cornell University Press, 1988). And Rorty's interpretation of Wittgenstein is instructively challenged by Alice Cary in Alice Cary and Rupert Read (eds), *The New Wittgenstein* (London: Routledge, 2000). Cary's discussion is reprinted as "Saving Wittgenstein from Conservatism (Richard

Richard Rorty

Rorty)" in Malachowski (ed.), *Rorty: Sage Masters of Modern Social Thought* (4 vols) (London: Sage Publications, 2002).

A quick way into Derrida's 'writerly approach' to philosophy is Christopher Johnson's *Derrida* (London: Phoenix, 1997). A more circumlocutory route, though one Rorty himself seems to approve (TP: 327–50), can be taken via Geoffrey Bennington's *Jacques Derrida* (Chicago, IL: University of Chicago Press, 1991). For those who find it hard to gain a philosophical foothold in the more recent (i.e. post-Sartrean) writings of the 'continental tradition', Samuel C. Wheeler's *Deconstruction as Analytic Philosophy* (Stanford, CA: Stanford University Press, 2000) should be helpful, as should Simon Critchley, *Continental Philosophy: A Very Short Introduction* (Oxford: Oxford University Press, 2001).

Chapter 4: Contingency

Contingency, irony, and solidarity has spawned a large variety of vigorous responses; however three key sources are: Alan Malachowski (ed.), *Reading Rorty* (Oxford: Blackwell, 1990), Robert Brandom (ed.), *Rorty and His Critics* (Oxford: Blackwell, 2000), and Malachowski (ed.), *Rorty: Sage Masters of Social Thought* (4 vols) (London: Sage Publications, 2002). A specialized, but wide-ranging, discussion that incorporates key figures from the 'continental tradition' can be found in John McCumber, *Philosophy and Freedom: Derrida, Rorty, Habermas, Foucault* (Bloomington: Indiana University Press, 2000).

Chapter 5: Liberalism

The articles in the final section of Alan Malachowski (ed.), *Reading Rorty* (Oxford: Blackwell, 1990) deal with Rorty's liberalism in some detail, as do those in volume 3 of Malachowski (ed.), *Rorty: Sage Masters of Modern Social Thought* (4 vols) (London: Sage Publications, 2002). An excellent collection of critical articles on most aspects of Rorty's political thought (published with his 'replies') is Matthew Festenstein and Simon Thompson (eds), *Richard Rorty: Critical Dialogues* (Cambridge: Polity Press, 2001). The point about needing to look more closely at Judith Shklar's work, in order to grasp why Rorty makes such a close connection between liberalism and the avoidance of cruelty, is well made (and graciously conceded

190

by Rorty in his 'reply') by David Owen in his contribution to the latter collection: "The Avoidance of Cruelty: Joshing Rorty on Liberalism, Scepticism and Ironism" (pp. 93–110). More details of Rorty's defence of 'anti-anti-ethnocentrism' are outlined in his article "Solidarity or Objectivity" (ORT: 21–34). An assessment of Rorty's approach to Rawls is now best made against the backcloth of Rawls's reiteration of his position in *Justice As Fairness: A Restatement* (Cambridge, MA: Harvard University Press, 2001).

Chapter 6: Some critics

Of the more substantial critical discussions of Rorty overlooked here for reasons of space, two that stand out are voiced in: John McDowell, *Mind and World* (Cambridge, MA: Harvard University Press, 1994) and Susan Haack, *Evidence and Enquiry: Towards Reconstruction in Epistemology* (Oxford: Blackwell, 1993). Responses to McDowell can be found in "The Very Idea of Human Answerability to the World: John McDowell's Version of Empiricism" (TP: 138–52) and again in Robert Brandom (ed.), *Rorty and His Critics* (Oxford: Blackwell, 2000), pp. 123–8. Rorty engages with Haack in Herman J. Saatkamp Jr. (ed.), *Rorty and Pragmatism: The Philosopher Responds to His Critics* (Nashville, TN: Vanderbilt University Press, 1995). An instructive account of the Madhyamika philosophy alluded to in this chapter can be found in Williams Magee, *The Nature of Things: Emptiness and Essence in the Geluk World* (Ithaca, NY: Snow Lion Publications, 1999).

Chapter 7: Rorty's legacy

There are currently six extensive collections of articles on Rorty's work (and the *Library of Living Philosophers* volume is on its way): Alan Malachowski (ed.), *Reading Rorty* (Oxford: Blackwell, 1990), Herman J. Saatkamp (ed.), *Rorty and Pragmatism* (Nashville, TN: Vanderbilt University Press, 1995), Robert Brandom (ed.), *Rorty and His Critics* (Oxford: Blackwell, 2000), Matthew Festenstein and Simon Thompson (eds), *Richard Rorty: Critical Dialogues* (Cambridge: Polity Press, 2001), John Pettegrew (ed.), *A Pragmatist's Progress? Richard Rorty and American Intellectual History* (Lanham, MD: Rowman and Littlefield, 2000), and Alan Malachowski (ed.), *Rorty: Sage Masters of Modern Social Thought* (4 vols) (London: Sage Publications, 2002).

Bibliography

Articles by Rorty

Books by Rorty are listed on page xxi.

1961. "Pragmatism, Categories, and Language", *Philosophical Review* **70** (April): 197–223.
1963. "Empiricism, Extensionalism, and Reductionism", *Mind* **72** (April): 176–86.
1965. "Mind–body Identity, Privacy, and Categories", *Review of Metaphysics* **19** (September): 24–54.
1970. "In Defence of Eliminative Materialism", *Review of Metaphysics* **24** (September): 112–21.
1970. "Strawson's Objectivity Argument", *Review of Metaphysics* **24** (December): 207–44.
1970. "Incorrigibility as the Mark of the Mental", *Journal of Philosophy* **67** (25 June): 399–429.
1970. "Wittgenstein, Privileged Access, and Incommunability", *American Philosophical Quarterly* **7** (July): 192–205.
1971. "Verificationism and Transcendental Arguments", *Nous* **5**: 3–14.
1972. "Indeterminacy of Translation and Truth", *Synthese* **23** (March): 443–62.
1973. "Criteria and Necessity", *Nous* **7**: 313–29.
1974. "More on Incorrigibility", *Canadian Journal of Philosophy* **4** (September): 195–7.
1976. "Realism and Reference", *The Monist* **59** (July): 3221–340.
1977. "Derrida on Language, Being, and Abnormal Psychology", *Journal of Psychology* **74** (November): 673–81.
1979. "Transcendental Argument, Self-reference, and Pragmatism". In *Transcendental Arguments and Science*, P. Bieri, R.-P. Hortsman and L. Kruger (eds), 77–92. Dordrecht: Reidel.
1980. "Freud, Morality, and Hermeneutics", *New Literary History* **12** (Fall): 177–85.
1984. "A Reply to Six Critics", *Analyse & Kritik* **6** (June): 78–98.
1986. "Should Hume be Answered or Bypassed?", *Human Nature and Natural Knowledge: Essays Presented to Marjorie Grene*, A. Donegan (ed.), 341–52. Dordrecht: Reidel.

Richard Rorty

1987. "Thugs and Theorists: A Reply to Bernstein", *Political Theory* **15** (November): 564–80.
1990. "Truth and Freedom: A Reply to Thomas McCarthy", *Critical Inquiry* **16**: 633–43.
1990. "Foucault/Dewey/Nietzsche", *Raritan* **9**(4) (Spring): 1–8.
1992. "What Can You Expect from Anti-foundationalist Philosophers? A Reply to Lynn Baker", *Virginia Law Review* **78** (April): 719–27.
1994. "Taylor on Truth". In *Philosophy in an Age of Pluralism: The Philosophy of Charles Taylor in Question*, J. Tully (ed.), 20–36. Cambridge: Cambridge University Press.
1995. "Towards a Post-metaphysical Culture" (interview), *The Harvard Journal of Philosophy* (Spring): 58–66.
1996. "Remarks on Deconstruction and Pragmatism". In *Deconstruction and Pragmatism*, C. Mouffe (ed.), 13–18. London: Routledge.
1996. "Response to Simon Critchley". In *Deconstruction and Pragmatism*, C. Mouffe (ed.), 41–6. London: Routledge.
1998. "A Defence of Minimalist Liberalism". In *Debating Democracy's Content: Essays on American Politics, Law and Public Philosophy*, A. L. Allen & M. C. Regan Jr. (eds), 117–25. New York: Oxford University Press.
1998. "Davidson Between Wittgenstein and Tarski", *Critica: Revista hispanoamericana de Filsofia* **30**(88) (April): 49–71.
1999. "Pragmatism as Anti-authoritarianism", *Revue Internationale de Philosophie* **1**: 7–20.
2000. "Foreword". In *Heidegger, Authenticity and Modernity*, M. Wratnall & J. Malpas (eds). Cambridge, MA: MIT Press.

Other references

Arcilla, R. V. 1995. *For The Love of Perfection: Richard Rorty and Liberal Education*. London: Routledge.
Bernstein, R. 1992. *The New Constellation: The Ethical–Political Horizons of Modernity / Postmodernity*. Cambridge, MA: MIT Press.
Blackburn, S. 1984. *Spreading the Word*. Oxford: Oxford University Press.
Blackburn, S. 1988. *Ruling Passions: A Theory of Practical Reasoning*. Oxford: Oxford University Press.
Brandom, R. (ed.) 2000. *Rorty and His Critics*. Oxford: Blackwell.
Clark, M. 2001. "On the Rejection of Morality: Bernard Williams' Debt to Nietzsche". In *Nietzsche's Postmoralism*, R. Schact (ed.). Cambridge: Cambridge University Press.
Conant, J. 2000. "Freedom, Cruelty, and Truth: Rorty versus Orwell". In *Rorty and His Critics*, R. Brandom (ed.), 268–342. Oxford: Blackwell.
Conway, D. W. 1999. "Of Depth and Loss: The Peritropaic Legacy of Dewey's Pragmatism". In *Dewey Reconfigured*, C. Heskins & D. Seipk (eds), 221–48. New York: State University of New York Press.
Davidson, D. 1984. "On the Very Idea of a Conceptual Scheme". In *Inquiries into Truth and Interpretation*. Oxford: Clarendon Press.
Davidson, D. 1987. "Afterthoughts". In *Reading Rorty*, A. Malachowski (ed.), 134–8. Oxford: Blackwell.
Derrida, J. 1976. *Of Grammatology*. Baltimore and London: Johns Hopkins University Press.
Derrida, J. 1994, *Specters of Marx: The State of the Debt, the Work of Mourning, and the Law of the New International*, P. Kamuf (trans.). London: Routledge.

Dickstein, M. (ed.) 1998. *The Revival of Pragmatism: New Essays on Social Thought, Law and Culture*. Durham: Duke University Press.

Dylan, B. 1987. *Lyrics: 1962–1985*. London: Jonathan Cape.

Edmundson, M. 1993. *Wild Orchids and Trotsky: Messages from American Universities*. New York: Viking.

Festenstein, M. & S. Thompson (eds) 2001. *Richard Rorty: Critical Dialogues*. Cambridge: Polity Press.

Foucault, M. 1996. "Philosophy and the Death of God". In M. Foucault (1999), *Religion and Culture*, J. R. Carreto (ed.), 85–6. Manchester: Manchester University Press.

Fyffe, R. 1996. "Conversational Constraints; Richard Rorty and Contemporary Critical Theory", Midwinter Meeting of the English and American Literature Section, ACRL, January.

Gadamer, H.-G. 1975. *Truth and Method*. London: Sheed and Ward.

Geertz, C. forthcoming. *A Word in Pieces*.

Gunn, T. (ed.) 2000. *Ezra Pound Poems*. London: Faber and Faber.

Hegel, F. 1977. *Phenomenology of Spirit*, A. V. Miller (trans.). Oxford: Oxford University Press.

Heskins, C & D. Seipk (eds) 1999. *Dewey Reconfigured*. New York: State University of New York Press.

Huntington Jr., C. W. 1989. *The Emptiness of Emptiness*. Honolulu: University of Hawaii Press.

James, W. 1978. *Pragmatism and The Meaning of Truth* (one-volume edition). Cambridge, MA: Harvard University Press.

Larkin, P. 1988. *Collected Poems*. London: Faber and Faber.

Lewis, C. I. 1956. *Mind and the World Order*. New York: Dover.

Lovibond, S. 1983. *Realism and Imagination in Ethics*. Minneapolis, MN: University of Minnesota Press.

Luban, D. 1998. "What's Pragmatic about Legal Pragmatism?" In *The Revival of Pragmatism: New Essays on Social Thought, Law and Culture*, M. Dickstein (ed.), 275–303. Durham: Duke University Press.

MacIntyre, A. 1999. *Dependent Rational Animals*. London: Duckworth.

Malachowski, A. (ed.) 1990. *Reading Rorty*. Oxford: Blackwell.

Malachowski, A. (ed.) 2001. *Business Ethics: Critical Perspectives on Business and Management* (4 vols). London: Routledge.

Malachowski, A. (ed.) 2002. *Rorty: Sage Masters of Modern Social Thought* (4 vols). London: Sage Publications.

Malachowski, A. 2002, forthcoming. "Rorty without Relativism".

Malachowski, A. 2002, forthcoming. "Imagination over Truth: Rorty and Quine".

Malachowski, A. 2003, forthcoming. *Truth in Progess: A Reintroduction to Pragmatism*. London: Routledge.

McCumber, J. 2000. *Philosophy and Freedom: Derrida, Rorty, Habermas, Foucault*. Bloomington, IN: Indiana University Press.

Merton, T. 1948. *The Seven Storey Mountain*. New York: Harcourt Brace Jovanovich.

Morris, L. 1950. *William James: The Message of a Modern Mind*. New York: Scribner's.

Murphy, J. 1990. *Pragmatism: From Peirce to Davidson*. Boulder, CO: Westview Press.

Nagel, T. 1997. *The Last Word*. Oxford: Oxford University Press.

Nagel, T. 1998. "Go With the Flow", *Times Literary Supplement*, 28 August, pp. 3–4.

Newell, R., 1986. *Objectivity, Empiricism and Truth*. London and New York: Routledge and Kegan Paul.

Richard Rorty

Nietzsche, F. 1954. *The Portable Nietzsche*, W. Kaufman (trans.). New York: Viking.
Nietzsche, F. 1967. *The Birth of Tragedy and the Case of Wagner*, W. Kaufman (trans.). New York: Vintage.
Nietzsche, F. 1995. *Human, All Too Human, I*, G. Handwerk (trans.). Stanford, CA: Stanford University Press.
Orwell, G. 1949. *1984*. London: Penguin.
Putnam, H. 1995. *Pragmatism*. Oxford: Blackwell.
Quine, W. V. 1953. *From a Logical Point of View: Logico-Philosophical Essays*. New York: Harper and Row.
Quine, W. V. 1990. "Let Me Accentuate the Positive". In *Reading Rorty*, A. Malachowski (ed.), 117–19. Oxford: Blackwell.
Rabossi, E. 1990. "La teoria de los derechos humanos naturalizada", *Revista del Centro de Estudios Constitucionales* (Madrid) **5**: 159–79.
Ramberg, B. 2000. "Post-ontological Philosophy of Mind: Rorty versus Davidson". In *Rorty and His Critics*, R. Brandom (ed.), 351–70. Oxford: Blackwell.
Ravitch, M. 2000. "Byron's Afterlife", *The Yale Review* **88**(2): 124–37.
Rawls, J. 1971. *A Theory of Justice*. Oxford: Oxford University Press.
Rawls, J. 1980. "Kantian Constructivism in Moral Theory". In *Collected Papers*, J. Rawls, 303–58. Cambridge, MA: Harvard University Press.
Rawls, J. 1985. "Justice as Fairness: Political not Metaphysical". In *Collected Papers*, J. Rawls, 388–414. Cambridge, MA: Harvard University Press.
Rawls, J. 1999. *Collected Papers*. Cambridge, MA: Harvard University Press.
Rawls, J. 2001. *Justice as Fairness: A Restatement*, Cambridge, MA: Harvard University Press.
Rée, J. 1998. "Strenuous Unbelief", *London Review of Books*, 15 October.
Russell, B. 1945. *A History of Western Philosophy*. New York: Simon & Schuster.
Said, E. 1999. "On Writing a Memoir". In *The Edward Said Reader*, M. Bayoumi & A. Rubin (eds) (2001). London: Granta Books.
Schact, R. (ed.) 2001. *Nietzsche's Postmoralism*. Cambridge: Cambridge University Press.
Searle, J. 1992. "Rationalism and Realism: What is at Stake?" *Daedelus* **122**(4) (Fall): 55–84.
Searle, J. 1995. *The Social Construction of Reality*. Harmondsworth: Penguin.
Sellars, W. 1963. *Science, Perception and Reality*. London and New York.
Sellars, W. 1997. *Empiricism and the Philosophy of Mind*. Cambridge, MA: Harvard University Press.
Shklar, J. 1984. *Ordinary Vices*. Cambridge, MA: Harvard University Press.
Stroud, B. 1969. "Conventionalism and the Indetermincay of Translation". In *Words and Objections: Essays on the Work of W. V. Quine*, D. Davidson & J. Hintikka (eds), 19–34. Doredrecht: Reidel.
West, C. 1989. *America's Evasion of Philosophy*. Wisconsin: University of Wisconsin Press.
Whitman, W. 1982. *Complete Poetry and Selected Prose*. New York: The Library of America.
Williams, B. 1985. *Ethics and the Limits of Philosophy*. London: Fontana Press.
Williams, B. 1995. "Nietzsche's Minimalist Psychology". In *Making Sense of Humanity and Other Philosophical Papers*, B. Williams. Cambridge: Cambridge University Press.
Williams, M. 2000. "Epistemology and the Mirror of Nature". In *Rorty and His Critics*, R. Brandom (ed.), 191–213. Oxford: Blackwell.
Wittgenstein, L. 1993. *Philosophical Occasions: 1912–1951*, J. Klagge & A. Nordmann (eds). Indianapolis: Hackett.

Index

absolute necessity 113–14
*Achieving Our Country: Leftist
Thought in Twentieth Century
America* (AOC) 173
ad hoc techniques 41–2
aesthetics 178
analytic philosophy xi, xiii, 12, 23–4,
  30–4, 64, 184
  critics of Rorty 141, 149, 165–6,
  167
  critiques of 38, 42
  Davidson 69
  dialectic of 70, 114
  epistemology-based 89
  Heidegger 92
  history 16–17
  Kantian foundations 56
  linguistic habits 102–3
  pragmatism 67–8, 84
  texts 87
  writing 85
anti-essentialism 2–3, 19, 62, 128,
  156, 180
  business ethics 186
  Dewey 92
  human nature 185
  pragmatism 83
  Wittgenstein 95
anti-theory 78
appropriation 42, 49–51, 67, 88–9
Aquinas, St Thomas 49
Arcilla, R. V. 122
argument 42–3, 63, 108–9, 116, 117
Aristotle 91, 100
art xii, 8–9, 148
Austin, J. L. 50
authority 4, 116, 142–3, 177
Ayer, A. J. 12, 92

behaviorism 42, 57–8, 176
beliefs 55, 58, 70–2, 115
  critics of Rorty 154, 164–5, 166,
  167–8
  Quine 53, 54, 145–6
  realism 146–7, 158
Berkeley, George 183
Berlin, Isaiah 110
Bernstein, Richard 44, 45, 47, 51, 68
Blackburn, Simon 141–8, 149, 168
Blanshard, Brand 50
Bloom, Harold 1, 170
Blumenberg, Hans 98
Boyd, Richard 80
Brandom, Robert 150, 175, 176–7,
  179–80
Brouwer, L. E. J. ix
business ethics 87, 186

Cage, John xii, 8, 179
Candrakirti 21
Carnap, Rudolf 47, 63, 92
Cartesianism 29, 47, 49, 82, 85
Cavell, Stanley 80
Chambers, Stephan xi
change 45, 53, 54
Christianity 25, 98
circularity 32–3, 117
Clarke, Thompson 81
community 108–9, 153, 179–80
Conant, James 179, 180
conceptual framework 70–1, 72
confirmation 57, 58
consciousness 12
consensus 152, 153
Consequences of Pragmatism (CP)
  11–12, 41, 67–96, 99, 125, 173
  Heidegger 18

197

Richard Rorty